After a medical check_____ _____ your doctor's supervision, you too may achieve significant loss of weight as many others have done by following the simple rules contained in this book.

Imagine losing weight with a diet that lets you have bacon and eggs for breakfast, heavy cream in your coffee, plenty of meat and even salad *with* dressing for lunch and dinner! No wonder Dr. Atkins calls it a "diet revolution."

This is the fabulous, controversial bestseller that explains the diet in infinite detail, includes meal plans, recipes, a list of foods to avoid and permissible foods.

DR. ATKINS'
DIET REVOLUTION

The #1 bestseller
that tells you how to lose weight

PUBLISHER'S NOTE

The Atkins Diet has become the subject of widespread discussion and controversy. On April 12, 1973, Dr. Atkins replied to criticisms of his diet in testimony before the U.S. Senate Select Committee on Nutrition and Human Needs. In order to alert as many readers as possible to the conflicting claims made about this diet and Dr. Atkins' answers thereto, the Doctor's formal statement to the Committee is reprinted beginning on page 299.

As this statement indicates, the charges which have been made against the diet by the AMA and others involve the possibility of various results and effects which may be adverse to the dieter's health. We therefore reiterate and reemphasize the importance of medical supervision prior to and during the utilization of this diet, as is indicated in the book and Dr. Atkins' statement.

DR. ATKINS' DIET REVOLUTION

THE HIGH CALORIE WAY TO STAY THIN FOREVER

ROBERT C. ATKINS, M.D.

Recipes and Menus by
Fran Gare and Helen Monica

DR. ATKINS' DIET REVOLUTION
A Bantam Book

PRINTING HISTORY
David McKay edition published September 1972

2nd printing .. October 1972	11th printing .. February 1973
3rd printing . November 1972	12th printing .. February 1973
4th printing . December 1972	13th printing .. February 1973
5th printing . December 1972	14th printing .... March 1973
6th printing . December 1972	15th printing .... March 1973
7th printing .. January 1973	16th printing .... March 1973
8th printing .. January 1973	17th printing .... March 1973
9th printing .. January 1973	18th printing .... March 1973
10th printing .. February 1973	19th printing ..... April 1973

Literary Guild / Time Inc. Book Club edition published
November 1972

Bantam edition / September 1973

2nd printing . September 1973	14th printing .... March 1975
3rd printing .. October 1973	15th printing ..... April 1975
4th printing .. January 1974	16th printing ...... May 1975
5th printing .. February 1974	17th printing ...... July 1975
6th printing .... March 1974	18th printing . September 1975
7th printing ..... April 1974	19th printing . November 1975
8th printing ...... June 1974	20th printing .... March 1976
9th printing . September 1974	21st printing ...... May 1976
10th printing . September 1974	22nd printing ...... July 1976
11th printing ... October 1974	23rd printing . September 1976
12th printing ... January 1975	24th printing ... January 1977
13th printing ... January 1975	25th printing ...... May 1977

26th printing

Condensations appeared in COSMOPOLITAN *and* WOMAN'S DAY

ISBN 0-553-11001-2

Published simultaneously in the United States and Canada

*Bantam Books are published by Bantam Books, Inc. Its trade-
mark, consisting of the words "Bantam Books" and the por-
trayal of a bantam, is registered in the United States Patent
Office and in other countries. Marca Registrada. Bantam
Books, Inc., 666 Fifth Avenue, New York, New York 10019.*

PRINTED IN THE UNITED STATES OF AMERICA

*This
book is
dedicated to
all
the diet
revolutionaries
who
are not
content merely
to follow
their
own diet,
but
who are
dedicated to
carrying
the message of
the diet
revolution
to
the world
which
needs it.*

ACKNOWLEDGMENTS

First of all, I should like to thank Ruth West for her inestimable help in the preparation of this book.

I also want to thank Fran Gare and Helen Monica for their creative work in producing the unique and delicious recipes. My thanks also to Dr. Ira Mason, my associate in practice; Dr. Harvey Sadow, for his invaluable criticism; Mr. Ernest Ash, my legal counsel; Mrs. Gloria Pann, my food consultant; Miss Judy Schrumpf, head nurse of my office staff; and Miss Mary Pyzik, typist.

CONTENTS

1

WHAT
THIS BOOK
WILL REVEAL
TO YOU

Millions of words have been written and spoken about over-weight. By now everybody knows everything about it—except what causes it and how to get rid of it.

I am constantly amazed at even how few physicians are treating the *real* cause of overweight. No wonder it doesn't go away.

REVOLUTIONIZE YOUR IDEAS ABOUT THE CAUSE OF OVER-WEIGHT. Are you thinking, "But surely it is caused by just overeating?"

Not so! This is one of those assumptions we have always taken for granted, one of the many myths about overweight that it is now time to unlearn.

METABOLIC IMBALANCE CAUSES MOST OVERWEIGHT. For fifty years, ever since the first best-selling diet book appeared, doctors and dietitians have been telling us that losing is just a matter of adjusting your calorie intake and eating a balanced diet.

But most people—and that includes doctors and dietitians—are totally ignorant of the metabolic imbalance that is the primary cause of *almost all* overweight.

The result of fifty years of prescribing a so-called "balanced diet" for patients who actually were suffering from metabolic imbalance is a raging national epidemic of overweight.

A REVOLUTION IN OUR DIET THINKING IS LONG OVERDUE. Overweight brings many problems with it. Our biggest health problem today—cardiovascular disease—is closely linked with overweight. So is diabetes, heightened accident and surgical risk, hyperinsulinism, arthritis, diseases of the kidneys, liver, gallbladder, even suicide.

HOW IS THIS A DIET REVOLUTION? If a revolution is a successful revolt against entrenched order, then the last eight years of my practice represents one. I'll be telling you more about how it all happened in the next few chapters, but to sum up, I've treated ten thousand patients for overweight in that time.

They have all lost weight without counting calories, without diet pills, *and most without feeling a single pang of hunger.*

They haven't lost by eating less of a "balanced diet." To begin with, this diet *isn't* "balanced." It is deliberately *unbalanced.* The reason—to counteract the metabolic imbalance that causes people to get fat in the first place.

You see, most balanced diets are around 50 percent carbohydrate, 30 percent protein, 20 percent fat. Overweight people usually have a disturbed carbohydrate metabolism, so they can't handle that much carbohydrate. In this diet we first cut out carbohydrates *altogether,* then keep them cut way down permanently.

THIS IS A NO-HUNGER DIET. One of the happy side effects of this deliberately unbalanced therapeutic diet is the fantastic change that it brings about in your hunger pattern.

My patients lose whether they eat more or less on this no-hunger diet. Most people eat less, but it's only because what they get on this diet so completely satisfies their hunger. They find they just can't eat as much as they used to.

But some have lost thirty, forty, one hundred, or more pounds, while consuming two to three thousand calories or more a day, enough to make the point that if you want to eat that much, you *still* can lose.

They've lost weight on bacon and eggs for breakfast, on heavy cream in their coffee, on mayonnaise in their salads, butter sauce on their lobster; on spareribs, roast duck, pastrami; on my special cheesecake for dessert. (See recipe, page 246.) And on this diet, cholesterol levels usually go down, and even more important, triglyceride levels (you'll learn about this in the recipe chapter) almost always go down. My patients have shed years along with the pounds. They have gained energy, cheerfulness, self-confidence. They're new people. And they no longer count calories.

This is because I don't believe that losing weight is a simple matter of counting calories and of just operating the body on a calorie deficit.

THE CALORIE-COUNTING APPROACH HAS FAILED. Orthodox medicine's conspicuous lack of success in treating overweight hasn't caused the profession to search widely for alternatives to calorie-counting approaches.

Instead, other events have taken place. A gigantic low-calorie food and drink industry has exploded into being. The drug industry has produced a multicolored Niagara of diet pills. Have all these appetite suppressants and all these low-calorie victuals and drinks turned us from a fat nation into a trim nation? You know the answer! Every year more of us worry about overweight, and rightly so, for every year in our increasingly sedentary society, more of us age and die prematurely from diseases linked with faulty diet and over-weight.

The calorie-counting approach to the problem of our national overweight has failed. (You'll read more about this in chapter 8.)

There are two major reasons why calorie counting has failed to trim us down. First, few people can tolerate the hunger that goes with a low-calorie diet long enough to succeed in losing much weight.

And, as I mentioned earlier, there is that other even more basic reason why calorie counting has failed us.

MANY OF TODAY'S DISEASES HAVE ONE PREDISPOSING FACTOR IN COMMON: CARBOHYDRATE INTOLERANCE. Over the years a large number of doctors and medical researchers have observed that the overweight person, the diabetic, the hypo-glycemic (that's a person suffering from a low level of blood sugar), the heart-attack prone, all have one thing in common: something is very wrong with the way their bodies handle sugar and other carbohydrates. These people are carbohy-drate intolerant—due to a metabolic imbalance.

What we need now is a diet revolution in which carbo-hydrate intake is cut to fit the tolerance of carbohydrate-intolerant people. Then—and only then—can overweight, with all its dangers, be controlled.

WHY HASN'T MEDICINE EXPLORED THE DEADLY ROLE OF CARBOHYDRATES? How can so many nutrition "experts" not be aware of carbohydrate intolerance?

Why have the medical "authorities" for so long ignored rather than explored this logical lead to the treatment of overweight?

What is the explanation for the blind eye that has been turned on the flood of medical reports on the causative role of carbohydrates in overweight, ever since the publication in 1864 of William Banting's famous "Letter on Corpulence"? Could it be related, in part, to the vast financial endowments poured into the various departments of nutritional education by the manufacturers of our refined carbohydrate foodstuffs?

WE'RE THE VICTIM OF "CARBOHYDRATE POISONING." The most killing diseases of the twentieth century stem from what I call "carbohydrate poisoning." What causes that? Mainly, sugar. In many cases, virtually a sugar *addiction*. As Dr. John Yudkin points out, "We consume more sugar now in two weeks than we did in a year two centuries ago."

For decades now Americans have been brainwashed by advertisers to start the day with processed cereals, and fill up in the hours afterward with soft drinks that contain no real nutritive value, only carbohydrates.

As cavemen, we humans evolved mainly on a diet of meat. And that's what our bodies were and are built to handle. For fifty million years our bodies had to deal with only minute amounts of carbohydrates—and *unrefined* carbohydrates, at that. Seven thousand years ago, when man learned to till the soil, the quantity of carbohydrates man consumed increased—but they were still unrefined. In other words these carbohydrates were not artificially concentrated by a milling or refining process. Only over the last century has a drastic change come about in what man eats and drinks, with the advent of a diet *predominantly* composed of refined carbohydrates.

The mechanism meant to metabolize the original tiny quantity we consumed has broken down under the killing onslaught of our Coke-cake-catsup-cookies-and-candy-bar culture. The result: overweight. Also cardiovascular disease, which accounts for the majority of deaths from *all* causes. Plus a whole spectrum of degenerative diseases previously unheard of.

THE NO-HUNGER RX FOR OVERWEIGHT: CUT CARBOHYDRATES, NOT CALORIES. Understanding the cause can point the way to the correct treatment. Removing carbohydrates from the diet is the most permanently effective treatment for overweight. One of the reasons that it is *remarkably* effective is because when you take away carbohydrates you take away hunger. (There's a biologic basis for this astonishing phenomenon, which you'll read about later.) There's no need to count calories. You eat and eat. To your heart's content. Never hungry, always losing.

You may be thinking, "But surely my body needs some carbohydrates?"

This is another of those preconceptions so deeply imbedded in our thinking (and I'm talking about doctors' minds here as well as patients') that it seems incredible that it isn't true.

WE NEED TO UNLEARN. But with our total body of knowledge exploding so in size, a big problem today for all of us is not to learn but to *unlearn*. And this idea about the *need* for carbohydrates is one of those old assumptions that just doesn't hold anymore, one of that legion of yesterday's "truths" that have become today's fictions.

"People and animals very likely can survive quite well on diets containing no carbohydrate, because the body can also use fats and proteins *directly* as sources of energy," we are told in the famous Department of Agriculture book, *Composition of Foods* (revised and reissued December 1963).

Philip K. Bondy, chairman of the Department of Internal Medicine at Yale University Medical School, and now the editor of Duncan's *Diseases of Metabolism*, the textbook that is virtually a bible for doctors in this field, writes: ". . . no carbohydrate is required in the diet . . . it has been shown experimentally that human beings can survive in good health for months on a diet of meats and fats."

And of course, carnivorous man survived for millions of years in a relatively low-carbohydrate world.

The total turnabout in man's diet, to the point where refined carbohydrates *dominate* it, has caused an evolutionary maladaptation that shows itself not just in adults but even in the young.

THE DAMAGE DONE BY CARBOHYDRATES STARTS EARLY. Arteries show damage startlingly early in life. Autopsies performed on many of the casualties of both the Korean War and the war in Vietnam showed grossly visible fatty deposits (atheromata) of the aortic wall in half these young men. *Their average age was twenty-two!* In other words their arteries already showed signs of serious damage which many recent studies attribute to years of overconsumption of refined carbohydrates along with a genetic predisposition to cardiovascular disease.

For carbohydrates—not fat—are the principal elements in food that fatten fat people. They do this both by preventing you from burning up your own fat and by stimulating your body to make more fat and by being used to make that fat. Protein and fat combinations alone do not do this.

So this diet is an anticarbohydrate diet, which takes off weight that low-calorie diets won't affect at all.

NINETY-THREE POUNDS LESS WEIGHT, MORE ENERGY. Lyn Duddy, who writes the music for the Jackie Gleason show, for years had tried every diet going without success, but then lost ninety-three pounds on his own personal limited edition of the anticarbohydrate diet. "I loathe fish. I hate cheese," he says. "So I lived pretty much on steak, chicken, and green salads. It wasn't difficult. For breakfast I had all the bacon and eggs I could get into me. And I could have mayonnaise on my lettuce and butter on my meat.

"I didn't know before I began that I had low blood sugar, but I did know that I didn't have much energy. I have a lot more now."

THE DIET THAT TREATS OVERWEIGHT AND ALL ITS DEADLY RELATIVES. *But this diet isn't just a reducing diet. It is the medical treatment of choice for most people with adult-onset diabetes, with cholesterol problems, with ulcer problems, with migraine, with heart and arterial disease, and especially for the fatigue and emotional disturbances that accompany hypoglycemia.*

All of these human scourges—and half a dozen others—can have their roots in a common cause: a metabolic disturbance resulting from the body's inability to deal with carbohydrates.

In the past we have found that uncovering the cause of a disease has made its control possible. This is no less true of these twentieth-century diseases.

IT TREATS THE CAUSE AS WELL AS THE SYMPTOMS. It is possible right now to control all these diseases, starting with the unsightly life-shortening condition of overweight.

I *know* this diet will work for you. It has worked on the thousands of patients who have come to me for treatment. More than that, it has apparently worked for thousands of patients who have not come to me for treatment but who have just read about the diet in the magazines and newspapers that have written about it—*Vogue, Harper's Bazaar, Town and Country, Cosmopolitan, Mademoiselle,* and *Fortune,* among others.

I KNOW THIS BOOK CAN CHANGE YOUR LIFE. Every time the diet has appeared I have received thousands of letters from all over this country and around the world. People write me that they find the diet easy to follow, that they are amazed and delighted at never being hungry. They write that they feel absolutely on top of the world, a great mood change. And they write that they are losing weight happily and effortlessly, that they *like* themselves now, that the diet has changed their lives.

I even hear from their doctors about diabetic and hypertensive conditions that the diet has corrected, about lowered cholesterol and triglyceride levels, in addition to dramatic losses in weight alone.

One thing I have learned is that there's no fixed formula that works for everybody. What I hope this book will do for you is steer you into an eating pattern that is best suited to *you:* your particular metabolism, tastes, habits, customs, likes, and dislikes. Because if you have a weight problem, then you have a problem for life. We doctors know this, but it's amazing how few patients can accept this self-evident fact.

2

THE DIET
REVOLUTION:
IT WILL
CHANGE YOUR
LIFE

THOUSANDS HAVE SUBTRACTED MANY POUNDS AND ADDED MANY GOOD YEARS TO THEIR LIVES WITH THIS ANTICARBOHYDRATE DIET REVOLUTION. Here are the highlights of it.

- With this diet you don't take pills because *you're never hungry.*
- Emotionally many people "fly high" from the very beginning.
- You don't count calories.
- You eat as *much* as you want, as *often* as you want.
- You eat *luxuriously*—heavy cream, butter, mayonnaise, cheeses, meats, fish, fowl (*and crisp green salads too*).
- Most people lose five to ten pounds the first week and two to five pounds a week after that.

- You lose inches even more dramatically than pounds.
- The second week you get a little of the carbohydrates you missed most (perhaps olives, wine, more vegetables).
- You get more carbohydrates in the weeks following until—
- You come to your *Critical Carbohydrate Level* (CCL). You know when this is reached because—
- Then your urine test sticks no longer turn purple. This means that—
- It's time to turn your carbohydrate intake *back* a few grams and then . . . that's *it*.
- You're on a diet so normal to stylish eaters that no one need ever know you're dieting.
- You're set to lose as much as you want and stay slim the rest of your life, because for the first time you know *exactly* how much carbohydrate *your* particular body can tolerate without being always fat, tired, hungry.
- Your appetite and metabolic system have normalized. Your figure has changed and so has your life.
- And by now you're *wedded* to eating this way and looking this way and feeling this way—fit, flat, and young—a whole cheerful new person.

Never mind about all those questions raised by what you've just read ("What *kind* of metabolic disorder?" "How can I possibly lose weight on mayonnaise and heavy cream?" "*What* urine test stick?"). I'll answer all these questions soon. First, let's get the difference between this and other low-carbohydrate diets straightened out.

THE VITAL DIFFERENCE BETWEEN THIS AND OTHER LOW-CARBOHYDRATE DIETS. You've heard of diets labeled "low-carbohydrate." Have you tried one? The Drinking Man's Diet? The so-called Air Force Diet? Carlton Fredericks's low-carbohydrate diets? Dr. John Yudkin's diet (*This Slimming Business*)? Dr. Blake Donaldson's diet (*Strong Medicine*)? There are many others—all a step in the right direction.

But there's a vital difference between those diets and this one. Most of those diets tell you to cut your carbohydrate intake down to sixty grams of carbohydrate a day. Right? There was a reason for this. On sixty grams of carbohydrate the body does not throw off ketones (little carbon fragments that are by-products of the incomplete burning of fat). You see, ketones were thought to be undesirable by the doctors who devised those diets. You'll read more about ketones later on. They are another one of those subjects about which a great deal has to be *unlearned*.

UNLEARN WHAT YOU'VE HEARD ABOUT KETONES FIRST. When a person is putting out ketones in the breath or urine, he is said to be "in ketosis."

Now for a carbohydrate-intolerant Mr. Fat to be in ketosis deliberately is a signal for rejoicing. It is a sign that the unwanted fat is being burned up as fuel. It is a sign of progress toward health, slimness, a stabilized blood sugar, lowered triglyceride levels . . . everything his heart desires —literally and figuratively!

Of course, if you are in ketosis after prolonged starvation or because you are a diabetic out of control, it has a different aspect. Then it indicates the presence of acidosis—and that is a danger signal.

Too many doctors have come to equate the two situations, although they are as different as night and day, and health and disease.

There is no acidosis when ketosis occurs as a normal concomitant of this diet.

I HAVE CHECKED THOUSANDS IN KETOSIS. Doctors who fear ketosis in a weight-reducing program such as this one have had no experience with the ketosis induced by a carbohydrate-free diet. I have, since this is my specialty.

For years I have regularly and carefully checked the well-being of thousands of people kept in ketosis for months on end. I have observed no ill effects and have never seen a state of acidosis as a result.

On the contrary, I have arrived at the conclusion that ketosis is a state devoutly to be desired, because while you are in this happy state (and I mean that literally, for an elevation of mood accompanies it as a rule) your fat is being burned off with *maximum* efficiency and *minimum* deprivation (since in ketosis your hunger disappears!).

NOT SIXTY GRAMS OF CARBOHYDRATES ON THE DIET BUT ZERO GRAMS. Here's how this diet is significantly different. During the first week on this diet, you cut your intake of carbohydrates down to what is biologically *zero*.

This creates a unique chemical situation in the body, the one favorable to the fastest possible burning of your body's stored fat. Ketones are excreted, and hunger disappears.

You see, *the first fuel your body burns for energy* comes from the carbohydrates you eat and drink. If any carbohydrate is available, your body burns this rather than stored fat—and maintains its old metabolic pathways. *But carbohydrates, as such, are not stored in the body beyond forty-eight hours.*

So when *no* carbohydrate is taken in, your body must draw upon the major reserve source of fuel—the stored fat.

It is forced to take a different metabolic pathway. In this process your body *converts from being a carbohydrate-burning engine into being a fat-burning engine.*

This is the diet revolution: the new chemical situation in which ketones are being thrown off—and so are those unwanted pounds, all without hunger.

GRADUAL ADDITIONS OF CARBOHYDRATE TO KEEP YOUR BODY BURNING ITS FAT FOR FUEL. We must *maintain* this chemical situation if you're to continue to lose without hunger. And if we add carbohydrate *very* gradually—in tiny amounts —we can do just this . . . *keep* your body converted into a fat-burning engine.

So that's just what we do. The second week you might

add a few more grams of carbohydrate to your diet. Every week thereafter a little more carbohydrate (around five grams) may be returned to the diet.

In this way—by a sort of chemical legerdemain—you're continuing to burn your own fat *just as hotly* as you did that first week on the diet.

How do we know this is so? We know because you're losing. We know because you're not hungry at any time. We know because you feel somewhere between more comfortable and absolutely marvelous. But we know for another reason, too.

DIFFERENCE NUMBER 2: "HEY, I'M TURNING PURPLE EVERY DAY." You see, while your body is burning off its fat at this clip, those substances I spoke of earlier, called *ketones,* are being thrown off both in the breath and in the urine. For dieters this is the happiest possible state to be in. It shows that the surplus body fat is being burned off.

It is easy to test the urine for the presence of ketones. An inexpensive test stick in the urine turns purple at one end when ketones are present. (The test sticks are available at any drugstore without prescription. You'll read more about all this later on.)

It is interesting—and very important—to keep track as you add your small increments of carbohydrates week by week. How can you be sure that your body is *still* converted into a fat-burning engine just as it was during the first week on this regimen?

Because with this diet you have an outward, visible (*checkable*) sign—the test sticks—that tell you you're burning off your fat at the healthy maximum rate. You can't be mistaken about whether your body is vigorously breaking down all those stored calories within you.

Also, ketones bring you another big bonus. The ketones in your urine and on your breath represent *incompletely burned calories.* This means that when you excrete or breathe out ketones *you are sneaking calories out of the body.* It's one of the reasons you can eat more calories than you burn up and—*as long as no carbohydrates are present*—*still* lose weight.

The ketones are the secret of this seemingly biochemical sleight-of-hand.

Hundreds of calories are sneaked out of your body every day in the form of ketones and a host of other incompletely broken down molecules of fat. You are disposing of these calories *not* by work or violent exercise—but just by breathing and allowing your kidneys to function. All this is achieved merely by cutting out your carbohydrates.

DIFFERENCE NO. 3: YOU'RE NEVER HUNGRY. YOU CAN EAT WITHOUT LIMIT SOLID "FATTENING" FOOD. On this diet you're allowed to eat truly luxurious foods without limit—for example, lobster with butter sauce, steak with Béarnaise sauce, and not merely hamburgers, but rich-tasting cheeseburgers, or even better, *bacon* cheeseburgers. Eating like this could be the reason why you're never hungry.

Yet oddly enough, it isn't. The weight loss of thousands of my patients proves that the basic reason you can lose on all this rich food is this fantastic fact: *As long as you don't take in carbohydrates, you can eat any amount of this "fattening" food and it won't put a single ounce of fat on you.*

A GENIE WITH THE INITIALS FMH KEEPS YOU UN-HUNGRY WHILE YOU LOSE. The basic reason that you lose without hunger on this diet is because of your altered metabolism. This kind of *un-hungriness* is a whole new experience.

You see, by cutting carbohydrates down to zero, you have summoned a powerful genie to your aid—a substance put out by the pituitary gland called the Fat Mobilizing Hormone (FMH) or FMS, as it was originally named.

This fat mobilizing material was not isolated as a pure substance until 1960, when three English researchers, Dr. T. M. Chalmers, Professor Alan Kekwick, and Dr. G. L. S. Pawan of Middlesex Hospital in London, were able to recover this substance from the urine of animals and humans who were on diets that contained *no* carbohydrates.

WHY DIDN'T PEOPLE LOSE ON A 1,000 CALORIE ALL-CARBOHYDRATE DIET? In search of the mechanism that caused this result, they analyzed the urine of the patients on varying diets and found no FMH (fat mobilizing hormone) present during the term of the diets containing carbohydrate but plenty of it in the urine during the terms of the diets composed either of all fat and/or protein and no carbohydrate.

In other words FMH is a natural substance of the human body that is only produced when the diet contains little or no carbohydrate. And its presence in the urine means that the individual is using up his fat stores as body fuel. What is in the urine is what is left over after it has done its work of tapping the fat stores.

Now we don't know precisely how this (or any other) hormone works. We can only observe what happens.

WHAT IS THE SIGNAL THAT SUMMONS UP THE GENIE? Apparently the signal for the pituitary gland to release the fat mobilizing hormone into the bloodstream is the absence in the diet of ready fuel—in other words, carbohydrate. When no carbohydrate is available, the body says to the pituitary, "I need fuel. Break down my fat so I can get some."

By cutting carbohydrates, this marvelous natural body substance—FMH—this magic bullet—is released by the pituitary and circulated in the bloodstream.

And the production of FMH is the whole purpose of this diet—and the reason it works when all other diets fail.

The presence of FMH circulating in your bloodstream guarantees that you are being *continuously* fed fuel which originates from your own unwanted stores of fat. This is so because the FMH makes your fat storage depots *continually* available to your body as fuel.

But remember, the magic key here is *no carbohydrates* to begin—and later, carbohydrates added only very gradually in tiny amounts as discussed earlier in this chapter, and explained more fully later.

THE FOURTH DIFFERENCE: EVEN THE MOST STUBBORN NONLOSER LOSES. It has almost never happened that a patient has come back at the end of the first week on the diet and said, "Doctor, I followed your diet—and I didn't lose." On the rare occasions when this has happened, we have always been able to find a correctible reason (see chapter 14).

But there is an enormous difference in the ease and speed with which different people lose. Singer Leslie Uggams is an easy loser. It only takes her a few days to shed pounds on the anticarbohydrate diet.

Doris Lilly, the author and columnist, is another easy loser. *She lost twenty pounds the first month—and has stayed slim five years.* One of my associates interviewed her using a tape recorder. This is how she tells about her weight loss:

"I was *struggling* into a size 16, and there aren't any size 18s except in the tent department. But I got taken out a lot. I sort of didn't notice. Then one night I was on the Merv Griffin show, wearing a new shiny Norell dress. It was a taped show. When I saw myself on the screen, I cried! I looked like a shiny silver tub. Fat, fat, fat! I went for dinner to the Uchitels (he owned El Morocco at the time) and I was crying, and she told me about Dr. Atkins.

"So I went to him and lost forty pounds, twenty of them the first month. No shots. No pills, except Dr. Atkins gave me megadoses of vitamins, including Vitamin C. That's because I don't have orange juice for breakfast, I guess.

"All it takes is guts. You certainly get plenty to eat. Of course I don't drink. That helps. Oh, I'll take one Scotch occasionally. Not more.

"He changed my whole habit of eating. I haven't had a loaf of bread in the house since. Like so many Americans, I used to have a sandwich for lunch. Now it's grilled meat and fish. No problem. I wear a size ten. My bra size went from 40D to 36C. Even my feet are smaller. I gave away all my shoes, in fact all my clothes but my handbags and fur coats. It's five years now, and I've never gained it back."

CALORIE COUNTING CAN'T HELP STUBBORN NONLOSERS. I see only a few lucky people who lose quickly and almost without effort. Most overweight patients have lived their lives entirely around a heartbreaking series of diets that haven't worked.

I love to see these patients at the end of the first week on this diet. I wouldn't give up that satisfaction for anything. They invariably have lost weight, and without hunger. A biochemical miracle has happened. They dare to hope again. For many, this week signals the beginning of a new life: a rebirth.

You can lose on this diet—even people who haven't been able to lose living on only 800 or 900 calories a day for month after month. I feel that people with this metabolic resistance to weight loss are *handicapped* people. This diet unlocks that resistance, while a low-calorie diet can't touch it. One of my patients, Perry Zenlea, is one of those handicapped people. But once he *stopped* counting calories and *started* counting grams of carbohydrate he came out of that category.

PERRY ZENLEA WAS A HEROIC DIETER—BUT FAT JUST THE SAME. Perry Zenlea, forty-five, is an engineer, and one of the most disciplined characters I've met in my practice. Even when he was nine, fat boy clothes had to be made especially for him. He's been fat all his life.

Such is Perry Zenlea's metabolic handicap that *he gains if he eats more than 1,100 calories a day*. This is unusual in a male, since male metabolism runs higher than female.

Most of his life he's been starving on 900 calories a day. So he would gain and lose, gain and lose, almost always hungry, feeling rotten, and with very poor future prospects indeed. Nobody can live that way indefinitely.

HE STARVED ON 900 CALORIES A DAY FOR MONTH AFTER MONTH. He had lost fifty pounds by existing miserably for months on a 900-calorie-a-day diet when he came to me. He had already regained 26 of those pounds and weighed 268¾ pounds. He rarely had a drink. He had never been an eater of sweets. How could he continue to stay this heavy?

Now he has been on the zero-carbohydrate diet for over a year and has lost ninety-nine pounds. His suit size went from 56 to 40.

His metabolic resistance to losing is so great that it has never been possible for him to lose when we tried adding any carbohydrate at all to his diet. So, he is still basically on the first week's diet—a biologically carbohydrate-free diet. And he still has weight to lose. But don't feel sorry for him.

HE LOST THAT NINETY-NINE POUNDS WITHOUT HUNGER AND WITHOUT COUNTING CALORIES! "This is the greatest thing that ever happened to me," he keeps telling me. "It's a new way of life. I'm never hungry. It's wonderful. I don't want to go off this diet—ever!"

Perry Zenlea eats such a big dinner (sometimes as much as one and one-half pounds of meat, salad or one-half cup of green vegetables, and D-Zerta) that he can't eat breakfast (except for a cup of coffee with heavy cream and sweetener). His lunch is usually bacon and two scrambled eggs. If he feels like it, he eats cheese between meals and before bed.

"I've been getting younger every week since I came," he says. "Not just that I look and feel younger. It's a physical fact. I am younger." And he's right.

Zenlea, the son of two diabetic parents, was a known diabetic. He was taking medication for this when he came to me. He was also a hypertensive, requiring more medication for that. I was able to get him off all his medications. His blood pressure and blood sugar are both now normal. His cholesterol, which was 335 on his first visit, fell to a normal reading of 215.

If, like Perry Zenlea, you have stuck to low-calorie diets in spite of the hunger and deprivation that goes with them, I can say to you that your worries are over. You have demonstrated that you have the personal qualities it takes to win. And combined with the technical know-how you'll find in this book, they should enable you to weigh what you'd like to weigh the rest of your life.

3

HOW

I ARRIVED AT

THIS DIET

REVOLUTION

I hope in this book to change your weight, your outlook on life, your life itself. Discovering this diet did all these things for me. Let me tell you how it came about.

I started off as a very thin child. When I got out of high school I was 6 feet tall and weighed only 135 pounds. I was the skinniest kid on the block. My parents had tried to get me to eat, and all of us were happy when I finally developed one hell of an appetite. At college I became the biggest eater on campus.

It finally began to take. I put on forty pounds by the time I graduated. Then I gained more weight in medical school, and during my internship and residency. I had the reputation of being the biggest chow-hound in the hospital. I was overweight, but my image of myself was that I was skinny, so it didn't bother me.

It wasn't until 1963, after another ten years of gaining, that I suddenly realized, seeing myself in a photograph, that I had three chins. The photo was on my identification badge for my new job as medical consultant for AT&T. I knew it was I because it had my name on it, but I thought I'd better double-check. "Do I really have three chins?" I asked the nurse. She nodded. So there it was. I was no longer a skinny kid. I was a fat man, and I looked fifteen years older than I really was.

EVEN THE IDEA OF HUNGER SCARES ME. Well, I guess I'd known it quite a while. But I'd been faced with another problem. I was literally afraid of dieting. I was afraid of being hungry. I think a lot of people don't go on diets because they fear hunger. There must be millions of people who react the way I do. Every overweight person has experimented at some point in his life with eating less—and then been defeated by hunger. For him this kind of dieting is a biologically improper adaptation.

I knew about diets. But the trouble was they all told me to stop when I had eaten seven or eight ounces of my steak. That's only half a portion. I knew from experience that halfway through a steak I was hungrier than when I sat down. I knew that I could never follow a low-calorie diet for even one day.

AND I HAVE ALMOST NO WILLPOWER. I have a big appetite, but I have very little willpower. If I am with a group of people waiting at a restaurant where the service is slow, I always did and still will call over the waiter and say, "Look, give me something to eat while I'm waiting to be served." I have no tolerance for hunger. However, since I had to carry that badge and look at those three chins every day, I decided I'd better try to do something about my extra weight.

Looking back at this period in my life I realize what a fortunate thing it was that my training had been in cardiology and not in metabolism. If I had been trained in nutrition and metabolism, I'd be parroting the same classical misconceptions that so many of my colleagues still hang on to. Being free of these misconceptions, allowed my mind then—and since— to approach the observable facts without prejudice. Anyhow,

I started out by researching the medical literature for some sort of a clue as to what I could do for myself.

ONE CAN FAST—YET NOT BE HUNGRY? One evening I read about the work that Dr. Garfield Duncan had done in nutrition at the University of Pennsylvania. Fasting patients, he reported, lose all sense of hunger after forty-eight hours without food. That *stunned* me. Incredible that I could find myself not hungry after going without food for forty-eight hours. How could that possibly be? That defied logic. I wanted to know why.

I WAS LOOKING FOR "THE HUNGRY MAN'S DIET." As I searched, I found more pieces of the puzzle. I read the work of two of those brilliant English researchers, Professor Kekwick and Dr. Pawan, who had shown that a fat-mobilizing substance was present in the urine when that diet had been free of *carbohydrate* for forty-eight hours. This and the presence of ketone bodies in the urine signified *that the body was satisfying its hunger by burning its own fat as fuel.*

NO CARBOHYDRATES ALSO MEANS NO HUNGER! Great news, I thought. If the absence of carbohydrate can switch one's body engine over from being a carbohydrate-burning engine to being a fat-burning engine, then perhaps I can eat all of my steak (which is carbohydrate free) and lose my fat at the same time! And a wonderful by-product could be that like Garfield Duncan's fasting patients, I wouldn't be hungry.

At the same time, I came upon some important information from the late Dr. Alfred W. Pennington, of the DuPont Company, who postulated that overweight is frequently explained by an intrinsic metabolic defect. He suggested a treatment for it that does not restrict calories.

DR. PENNINGTON HAD PROVED IT ON DUPONT EMPLOYEES. He had proved that his treatment worked shortly after World War II, when the medical division of the DuPont Company gave him the job of trying to find out why low-calorie diets failed with so many of their staff members. As a result of his studies, Pennington decided that overweight could be caused, not by overeating, but by a metabolic defect—an inability of the body to utilize carbohydrates for anything except making fat.

So he designed a test diet. Twenty staff members volunteered to try it. The diet eliminated sugar and starches and gave protein and fat instead. This, of course, was a ketogenic diet—which means that the absence of carbohydrates caused ketones to be spilled over in the urine, a sign that the fat-mobilizing hormone is circulating in the bloodstream.

There was no calorie counting on Dr. Pennington's diet. The basic diet allowed 3,000 calories a day but anyone who was hungry was free to eat without limit.

During the test period, all twenty of his dieters reported that they felt well and were never hungry. And at the end they had lost an average of twenty-two pounds in an average of three and one-half months. Those who had high blood pressure discovered happily that it had dropped, parallel to their drop in weight.

I READ ABOUT A DIET I FELT I'D LIKE TO TRY MYSELF. Finally I read about the ketogenic diet that Dr. Walter Lyons Bloom of Atlanta, Georgia, reported on. The purpose of the diet was merely to test the metabolic changes in a no-carbohydrate diet, *not* to treat patients. He was able to show that the same remarkable disappearance of hunger that occurred during a fast also occurred on a no-carbohydrate diet. And because absence of hunger was what I was looking for, I was fascinated with Dr. Bloom's diet.

It sounded delicious to me—bacon and eggs for breakfast, plenty of meat, and even salad for lunch and dinner.

After each of the papers that I mentioned appeared, it always was followed by a rash of others fiercely disputing these findings. But in spite of their critics, these new concepts sounded to me like logical and promising alternatives to low-calorie dieting.

In 1963 I decided to try Walter Bloom's diet. It's very

easy for me to remember when this happened. At that time I had been working with a diagnostic clinic that I thought was going to contribute enormously to medicine in New York. Then the hospital where we were practicing was sold, and the clinic folded. Everything in my life seemed to be breaking wrong. It was in the midst of this depression that I decided to go on this diet. I don't know where I found the courage. I guess it wasn't courage. It was desperation, really. I began on this ketogenic diet in spite of having read a great many medical papers telling me that it wasn't sound, that it wouldn't work.

I BEGIN MY HUNGRY MAN'S DIET—AND CHECKING FOR KETONES. Of course it was easy for me to check for the presence of ketone bodies in the urine. I had known how to do that since my second year in medical school. An ordinary urine test stick, or tablet devised for this purpose, and available at any drugstore for the asking, turns purple on testing when ketone bodies are present.

I soon discovered that even if I added ten or fifteen grams of carbohydrate, after a zero carbohydrate start, the test tablet still turned purple. This meant that my body was continuing to burn up my fat. I could snack on cheese, cold cuts, cold shrimp, cottage cheese, and have a filling salad with each meal. For dessert I discovered creamy ricotta cheese, which I enhanced with artificial sweeteners and flavored many different ways (see recipe section for some of them).

NOT HUNGRY EVEN ON FORTY GRAMS OF CARBOHYDRATE. By trial and error I found as time went on that I could have thirty-five to forty grams of carbohydrates a day and still lose, without hunger, if I added them *gradually* enough. That meant some vegetables, sometimes melon, big fresh strawberries smothered in whipped cream. I even found that I could resume an occasional Scotch and water before dinner.

And I was eating all day. Small meals—but eating. I made it a point to go home from the hospital three times or so a day to fill up again.

When I started being my own guinea pig, I knew I was going to eat a lot of food and felt that I would be lucky to lose three or four pounds in a month. I was truly surprised—in fact it was probably the greatest surprise of my life—*when at the end of six weeks on this diet I had lost twenty-eight pounds!*

I FELT AN ODD COMBINATION OF MIXED EMOTIONS AT LOSING SO MUCH SO FAST. Of course I was delighted. But that wasn't all. What I felt actually was a combination of exhilaration and resentment: exhilaration because of the gratifying amount of weight I had lost, and resentment that I had been duped so long by the misinformation given me in the medical literature.

What I had read was the same tired, fifty-year-old nutritional dogma that is still being dished out today: that there is only one way to lose weight—a low-calorie diet.

With my big appetite, of course, that was always out for me. Now I thought, "How can so many experts be so wrong for so long? Because I lost that weight not on a low-calorie diet but on a carbohydrate-free diet of high-calorie foods, eating all I wanted."

THE MORE I ATE, THE MORE I LOST. I actually ate this weight off. I spent more time eating during those six weeks than usual. This was because the very idea of dieting made me afraid of being hungry. I never was hungry. I was just afraid that I would be hungry, so I kept eating. And it didn't seem to slow me down.

The thing I remember most about those days was waking in the morning an hour or so before my alarm rang because I wanted to feel my belly, feel how it was smaller every day. I used to jump out of bed at six in the morning in a frenzy of excitement to find out whether I had lost another pound or two. And invariably the scale showed that I had.

Later I found that this early wakening might not just have been the excitement of seeing my body image change. It was probably due to the fact that my blood sugar was being stabilized by my very low-carbohydrate diet. This always results in a big lift in energy and spirits.

Thinking back on that time, I didn't realize how sleepy, tired, and lazy I had always been until I went on my diet. I thought I felt well before I started the diet. It was only after I had been on the diet that I noticed the improvement and suddenly realized that I really hadn't been feeling up to par. This is a phenomenon I invite all readers to experience.

SIXTY-FIVE AT&T EMPLOYEES TRY MY DIET AND LOSE WEIGHT. Of course my new colleagues in the medical department at AT&T noticed those twenty-eight pounds drop off. And they noticed how much I was eating, how good I was feeling. It wasn't hard to convince everybody that a weight-control pilot study would be good preventive medicine for our personnel.

We ended with sixty-five people on my diet. The results were astonishing. Without a single exception, every individual who started on the program not only got down to his ideal weight but remained there. Nobody ever complained of being hungry. Some volunteered that they had never eaten so much. Most averaged a loss of eighteen pounds in the first month.

One executive lost sixty-six pounds in four months, felt that he "had been physically and mentally rejuvenated." Another, who lost fifty-four pounds in five months, especially liked the fact that the weight loss "fixed the trouble I had with my feet, which prevented my walking more than half an hour without great pain. I'm now able to go hiking . . ." Still another, who lost twenty-eight pounds in five weeks, said he felt "like a new man. I do more walking, running, exercising than ever before."

HOW THIS DIET DIFFERS FROM OTHER "LOW-CARBOHY-DRATE" DIETS. It was in 1964, while I was testing this diet program at AT&T, that a rash of diets featuring sixty grams of carbohydrates became popular: the Air Force Diet, the Drinking Man's Diet, the Martinis and Whipped Cream Diet.

Carlton Fredericks came out with a sixty-gram diet. So did a man I have mentioned admiring greatly, John Yudkin.

Everyone said, "Hey, look, they've got your diet, doc." I said, "Well, I don't know."

I knew that if my patients were to keep losing they had to be kept in ketosis—so that the urine test sticks turned purple. In contrast, all the sixty-gram diets were designed specifically to cut carbohydrate intake but *prevent* ketosis. Many people can use a sixty-gram diet for maintenance after they've lost weight, and of course the person who cuts his carbohydrate intake suddenly—from a habitual four or five hundred grams to sixty—is going to get a pretty dramatic response at first. But for the sophisticated dieter or the reasonable eater who has been cutting down on carbohydrates already, there's not much weight loss on a sixty-gram diet.

THIS DIET WORKS 100 PERCENT OF THE TIME! I think the important thing was that right from the start I knew with great certainty that I was working with a diet that worked dramatically and worked all the time. This of course has given me a great deal of personal strength in dealing with patients. When a patient says the diet doesn't work, I know that it does. That it *has* to work. And therefore that something is being done wrong. Eventually patients accept this. We discover what is being done wrong, and the diet always works.

I hope the same thing will happen as you read this book. You're an expert on diets, I know. Why not try this diet and compare your reactions? Judge for yourself whether or not you feel better on it, have more energy, feel less hungry . . . just generally enjoy the whole experience more. I question all my patients on this score. I have learned from them that when people have tried both a good low-carbohydrate diet and a good low-calorie diet, 95 percent of them will report that it is far easier to go without carbohydrates than calories!

I BLEW BLOOM'S DIET WIDE OPEN SO THAT YOU CAN EAT THIS WAY ALL YOUR LIFE. This isn't a short-term approach; it's a lifelong way of eating. You'll end up with a diet that's as personal to you as a pair of contact lenses. It's the happy way of eating—plentiful, palatable, varied.

I quite deliberately opened up Bloom's test diet so that this should be so. His was a three-day diet. And, as I said earlier, it was designed merely to observe the metabolic effect of a zero carbohydrate diet. It was bacon and eggs, meat and salad, period.

This was his purpose—fine for a short-term experimental diet. But what I wanted was a diet I could live with and enjoy the rest of my life. So I evolved this diet, by trial and error. I added mayonnaise, butter, and the other fats I loved.

I also added the concept of gradually adding carbohydrates until the break-off point—*the Critical Carbohydrate Level*—is reached.

It makes all the difference in the world, psychologically, to be able to eat luxuriously and substantially on a diet—to have heavy cream in one's coffee, whipped cream on berries, mayonnaise, fried foods, fatty meats such as pastrami and pâté, butter sauces—and to be able to have all the good desserts you'll read about in the recipe section of this book (especially my cheesecake, which is the staff of life to most of my patients!).

ITS FLEXIBILITY IS JUST ABOUT INFINITE. There's no limit to its flexibility. And it's the only way of eating that will keep you unhungrily slim for the rest of your life. To your over-worked pancreas (or your recurring overweight), carbohydrates are poison. Perhaps you will have to *ration* your poison the rest of your life. But with the lessons to be learned in this book, it can be done with less sacrifice, less willpower, than you think. I have told you how little willpower I have, yet despite this minute amount of willpower I have been able to stay on my diet all the years since I first devised it.

There's no need to set any speed records in weight loss. What we're aiming at is a comfort record—a *lifetime* way of eating.

And the reason that this is a diet revolution is that you *can* eat this way comfortably, luxuriously, without deprivation, without a single hunger pang all your life—*losing* in pounds and inches, *gaining* in energy, happiness, health.

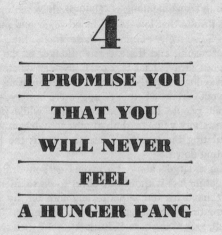

4

I PROMISE YOU
THAT YOU
WILL NEVER
FEEL
A HUNGER PANG

"I don't have any willpower. Is it really true that one can lose weight on this diet without hunger? And without pills either?"

I hear this question very often. My answer is—absolutely! There's no question about it. Hunger is what takes place when people try to cut down the quantitative intake of food in order to lose weight.

But quantity cutting is not the only way to lose weight. The other way, the more natural way, is merely by eliminating the carbohydrates. Then it is not necessary to worry about how much you eat. When you can eat as much as you want at any hour of the day or night, how can you ever get hungry?

WHEN IN DOUBT—EAT! "How can you eat as much as you want and still lose weight?" I hear this question, too, from

31

new patients. I explain to them, if you understood more about the physiology of overweight you'd know why. You see, virtually all overweight people have one very important disturbance in their metabolism. They produce too much insulin. And it is insulin that lowers the blood sugar and makes people hungry. Selectively eliminate those foods that trigger the release of insulin and the excessive hunger of the overweight person goes away. That is why I say—eat whatever it takes to satisfy your hunger—except insulin-stimulating foods, and if you're not certain whether or not you're hungry, eat anyway!

What people fail to realize is that while proteins and fats have satiety value, carbohydrates actually provoke hunger by stimulating the insulin release that sends the blood sugar plummeting down.

Even a large eater who avoids carbohydrates will find himself eating less without any effort to do so, merely because he won't have his old appetite anymore on my diet. That's how dramatically satiating this way of eating is.

Well, look at the case of Ruth S.

RUTH WAS SO DESPERATE TO LOSE THAT SHE HAD PUT HERSELF IN A HOSPITAL. Ruth was twenty-seven when she came to see me two years ago, a tall good-looking brunet who weighed 283 pounds. She had a good job, good friends, a good psychiatrist, but a sad history as to overweight. Even in college she weighed 182 pounds. For six years she lost and gained, lost and gained with pills. When she weighed 266, she went to Weight Watchers, lost 30 pounds slowly, and quickly regained it. Then she grew desperate. She put herself in a hospital. In six months she dropped from 263 to 196. Six months later she weighed 263 pounds again.

She was almost without hope when she came to ask me whether there was any point to starting another diet program. When I saw her, she was the heaviest she had ever been. There was no history of diabetes. She was just plain fat. She had a 300-pound sister, a 230-pound mother, and a bottomless capacity for potato chips and Cokes.

"I was disgusted, and low, so utterly demoralized when I came to see you," she says.

I had hope, however. Ruth was clearly a tryer. Cutting yourself off from food and friends in a hospital at twenty-five takes guts.

WHO WOULD BELIEVE SHE WAS DIETING? "Eating this new way was hard in the beginning," she says. "Just the change. But you build up flexibility as you go along with it. I could change because I was always perfectly satisfied. I was never hungry. I never counted calories.

"I felt guilty, though. There I would be in a restaurant, weighing 280 pounds, which is no small bud. And I would order scampi for an appetizer, then a salad and maybe frogs' legs in garlic butter. And I would have cream in my coffee. People watching me were bound to think, 'Why doesn't she go on a diet?' And I *was* on a diet!

"I don't feel that it's a diet though. It's just a different way of eating that I love. I always used to be exhausted and depressed. The weight would trigger off one depression after another. Now I have so much more energy. I still have more to lose but I feel so much confidence in myself. The pressures are off. I enjoy walking along the street and seeing the men turn around to look at me. It's a great feeling."

SHE LOST 120 POUNDS WITHOUT ONCE FEELING DEPRIVED. The 120 pounds she lost didn't come off quickly. But the point is that by now she knows the score. "I can never again eat the way most people do," she says. "But I enjoy the way I eat. I've never deviated. I just couldn't. As a matter of fact, I eat better than most people do. I believe in that. Never have a plain hamburger—have a cheeseburger; have chicken breasts with mozzarella, Béarnaise on your fillet. And I love Swiss cheese and lox. How can I feel deprived?"

AS STRONG AS DIET PILLS—WITHOUT THEIR BAD SIDE EFFECTS. This absence of hunger is a major advantage of the carbohydrate-free diet. Patients report that the action of the diet is as strong as that of diet pills in suppressing appetite. Yet there aren't any of the pills' sleep-destroying, nervousness-making, addicting side effects. However, there is a uniform and dramatic decrease in appetite. This is reported by at least 90 percent of all patients who go on the carbohydrate-free diet. They comment voluntarily that they can't understand what happened to their appetites. "I can't even finish what's on my plate these days and it used to be that I always had seconds."

I DON'T BELIEVE THAT MOST OVEREATING IS "PSYCHO-LOGICAL." It's my opinion that overeating is not as psychological in origin as it's cracked up to be. I don't believe that many people want to eat huge quantities of food because they need the psychological balm that food provides. They overeat merely because their own metabolic abnormality makes them feel that degree of hunger.

When the metabolic pathways are rerouted through this special diet, this excessive appetite goes away. Then many of these same people have quite a small appetite, I have found.

CRAVINGS FOR SWEETS ARE OFTEN A SYMPTOM. Have you ever had dinner with a big dessert and almost immediately afterward had a terrific craving for candy? Such untimely hunger cravings are (like fatigue) one of the symptoms of a deranged carbohydrate metabolism. On the diet in this book these cravings disappear.

And this freedom from bizarre hunger is another one of the built-in punishment and reward features of the diet that makes it easy to live with. It's so good to enjoy food but never to suffer a hunger pang while sloughing off the pounds. And as long as one stays completely with the diet, that's how life is.

On the other hand if you cheat, if you start loading in carbohydrates, suddenly you're starved. You hate yourself but you can't stop eating. The pounds and bumps and bulges pile back. Up goes your weight, down goes your energy.

WHAT ABOUT COMPULSIVE EATERS? On a first visit patients frequently tell me, "I can't stop eating. Whenever I'm upset, I go to the refrigerator and eat. How can you possibly help me if that's the kind of person I am?"

I say, "Great!" That's exactly what I want you to keep on doing. Every time you're upset I want you to go straight to the refrigerator and eat some protein food. I don't want to take away the role that food plays as a salver of injured feelings or a lifter of depression. I merely want you to make sure that the food is not carbohydrates. But I think going to the refrigerator and eating a piece of cold fried chicken from yesterday, or having some of your favorite cheese, or one of the "safe" desserts we tell you how to make later in this book —that's exactly what you should do when you're upset.

AVOID BEING "ANY KIND OF HUNGRY." People who eat when they're upset don't worry me because on a protein/fat diet there's a satiety carry-over of twenty-four or even forty-eight hours. So even stuffing yourself one day on protein/fat isn't so terrible, because invariably there's a diminished intake the following day, I have discovered.

What's bad news is being hungry—"any kind of hungry," emotional or physical. Every time a person has to contend with hunger the possibility of long-range success in weight loss becomes very questionable indeed.

No patient on this diet can be hungry. When a patient comes back after the first week and reports being hungry I say, "Then, eat more! Eat enough protein so that you're not hungry." And, of course, the following week he's back reporting that he ate more, wasn't hungry—and yet he has lost weight.

WATCH OUT FOR PREHUNGER SIGNALS. I hear people say, "Well, I'm never hungry, I'm just a compulsive eater." Most of these people do most of their eating between meals, especially just after dinner. I contend that this so-called compulsive eating is in reality a response to a prehunger signal—an inner prompting that is not easily recognized as hunger because the stomach is full—even though the blood sugar is plummeting. When these "unhungry" overeaters go on the carbohydrate-free diet, the nonstop nibbling pattern ceases abruptly. The early hunger signal is apparently wiped out by the diet's appetite-killing, blood-sugar-stabilizing effect.

"It's a mystery," patients tell me. "I've been a big between-meal eater all my life. And now suddenly I'm not. It's spooky. Did you hypnotize me on my first visit? Are you sure those vitamins you prescribed aren't diet pills?"

DON'T CALORIES PLAY ANY ROLE IN A CARBOHYDRATE-FREE DIET? Counting calories in this context serves very little purpose. On the contrary, it merely increases the likelihood of breaking the diet (as you'll read in chapter 8). Of course there's no question but that a 1,500-calorie, ten-gram carbohydrate diet will take off weight more quickly than a 2,000-calorie, ten-gram carbohydrate diet. If the carbohydrate levels remain unchanged, then the extra calorie intake does make a difference, but it is not of great magnitude.

People who eat double portions out of habit sometimes continue on a very high calorie intake. Overeaters, unfamiliar with the new level of satiety to be achieved on this diet, sometimes think they still have to eat double portions. If they'd try eating less, they'd find they were just as comfortable.

If you're in a hurry to lose, you are better off to restrict quantities, but not when it gets to the point where you have to put up with feeling deprived. Then it just doesn't pay.

HE LOST TWENTY-THREE POUNDS IN TWENTY-EIGHT DAYS ON 2,500 CALORIES A DAY. However, there are studies showing that even if you eat 2,500 or 3,000 calories you can lose weight on a carbohydrate-free diet—and not just for the short haul.

I remember one of my very first patients. He was an accountant; he tabulated everything he ate to the ounce, made the proper conversion into calories, and submitted to me the documented record. In a month (twenty-eight days) of eating 2,500 calories a day he showed a twenty-three-pound weight loss.

Now that is more than a short-term loss—and this was not just a loss of fluid. The man had gone down two suit sizes in those twenty-eight days. And this is not an isolated case. I have treated thousands like him. Take Max S., for example.

HE LOST FIFTY POUNDS ON 5,000 CALORIES A DAY. Being a three-hundred-pounder whose catering job gives him free and easy access to food, Max took me quite literally when I said, "Eat all you want." When my curiosity made me ask him to weigh the quantities of meat he was consuming, it came to four pounds of meat per day—at least 5,000 calories. On these quantities, Max still lost fifty pounds!

HE LOST ONE HUNDRED POUNDS WHILE EATING ENOUGH FOR FOUR PEOPLE. Every day I talk to many other patients who lose while eating really fantastic amounts of food. Marc Eletz is one of these. A tall (5 feet, 11 inches) young tax consultant, he was twenty-six when he came to me in November a year ago, and he weighed 302 pounds. At seventeen he weighed 190. He had been to six doctors during his teens. His weight would go up and down, up and down.

About four years before he had spent almost nine months at Duke University on its rice diet—a test of fortitude and real immolation for any young man, especially one who likes to eat as Marc does. It took him nine painful months to lose forty-nine pounds there, and he gained it back, of course.

Then he tried his sixth diet doctor, the one who gives the most pills of all. He lost, then he gained. In the six weeks before he came to see me he had regained thirty pounds.

"How long can you expect to live?" I asked him. "Why eat enough for four people?"

"Because if I ate enough for three people, I'd still be hungry," he said. "And I couldn't take being hungry anymore."

Marc hasn't finished losing yet, but in the year that he has been with me he has lost just one hundred pounds. That isn't so remarkable. What is remarkable is the record I asked him to keep of what he was eating while he was losing that hundred pounds.

Marc ordinarily eats only two meals a day. He has breakfast around eleven o'clock. On weekdays it's usually a three- or four-egg cheese omelet, plus a cup of cottage cheese with sour cream. Dinner on weekdays is around four or five o'clock. Here are a few dinners at random from his daily record:

22 June 1970:	Six lamb chops, salad.
23 June 1970:	Seven frankfurters and sauerkraut.
24 June 1970:	Two and one-half pounds of lobster, string beans.
24 July 1970:	Two dozen spareribs, steak, cheese, a big salad.
25 July 1970:	Three eggs with cottage cheese, one dozen spareribs, one pound of chicken.
26 July 1970:	One and one-half pounds of chuck steak with fried onions.

On weekends, both meals are later and considerably bigger.

Marc Eletz isn't a fantasy. He is a fact, a living proof that it isn't the *number* of calories but the *kind* of calories that count.

He is able to stay with this diet because he is never hungry. He can indulge his outsized appetite and lose weight steadily because he keeps below his Critical Carbohydrate Level. And that means he is not depositing fat, he is using up his own fat at the rate of a couple of pounds a week even on these gargantuan meals.

What makes this diet work for him is not only its nature but its flexibility.

But these are extreme cases. A more typical case history might be that of Milton Braten.

HE LOSES, AND HIS CHOLESTEROL DROPS ON EGGS AND HUGE STEAKS. Milton Braten (5 feet, 10½ inches and thirty-six years old) is one of those born-hungry people, who continues to eat a lot even under the appetite-quelling regime of an almost carbohydrate-free diet. Though neither his father nor mother are overweight, he has always been heavy.

His diet breakfast every morning: a two-egg cheese omelet and coffee with heavy cream. He has his big meal at noon, a really huge steak, often a full pound, with lettuce and blue cheese dressing. For dinner he has more beef—usually three-fourths of a pound of chopped steak—more salad (or a green vegetable), D-Zerta (sometimes), and coffee.

Milton lost twenty pounds in two months eating this much—lost slowly, steadily, and needless to say, without hunger.

What is just as important for his future prospects, in these two months of eating all these eggs and all this beef, is that his triglyceride level went down from 180 to 90, and his cholesterol level from 317 to 213.

MILTON BRATEN EATS A LOT, SUSAN HEILBRON EATS VERY LITTLE—BUT NEITHER ARE HUNGRY ON THE DIET. Young Susan Heilbron has always been fat. As my patient she has lost ninety-four pounds in seven months. And this is the first time she has ever lost more than thirty-five pounds. Nevertheless, I would prefer to see her eat more. But she's a one-meal-a-day girl. (No breakfast, a can of diet cola for lunch, then fish or meat with salad—all she wants—for dinner.) But she is so happy and says, "I know I can eat if I want to, so I never feel deprived. But I just don't feel hungry."

In seven months this eating pattern has stabilized. Her health is good (the diabetes she demonstrated when she came to me is now no longer detectable), her energy is high. So I accept the fact that this is how she is, and no two people are alike. She says, "It makes eating the old way seem insane. I feel positively guilty losing because I'm so happy with what I eat." And, "It's as if I'd been in a wheelchair all my life and suddenly I find I can run and walk. I love living so much now that it's just incredible." And, "Food is not on my mind anymore, and it used to be all I ever thought of."

Well, anyhow, I can't doubt but that Susan on her one meal a day is as unhungry as Milton is on his three big Squares. The conclusion: You can eat a lot or a little and still lose without a moment's hunger as long as you cut down carbohydrates low enough.

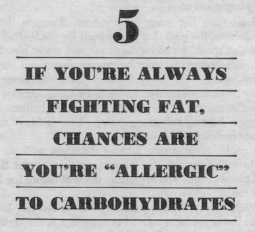

5

IF YOU'RE ALWAYS
FIGHTING FAT,
CHANCES ARE
YOU'RE "ALLERGIC"
TO CARBOHYDRATES

DEFINITION OF THIS MOST COMMON OF ALL "ALLERGIES." How do I define this phrase I find convenient—"an allergy to carbohydrates"? It is not a true allergy as we doctors know it, but it is a sensitivity to carbohydrates in the diet, which results in an overproduction of insulin (hyperinsulinism). In other words—and remember this, because it is a basic reason for your overweight—if you are "allergic" to carbohydrates, *carbohydrates taken into your body release* a flood of surplus insulin in your bloodstream.

This doesn't mean that you are seriously ill. It simply means that your body overreacts to carbohydrates just as another person's may overreact to seafood. You don't break out in a rash, you break out in rolls of fat (also perhaps in fatigue, depression, a craving for sweets, and a raised level of triglycerides).

41

"ALLERGY" HERE MEANS A DISTURBED CARBOHYDRATE ME-
TABOLISM. Most overweight people have a disturbed metabolism. (Metabolism is the process by which food is changed into
the chemicals your body can use for energy or to form body
tissues.)

Metabolism has many subdivisions. There is the basal
metabolic rate, the part that is governed by the thyroid gland.
But we also speak, for example, of salt and water metabolism,
protein metabolism, fat metabolism—all describing the processes by which your body handles these substances. The
category of metabolism that seems to be most sensitive in the
overweight person is the carbohydrate metabolism. If you
are always fighting fat, the primary cause is likely to be a
disturbed carbohydrate metabolism.

A conservative doctor I know disagrees with me about
this. He maintains it's the overweight that causes the disturbed metabolism. "You're putting the cart before the horse,"
he tells me.

"Well," I say, "when patients come to see me, both the
cart and the horse have arrived in the office at the same time.
What difference does it make to them which came first?"

Whichever came first, because it is carbohydrates that
trigger the trouble, there is just one maximally effective treatment for such people: Cut carbohydrate intake right down to
the bone.

I GET ANGRY OVER THE NEEDLESSNESS OF OVERWEIGHT.
For millions who suffer the endless physical and emotional
miseries of being fat, it is a tragedy that so few authorities
understand most overweight for what it is—a disordered carbohydrate metabolism, which affects some people and not
others, that is quite apart from the amount of food, or calories,
consumed. I get angry when I think of the useless, needless
deprivations imposed on fat people by most diets.

Deprivation isn't all that overweight people with a
disturbed carbohydrate metabolism have to bear. They usually
suffer also from periods of extremely low energy, the most

common symptom of low blood sugar. Unhappily the usual handy-dandy "remedy" for that utterly all-gone feeling is a quick fix of the same poison to which overweight people are usually both "allergic" and addicted: sugar. (In some of the people some of the time, it's alcohol.)

HOW THIS VICIOUS CYCLE WORKS. DO YOU SEE YOURSELF HERE? Let's suppose that you've learned from experience that you tend to run down around 5 P.M. to the point where you know you need a lift. And you've learned that a candy bar gives you a quick pickup in energy. Perfectly normal, isn't it? Wrong. The normal person is expected to have the proper biologic machinery to keep his blood sugar in the symptom-free range. The fact that the sugar in the candy bar changes the way you feel shows that your blood sugar level falls too low.

But what happens after that candy bar? Why doesn't the lift in energy last very long? Here's what happens. The candy sent the blood sugar level up only briefly, just long enough to signal the oversensitized pancreas to release an oversupply of insulin.

UNDERSTANDING INSULIN IS THE KEY TO UNDERSTANDING YOUR OVERWEIGHT. Because insulin plays such a vital role in your metabolism, let's talk about it for a moment. Insulin is the hormone manufactured in little clusters or cells within the pancreas, called islets of Langerhans. Its principal function is to act upon the carbohydrate in the bloodstream, which is in the form of glucose, and chemically deliver it to the body's tissues to be used as energy or to be converted into fat for storage of energy. If there is a surplus of glucose it is converted into stored energy or fat. In delivering the correct amount of glucose to the tissues to be used as energy, it is useful. In delivering the surplus, it is bad for the person with a weight problem.

It is important to know that insulin differs from other

hormones in that the quantity circulating in the bloodstream changes on a minute-to-minute basis. (Half of the insulin is removed from the blood within seven minutes of its release.) Thus, the level of sugar in the blood can change from minute to minute. When people tell you they have high blood sugar or low blood sugar, the answer should be, "When?" Many people vary from one extreme to the other within a few hours.

When you eat your 5 P.M. pickup candy bar, the insulin it calls for causes the blood sugar to plummet down—lower than it was before you ate it. Usually, it takes only an hour for your energy to nosedive this way, and in some people the effect is even faster and more dramatic.

When your blood sugar is too low, your energy drops. The candy bar buys you a tiny interval of energy, but the price is too high. It leaves you in worse shape than before you ate it. *Now* you're *so* exhausted that you think, "I need *two* candy bars and perhaps a drink." Well, that's not how you lose weight, is it?

But there's an even more serious penalty. It's this: Each candy bar (and the insulin flood it triggers) aggravates your permanent sensitivity to carbohydrates. In other words, the more sugar you eat in your lifetime, the more abnormal your response to sugar becomes. That has been demonstrated in many ways by a variety of medical studies.

BESIDES LOWERING YOUR BLOOD SUGAR, INSULIN INCREASES YOUR TRIGLYCERIDES. For years, some of the most eminent medical researchers (among them Dr. John Yudkin; Dr. Peter T. Kuo and Dr. D. R. Basset, both of Philadelphia; and Professor Margaret J. Albrink of the West Virginia School of Medicine) have been warning us that sugar in the diet leads to heart disease, but the entrenched medical establishment has ignored the body of evidence offered.

There is, however, increasing recognition that there is a strong correlation between high levels of insulin and high levels of triglycerides in the blood. The fat that we store in our fat cells is stored in the form of triglycerides. It has also been observed that there is a strong correlation between high triglycerides and coronary heart disease.

Not long ago, the big villain here was thought to be cholesterol. But it now appears that the correlation with heart attacks may be even higher with elevated triglycerides than with high cholesterol levels. Insulin is a mediator of the manufacture of triglycerides, so that the greater the insulin levels, the greater the triglyceride levels.

INSULIN HAS BEEN CALLED "THE FATTENING HORMONE." And most important, we come to the role that insulin plays in the metabolism of fat. Insulin has been called "the fattening hormone." It promotes the conversion of sugar (glucose) into fat by initiating the manufacture of fatty acids. And it somehow *prevents fat from breaking down so that it cannot be used up as the reserve source of fuel it was meant to be.*

The theory is that insulin indirectly reduces the activity of a group of substances called lipid-mobilizers. They control the movement of fat out of the unsightly spare-tire places it is kept. One of these fat-mobilizers was mentioned earlier, the FMH (fat mobilizing hormone) of the pituitary gland.

What all this means to you fat fighters is that the more insulin you produce (that is, the more disturbed is your metabolism) *the greater resistance you have to breaking down your fat.*

So if it's more difficult for you to lose weight than it is for some people, you probably can blame it on a tendency to readily overproduce insulin. But don't give up. It may be more difficult for you to lose, perhaps, but it is never impossible with a diet low enough in carbohydrate. Almost half of my successful losers have shown this metabolic resistance to losing weight, but they all lost nevertheless.

WHAT ARE THE IMMEDIATE COMPLICATIONS OF CARBO-HYDRATE POISONING? You probably wouldn't be reading this book if weight gain weren't the immediate complication of carbohydrate poisoning that most disturbs you. You may not like the idea that in order to lose your fat you are going to have to cut down sharply on your consumption of carbohydrates (your favorite foods, perhaps!). It may be a new idea to you, and even the loathsome alternative of starving may seem preferable to you at first. But that's only because you haven't been exposed to the advantages that a low-carbohydrate diet presents.

But I'll promise you this: From my experience with thousands of patients I can assure you that cutting carbohydrates is infinitely less painful than cutting calories. That's what my patients tell me. That's what I found out for myself —and live by. This is partly because you're never hungry, partly because your food preferences change, and partly because once you understand what carbohydrates do to you they become, in your own mind, your enemy. You not only don't want them, you feel downright hostility toward them. "Nothing could ever make me eat that junk again." I hear that over and over from ex-carbohydrate eaters.

EVEN NONSTOP EATERS CAN LOSE, WHEN THEY SKIP CARBOHYDRATES. Selma Zisk is one of these ex-carbohydrate eaters. She has lost sixty pounds. She's thirty-eight, 5 feet, 4 inches tall, a cheerful brunet who weighed 118 when she was married, but gained after each of her four children was born so that she weighed 209 when she came to see me. She had lost weight exactly twenty times with diet pills. After each diet she gained back more than she had lost.

As my patient she lost thirty-six pounds in the first twelve weeks. Then she continued to lose more slowly but steadily, week after week until she got down to a respectable weight again.

She has often reminded me of what I told her on her first visit: "You'll never live to see your children grow up at the rate you're gaining."

She now says, "I never had willpower, but I stuck to the diet for three reasons: because it's so easy to live with, because you scared the hell out of me on that first visit, and because of the compliments I've received as I have lost. My family is thrilled. It's a fantastic way of life for me."

SELMA HAD NEVER BEEN ABLE TO STAY WITH THE USUAL DIETS. Selma, like so many overweight people, has low blood sugar of diabetic origin. Besides diet pills she has tried shots, the meat-and-water diet, as well as diet-group therapy. Her weaknesses are cola beverages, cake, and cookies.

"I'm the kind that likes to eat all day long," she says. "What I ate between meals on the other diets—carrot sticks, celery, pickles—never satisfied me emotionally. I loved being able to have a big dish of diet Jello-O with whipped cream and almonds instead. Or a chicken salad with lots of mayonnaise."

She has good ideas for varying her diet: shish kebab, well marinated beforehand in Italian dressing and white wine; salmon croquettes made with eggs and no bread crumbs; veal birds. A favorite canapé is water chestnuts wrapped in bacon.

"The whole thing is a marvel," she says. "I just took each day as it came. 'You did great today, kid,' I told myself. 'Just take tomorrow when it gets here.'" What Selma has learned is that all her many todays have made tomorrow a habit.

Selma with her blood sugar disòrder is a good example of metabolic overweight.

WITH AN ABNORMAL METABOLISM, FAT MAY BE MANU-FACTURED EVEN WITHOUT FOOD. Harvard's Dr. Jean Mayer notes in this connection that "an animal with metabolic overweight will make more fat even though it may not overeat. In fact, it will make more fat *even while fasting.*"

Think about this a little. It certainly brings home the point that with a disturbed metabolism just eating less food isn't the answer, doesn't it?

This isn't bad news. It's good news. Once you understand why this happens, then for the first time you can hope to win for good against overweight.

WHAT ALL THIS MEANS TO YOU. Overweight is not only an illness in itself, but is a symptom of illnesses ranging in seriousness from minor to fatal. Sometimes, I shock patients when I tell them, "You'll be dead in two years if you continue eating and gaining the way you do." According to Metropolitan Life Insurance studies, the death rate for overweight men is 75 percent higher than for those of normal weight. The death rate for overweight women is 61 percent higher.

You may think that you'd like to lose some weight just so you will like what you see in the mirror better, but what's at stake is much more.

A TREE WITH DEADLY BRANCHES. There is a tree. For a minute we won't give the tree a name. Its branches are called Diabetes, Heart Disease, Overweight, Low Blood Sugar, Peptic Ulcer, Migraine, Allergy, and half a dozen other diseases that are so common nowadays.

The name of the tree might be, A Disturbed Way of Handling Carbohydrates.

IF CARBOHYDRATES ARE YOUR PARTICULAR POISON . . . We know that some of us are susceptible to complications of carbohydrate consumption, especially from sugar, and some of us are remarkably free from them.

But suppose that you are one of the carbohydrate-sensitive people, and the carbohydrates you take in stimulate an overproduction of insulin. We know from experiments done with animals by Dr. R. W. Stout of Belfast that adding insulin will speed up the formation of atherosclerotic deposits in key blood vessels. And we know that this can be the forerunner of many serious ailments.

HYPERINSULINISM AND HEART DISEASE. Of course, hyperinsulinism isn't the *only* contributing factor in cardiovascular complications. They are also aggravated by stress, smoking, too little exercise, and perhaps, in some people, are the physiological result of a special sensitivity to fats in the diet.

However, Dr. Yudkin has pointed out that increased sugar consumption may be the most significant factor. He maintains that even when fats have been blamed as the chief culprit in coronary problems, the diet eaten by the subjects studied also proved very high in sugar.

THE MORE SUGAR IN THE DIET, THE MORE HEART DISEASE. He cites the Masai and Samburu tribes of East Africa, where the diet is high in fat but low in sugar. There the rate of coronary heart disease is extremely low. Among the residents of the island of Saint Helena, on the other hand, where the diet is high in sugar and low in fat, the rate of coronary heart disease is high.

CUTTING CARBOHYDRATES PREVENTS WHAT CAN'T BE CURED. By cutting carbohydrates in your diet, we are not just treating you for that unbecoming fat you want to lose, but are probably prolonging your life.

ARE ALL OVERWEIGHT PEOPLE A LITTLE BIT DIABETIC? This is not primarily a book for diabetics. But it is a book for people who have some weight to lose because their bodies produce an oversupply of insulin. I am not alone in the view that such people are perhaps a little bit diabetic; prediabetic, at least. So it's important to understand a few things about this condition.

The amount of sugar (glucose) needed to keep the nervous system and brain functioning well is approximately two teaspoonsful circulating constantly in the blood. This is the amount the blood of a normal person contains. When the blood persistently contains more sugar than normal, the condition is described as diabetic.

The direct connection between diabetes and the amount of sugar you eat was demonstrated in England during World War II. When sugar was rationed there then, deaths from diabetes dropped more than 40 percent!

And when sugar was added to the diet of the nomadic Jewish people of Yemen after they moved to the Israeli cities following World War II, the incidence of diabetes there increased dramatically. And with it, heart disease, almost unheard-of before, became just as prevalent as in the rest of urbanized Israel.

CAUSES OF DIABETES. The whole story of what causes diabetes is not known. There are two quite different types. The kind that children have is so different that it may not even be the same disease. It is a far more severe illness and it requires insulin therapy, because insulin is deficient. The kind that begins in overweight adults can be much less dramatic, and almost always can be prevented from progressing to a point where insulin is required.

HEREDITY PLAYS AN IMPORTANT ROLE. We do know that in both types your heredity is important. If someone in your family had diabetes, you must be on guard all your life against it. If one parent had it, you have a 50 percent chance of having it. If both parents had it, you are, by definition, a prediabetic (meaning that theoretically there is a 100 percent probability that you will have it eventually).

Age is another critical factor. As people get older, the rate at which the system removes sugar from the blood falls to such an extent that it is estimated that nearly half those sixty years old would be classified as chemically diabetic if the testing standards used on younger people were applied to them.

The third factor is prolonged overeating of refined carbohydrates. This often brings about hyperinsulinism and a breakdown in your body's ability to metabolize carbohydrates.

If the adult-onset diabetic's diet had been carbohydrate-free from babyhood on, would that diabetic gene ever have manifested itself? We can only speculate, but we know that diabetes does not exist in cultures where refined carbohydrates are not consumed.

"BUT ISN'T DIABETES LICKED SINCE INSULIN WAS DISCOVERED IN 1921?" Far from being one of our conquered diseases, diabetes still affects 6 to 10 percent of America's population. There are said to be more than one million undiagnosed and untreated diabetics in this country, but my own laboratory incidence statistics indicate that there may be millions more than that.

WHEN THE DISTURBANCE IS NEGLECTED. Yet diabetes is one of life's easiest illnesses to control. One need only to have it diagnosed when it is in the early, "chemical," or latent stages, and stop eating the carbohydrates without which it cannot progress.

Don't wait for symptoms (the classic ones are increased thirst, increased urinary output, and unexplained loss of weight), because by then it is rather late. The symptoms of *early* diabetes are probably overweight itself and the signs of low blood sugar, described elsewhere in this book. Low blood sugar might, in fact, be the first recognizable stage of diabetes.

DO-IT-YOURSELF DIABETES SCREENING TEST. To screen a patient for diabetes, too many doctors merely take a single blood sugar test in the morning before a patient has eaten, or rely on a casual urine specimen, during a routine checkup. But my studies show that 90 percent of all cases are missed that way. I recommend a standard glucose tolerance test interpreted by the criteria of the American Diabetes Association. Of the 2,000 patients I have found who exceeded these limits and were therefore early diabetics, 1,900 had no inkling of this fact, yet almost all had been given regular checkups by their own physicians!

Because one out of five of my office patients show sugar in their urine after a standard dose of glucose, I assume that the same percentage may well apply to my readers. Before you start this or any diet, you should do the following screening procedure as a minimum effort.

HOW TO GIVE YOURSELF A GLUCOSE TOLERANCE TEST (GTT). The first thing you need is a "dose" of glucose. To prepare this, purchase a bottle of Glucola or Paladex at any drugstore (two bottles if you weigh over 225 pounds) or an equivalent (one-half cup of cola syrup diluted with as much water or soda as you please also does nicely). At the same time, buy a few urine glucose testing strips (Tes-tape will turn green, Clinistix will turn blue if sugar is present). No prescription is needed for any of these.

Eat your usual diet, making sure that for three days you have had at least six hundred calories a day in the form of carbohydrates. At the end of the third day, do not eat after retiring.

First thing in the morning of the fourth day, quickly drink the glucose. Void your urine as often as you can and test every specimen for glucose. If it turns positive, you are a prime diabetic suspect and *must* arrange for a glucose tolerance test by a laboratory or a doctor.

To learn more about yourself, continue to go without eating for six hours, and pay attention to how you feel. If you get dizzy, clammy, tired, irritable, headachy, light-headed, emotional, tearful, or feel any of the other symptoms you have suffered from, then you are probably experiencing low blood sugar.

This home-screening test tells you that you must get the full glucose tolerance test to confirm this diagnosis. If you experience these symptoms, it is essential that you see your doctor and insist upon being given a careful test by him. Do not accept a yes or a no about the diagnosis, but ask for the numbers in your glucose tolerance test. Is there a difference of 100 or more points between the high and the low reading? Does the sugar level drop more than 50 points in any one hour? Does the low reading drop 30 percent or more below the starting point? In my experience, these are just *some* of the findings that correlate with the clinical symptoms of low blood sugar.

YOUR OVERWEIGHT, LOW BLOOD SUGAR, AND DIABETES ALL HAVE A COMMON DENOMINATOR. "But isn't low blood sugar the opposite of diabetes?" patients ask me. "No," I always answer, "the opposite of diabetes is normal."

Roughly, here is the way that overweight, low blood sugar, and diabetes relate.

Stage one begins with a genetic defect in your carbohydrate metabolism. You literally have a "carbohydrate allergy," demonstrated by your being overweight, but your glucose tolerance is still normal.

In stage two the pancreas continues to overwork and overproduce insulin. The result—more overweight, and low blood sugar can be demonstrated.

In stage three the pancreas continues to overwork, but the insulin can no longer immediately control the blood sugar balance. The result—overweight, symptoms of a low blood sugar, and a glucose tolerance test that shows both diabetes and a low level of blood sugar. (This stage is found as frequently as any other among my patients.)

In stage four the pancreas, although still releasing large amounts of insulin, cannot produce enough of the hormone to handle the increasing demands on its supply. The result— overweight and a chronically high level of blood sugar, that is, overt diabetes.

This is an oversimplification, and the phases may all occur at once, so that not all stages are found in every diabetic's past history.

But the common denominator here is the trio—overweight, low blood sugar, and diabetes. Excessive insulin is the common enemy.

I ask you to make this connection clear, for if you understand that overweight is a sickness, and see how it threatens your mobility, personality, youthfulness, and even your life, you'll decide that cutting down on carbohydrates for the rest of your life is something you *want* to do. And to eat the way you *want* to really requires no willpower.

CONTROL OF DIABETES IS OFTEN JUST THIS DIET. I have treated two thousand stable, adult diabetics. *I have never yet had to begin giving injections of insulin.* The diet described in this book has been effective in bringing both the diabetes and the overweight under control in every one of those two thousand cases. I suppose it can happen that one day someone will walk in and be an exception, but so far it hasn't occurred.

6

WHAT
CAUSES THIS
TWENTIETH-CENTURY
PLAGUE?

We tend to take it for granted that the way we eat now is the way we always ate. Nothing could be further from the truth. For most of man's fifty million years on earth, we have lived off the flesh and fat of other animals. When times were hard, the women would gather roots and berries. This might have amounted to fifteen grams of carbohydrate a day, perhaps half an ounce. But man was a hunter and our eating habits were largely carnivorous.

It is important to remember that the body you live in now is the fifty-million-year-old body that evolved on this diet. No orange juice for breakfast, yet that body not only survived, it flourished. Weaklings who couldn't maintain health, stamina, and agility on this virtually no-carbohydrate diet were quickly bred out of existence.

HOW MAN'S DIET CAME TO HAVE A PROFOUNDLY DAMAGING EFFECT ON HIS HEALTH. Step one: Around 7000 B.C. (a few minutes ago, anthropologically speaking), Neolithic man began to plant grains and roots, and settle down. His diet began to contain a higher percent of unrefined carbohydrates. For those who couldn't adjust to this, the mortality rate was undoubtedly high.

NEXT CAME THE FOOD-PROCESSING REVOLUTION. The second step was much more recent—about two hundred years ago —and grew out of man's ambition to store grain, so that he would have it on hand between growing seasons. This was and still is achieved by making grain products so nutritionally sterile that even pests and other microorganisms couldn't live on them. Rice was polished, flours were degerminated and bleached. The result was a loss of most B vitamins and other essential nutrients, and an increased consumption of refined carbohydrates.

THEN CAME REFINED SUGAR—THE KILLER CARBOHYDRATE. Sugar has been important in our diet for less than a hundred years. The Crusaders introduced it to Europe, but for centuries only apothecaries had it to sell. And they sold it by the ounce. Only the richest could afford it, and then it was reserved for state occasions. But by 1750, it is estimated that the average Englishman ate four pounds a year, and by 1840, it still was only twenty pounds.

It is difficult to calculate just how much sugar we consume in the United States today. What we use right from the bowl on fruit and cereal, in tea, coffee, and cooking, is a small part of the total. Three doctors doing research at the State University of Iowa, Mohamed A. Antar, Margaret A. Ohlson, and Robert E. Hodges, estimate that we take in as much as 110 pounds of sugar and syrup per person a year, in everything from soups and salad dressings to soft drinks, desserts, and candies. We also eat another 60 pounds of simple carbohydrates in honey, fruit, and milk, bringing our consumption of various kinds of sugar to a grand total of 170 pounds a year.

And in the year following the unfortunate and, I feel,

unjustifiable ban on cyclamates—the per capita consumption of sugar escalated another five pounds.

THE BIGGEST DIETARY CHANGE IN FIFTY MILLION YEARS. *From 4 pounds of sugar—the most concentrated of carbohydrates—to 175 pounds per person a year in eleven generations! This may well be the most drastic dietary change in man's environment in his whole fifty million years of existence!*

So what? Sugar makes us fat. It makes dentists rich. One doctor asks, "If simple sugar can rot and crumble away to nothing the hardness of teeth, what ruin is it wreaking on the rest of the body?"

But what is the evidence as to other damage caused by sugar? Let's take the least, first.

SUGAR CAUSES A VITAMIN B DEFICIT. In order to assimilate carbohydrates, large quantities of Vitamin B are required. Sugar, of course, contains no vitamins or nutrients of any kind, except sucrose. So the body is forced to draw on its own Vitamin B reserves. The more sugar you take in, the greater the Vitamin B deficit imposed on your body. It is important, then, to understand that sugar has *antinutrient* properties.

This is true to a lesser extent of all carbohydrates that you take in. Starch is the major source of hidden sugar, because the body turns starch into sugar while it is in the stomach. In order to know the truth about your sugar intake, you must visualize *all starchy food* as servings of sugar.

SUGAR CAUSES BASIC METABOLIC DISTURBANCES. Since it was only four or five generations ago that we began eating a diet moderately high in sugar, there hasn't been enough time for natural selection to evolve a human genetic system able to deal satisfactorily with today's tidal wave of refined sugar and starch.

Given this deluge of sugar and refined carbohydrates, the pancreas is forced to behave hysterically. It overreacts to the repeated signal for insulin release that carbohydrates cause, and floods the bloodstream with this blood-sugar-lowering hormone, until the blood level of sugar is lower than when the signal was first received (that's hypoglycemia). After this has gone on long enough, in the genetically predisposed individual, the insulin becomes less and less effective until eventually diabetes is the result, as we have seen.

Because it takes all kinds of bodies to make a species, we all know some lucky people who can eat anything and not gain. They happen to have bodies that can deal with carbohydrates, but they are in the minority.

NOW LET'S LOOK AT YOUR INDIVIDUAL SITUATION. Let's consider what in your family history and life pattern may be causing or contributing to the possibility that you are carbohydrate sensitive.

BEING CARBOHYDRATE INTOLERANT IS LARGELY A MATTER OF GENES. Mark Twain wrote, "When you're born, you're finished." A joke? My records show that *forty-eight out of fifty patients who have come to me for overweight* have relatives who are either diabetic or overweight—two of the surest signs of carbohydrate disturbance.

Most fat babies have fat parents. A survey of several thousand overweight children in the Boston area showed that only 10 percent had parents of normal weight. Similar surveys in Chicago, Philadelphia, Edinburgh, and Vienna showed the same results.

This doesn't mean that you're "finished" if you have diabetes or overweight in your family background. There is something you can do about it—this diet will fight both.

MOTHER LOVE IS NOT THE VILLAIN OF THIS STORY. You will hear it said that the reason for this is because the mother constantly forces food on the child. I don't believe this. I think mothers, particularly those who are themselves overweight, are very sensitive to the suffering and heartache that overweight causes. It is my belief that as a rule they do not overfeed their children. Quite another factor is involved.

These children are born hungrier. The metabolic defect they suffer from is apparent from the crib as increased hunger. Children like this show they are not satisfied by the quantity of formula presented to them. Even after a feeding they may still cry and scream. Mothers today have been indoctrinated into the concept of demand feeding. So they relent and give their offspring a little more of the formula. They are not force feeding. They are barely satisfying the baby's very real hunger.

Although *over*feeding in infancy is not likely to take place, *incorrect* feeding may well be the cause of childhood-onset obesity. After all, what is the first extra "nutrient" added in our culture when the basic milk formula is expanded upon? You guessed it: sugar! Sweetened orange juice, strained bananas, applesauce, and sweetened cereals are all added early in an infant's feeding program, and when he is not much older, cookies and candy become his principal reward. By the time he is old enough to think for himself, his carbohydrate-susceptible body is already ravaged by his well-meaning parents, with the support of the nutritional "authorities."

A study should be done to demonstrate what the strict avoidance of refined carbohydrates from infancy on can do to prevent childhood-onset obesity. I am confident the results would be startlingly successful.

A RESISTANCE TO LOSING CAN ALSO BE INBORN. Our fifty-million-year-old body naturally contains a few odd bits and pieces for which it has no further use. These leftovers from primeval life-styles can be troublesome. The appendix is one example. Another, recently discovered by Dr. Jerome Knittle and Dr. Jules Hirsch, both of Rockefeller Institute, is an overgrowth of fat cells. This overgrowth of fat cells is nestled in the tissues between the skin and the muscles, especially on the abdomen.

Back in our primeval days, when long periods might elapse between meals, those fat cells were a survival mechanism. Today they're the opposite! It is absolutely vital to learn to eat our way around this hazard.

IS AN OVERGROWTH OF FAT CELLS HEREDITARY? Even thin people have some of these cells—tiny storehouses of fat and potential energy. But fat people have an overgrowth of them, often from babyhood. In the first few months of life, they can triple or quadruple in number, Knittle and Hirsch discovered. And once these fat cells appear, they remain for life.

At an age up to adolescence this overgrowth of fat cells can appear. Then the prognosis for ultimate control of the child's weight problem into adulthood is poor. Dr. Knittle feels that it is "nearly hopeless." However, in my own practice, I have treated hundreds of such cases of childhood overweight. And by living on the diet in this book they have managed to control their weight. (See Perry Zenlea's story in chapter 1.)

The reason for the poor outlook in these cases is the metabolic effect of fat cells themselves. Fatty tissue is not the inert accumulation of blubber that it seems to be, but rather is an active organ of metabolism. Among other functions, the membranes of the fat cells, by resisting the action of insulin, cause an increased production of this hormone. So even if starvation should reduce the cell size, the more fat cells, the more cell membranes, and therefore the greater the production of insulin.

AGE, IN ITSELF, CAN MAKE YOU ALLERGIC TO CARBOHYDRATES (WHICH MEANS FAT!). Even if you didn't have overweight parents, even if you didn't begin life as a plump baby chock-a-block with fat cells, there is no guarantee that you won't be overweight and oversensitized to sugar by the time you've been eating and drinking for sixty years or so in our carbohydrate culture.

There are exceptions, but in general the ability of our bodies to handle carbohydrates lessens as we grow older, and so we get fatter.

STRESS AND ANXIETY CAN MAKE YOU ALLERGIC TO CARBOHYDRATES (WHICH MEANS FAT!). Stress, anxiety, and emotional tension tend to make carbohydrate-sensitive people fat! Here's why. When we are under strain, our bodies put out adrenaline. And adrenaline raises blood sugar levels. This in turn triggers off a flood of insulin, so that the blood sugar ends up lower than it started. (It is important to note that insulin's lowering effect on the blood sugar is more potent and longer-lasting than is adrenaline's opposite effect.)

It is at this low point that we eat and drink for energy, for comfort, to rest and calm our fears, anger, and tensions. And these high-carbohydrate pick-me-up feedings lay on the pounds.

Being anxious causes low blood sugar. And low blood sugar causes feelings of anxiety many of us satisfy with high carbohydrate food and drink.

Happily there is a way to break this vicious cycle—the diet in this book. It allows for *protein and fat pick-me-ups* as often as you like.

You see, protein/fat combinations tend to be insulin stabilizers, biologically speaking. That is, they, *unlike carbohydrates,* do not dramatically affect blood sugar levels, and thus do not trigger the insulin flood.

On this diet, your blood sugar is gradually brought into the normal range, where it stays, because nothing is eaten which triggers off an insulin deluge. And in this tranquilizing metabolic climate, stress and anxiety can fade away.

JENNY O'HARA CAME TO ME AT AN ANXIOUS TIME. Jenny O'Hara was just beginning her turn as star of the Broadway hit *Promises, Promises* when she came to see me in August 1971. She is 5 feet 6 inches tall and she weighed 142¼. "That is too much for a civilian and it's far too much for an actress," she says. "But I dreaded the thought of going on a diet—just at this hectic time. I thought, 'It will make me nervous and irritable and tense and tired and miserable the way diets always do. How will I ever stand it?'

"And then it wasn't so at all. I feel fantastic. I never had so much energy in my life. Yet before I started on this diet I used to sleep hours in the day, I was so tired. So then I'd go on that horrible sweet cycle; you know, eat sweets for a lift, then find my energy had dropped way below where it was when I ate the sweets."

Jenny's parents are very much overweight and she was a fat child, a fat teen-ager. Her top weight was 160 (when she was seventeen). And she has hovered between 145 and 150 most of the time.

"I'M A PASTRY MAVEN," JENNY ADMITS. Now she hovers between 120 and 125, which is just where she wants it. "And the inches have come off like crazy," she says.

She had tried (and failed) with many diets. "I'm a pastry buff," she confesses. "I have a craving for sweets of all kinds. That was what would always ruin me.

"It's such a strange and wonderful thing that on this diet I'm not hungry for all those things I'm not supposed to eat. What does it, I think, is being able to have butter and sour cream and mayonnaise. I love grilled chopped steak mixed with a little garlic and topped with sour cream and pepper. M'mmm! And steak with a square of sweet butter sitting on it. I love quiche Lorraine, which is perfectly legal. One just leaves the crust. I've got a lot of enjoyment out of the cheese-cake. And I invented a pumpkin soufflé, made with heavy cream and sweeteners and spices that's just great."

Between meals Jenny munches on macadamia nuts and cheese (Cheddar is her favorite). For lunch she loves all-beef hot dogs, and for breakfast (with her eggs) Jones sausage, one of the brands without filler.

JUST BEING A WOMAN MAKES YOU ESPECIALLY SUSCEPTI-BLE TO "CARBOHYDRATE ALLERGY." Even women who are not usually hypoglycemic frequently develop periodic low blood sugar in the week just before menstruation. This state of affairs can account for those feelings of depression, irritability, and emotional instability that trouble so many women.

That "all-gone" feeling also leads to the eating of "comfort" foods, such as cookies, candy, cake. All the weight that women gain before their periods isn't always merely water weight. With many women each period is followed by a week of crash dieting.

Women also are peculiarly vulnerable to a common disorder of body fluid retention, called idiopathic edema of women. This, too, is a known disturbance of carbohydrate metabolism.

Often, too, hypoglycemia and overweight begin with a woman's first pregnancy, and increase with each pregnancy thereafter. Pregnancy and childbirth add enormously to the stresses and anxieties under which a woman lives. And they act as triggers that can initiate a permanent metabolic disturbance. Also, during pregnancy a woman's body is flooded with female hormones, which set off an excess secretion of insulin.

Modern obstetricians are aware that hypoglycemia, lingering on, can be the cause of postchildbirth depression as well.

CAFFEINE ALSO AGGRAVATES CARBOHYDRATE INTOLERANCE. The caffeine in our coffee (and even the theobromine in our tea) also can lead to an excess insulin production. Our national consumption of soft drinks (many of which contain significant amounts of caffeine as well as sugar) has contributed importantly to our national vulnerability to overweight, hypoglycemia, heart disease, and diabetes.

But, if I had to pick the single causative factor most responsible for the obesity epidemic that has spread through all Westernized countries, it would be the overconsumption of refined sugar. I think something should be done to correct this situation *now*.

Candy bars and soft drinks should carry a warning statement equivalent to that on cigarette packages stating that "cigarette smoking is dangerous to your health."

Packages of sugar-containing products might read: "Warning: This product contains sugar and may be physically injurious to some individuals. Consult your physician before purchase and use."

OTHER AGGRAVATORS: THE PILL AND ESTROGEN REPLACE-
MENT THERAPY. The Pill for birth control and the estrogen
used as menopausal hormone replacement therapy have the
same kind of effect as a pregnancy. They increase the severity
of hyperinsulinism and therefore aggravate hypoglycemia,
diabetes, and overweight. (If you are on these medications,
you would not be expected to do well with this or any other
diet. In other words, you may be forced to choose between
the female hormone and being slim and having normal blood
sugar levels.)

MEN ARE REALLY NO LUCKIER. Men are not by any means
exempt from the havoc wreaked by refined sugar and starch.
One Swedish study showed that in men carbohydrate intolerance went up steadily every decade from the age of
twenty on.

In women, this change doesn't occur until the menopause
is reached.

This data correlates with the fact that men are suscepti-
ble to heart attacks from their twenties on, but that women,
unless they are diabetic, are far less likely to get heart disease
until after the menopause.

DOES WHAT YOU'VE JUST READ SEEM LIKE A FLAT CON-
TRADICTION? How can I tell you that the Pill and estrogen
replacement therapy aggravate hyperinsulinism and all its
train of connected disorders—and then in the next breath tell
you that postmenopausal women who have lost most of their
estrogen become as vulnerable as men to these same disorders?

Sounds like a flat contradiction, doesn't it? It's not,
though. It merely points up one of medicine's many remaining
mysteries. We know that these seemingly contradictory states
of affairs exist. So we can come to only one conclusion:
Estrogen alone is not the protective agent.

There are other hormones, other factors at work in the
natural hormonal balance of the premenopausal woman. We
don't really know which element plays the protective role

here. We can only assume from our observations that such a factor must exist.

THE MORE POTENT PSYCHO DRUGS CAUSE WEIGHT GAINS. In these take-a-pill-for-whatever-ails-you times, it is hardly a surprise that some of our drugs designed to "help" people have side effects that do just the opposite. A good example: the more potent psycho drugs. The major categories of such potent medicines are the phenothiazines (such as Thorazine and Compazine) and the psychic energizer groups (Elavil and Sinequan, for example). My own clinical observations, as yet unproven, suggest that both seem to increase insulin output and lead to weight gain and hypoglycemia. (This may not be true of the milder drugs such as Librium, Valium, Meprobamate.)

Now, because hypoglycemia is so often the root cause of psychoneurotic symptoms such as depression and anxiety, it is hypoglycemics who are very likely to receive these drugs. You can see how such drugs, useful as they are, can, if your problem is really hypoglycemia, provide more harm than benefit.

I'm not a psychiatrist, but I have worked with hundreds of psychiatric patients and I have found that this diet has sometimes been more effective than the drugs in stabilizing the mental symptoms my patients have been suffering. In many cases, working with the patient's psychiatrist, we were able to reduce the dosage of these potent drugs, and, in some cases, discontinue them completely, as patients began to show a sometimes miraculous and dramatic improvement in their depression, anxiety, and adjustment problems.

7

IT'S A NEW ENERGY DIET— BOTH PSYCHOLOGICAL AND PHYSICAL

To me the most gratifying and extraordinary thing about this diet is the way it can completely transform a patient's personality. I continually see this happen and never cease to be amazed and delighted by this miracle.

On the *first visit* most people come in depressed, defeated, lethargic, looking years older than their age. How can so simple a thing as a change in diet transform them within a few months into the energetic, youthful, self-confident individuals they become? Well, it does! This is one of the reasons I have become such an evangelist about this diet. Why can't *everyone* change this way?

Of course *most* fat people who lose weight by any reasonable method look and feel a lot better and younger *while the weight loss holds*—which, alas, isn't usually very long on most regimens.

But the physical and emotional changes this diet brings about are different. So much more is accomplished than merely the weight loss. *The physical, mental, and emotional symptoms of a low level of blood sugar are relieved. The result is an upsurge of mental, sexual, and physical energy, wonderful to feel and wonderful to behold.*

Take the case of Hal Linden, the actor and star of *The Rothschilds* on Broadway, who weighed 188½ when he came to see me. Because he is 6 feet, 1 inch tall, he didn't have any vast amount to lose. "But," says his wife Frances, "my husband loves to eat. He can eat his meat and mine too—anytime! And he's a fast regainer."

So for Hal Linden getting, and keeping, even those few extra pounds off had been a problem for quite a long while. On this diet, however, which is designed for people (like me!) who love to eat, the weight came off easily. And he has been able to keep it off without any difficulty. It's the first time in his life that this has happened. Naturally, he is delighted. "And his energy has tripled," says his wife. "It's fantastic."

AT STAKE IS ENERGY VERSUS FATIGUE, CHEERFULNESS VERSUS DEPRESSION. All these good new feelings of youthfulness, optimism, and energy make a big difference in a patient's desire to stay on the diet. It's not just, "If I have this piece of birthday cake, I'll gain," it's, "If I have this piece of birthday cake, I'll gain and also I'll find myself sliding downhill on that old toboggan emotionally—back to being tired, depressed, and irritable."

This good new zest and well-being isn't just because your figure is shaping up to suit you. It is the biochemical result of the fact that your blood sugar (the source of your brain and body fuel) is no longer falling to intolerable levels, but is being stabilized to near normal by this diet.

Next to the complaint about being overweight, complaints about fatigue are what I hear most often on the first visit.

DEPRESSION IS OFTEN A SYMPTOM OF LOW BLOOD SUGAR. Because I am not a psychiatrist, few patients start out by dwelling on their depression. But it becomes clear very shortly that along with the fatigue there is depression—a well-known symptom of low blood sugar.

I hear variations on this depression theme toward the end of almost every first visit. "I'm so disgusted with myself." "I feel absolutely desperate." "I cry myself to sleep." "I don't belong." "I'm a mess and I know it."

Most overweight people rather expect to be depressed, because overweight in our society is a social and sexual handicap, a constant ego punishment. But they don't take fatigue as much for granted. They often seem surprised about it.

"I don't know what's the matter with me, but the minute I've finished dinner, I can't keep my eyes open."

"I love that course, but can't seem to help sleeping through most of the classes."

"I could just die in the afternoons I get so sleepy. It's *torture* to stay awake. Why is that?"

"I don't get up all that early, yet by eleven o'clock at night I'm out on my feet as if I were an old, old person."

Is this the kind of thing you hear yourself saying?

I ask, "When are you most tired? At what hours?"

"Well, I think it's worst around eleven to twelve and between four and six in the afternoon," is what I am most often told.

ARE YOU FAMILIAR WITH THIS FATIGUE PATTERN? Most people have fatigue at one time or another in the course of the day. You accept it as normal. You've done all this work, you've worried so much, or your life presents many problems, so why shouldn't you be tired?

Yet almost all of us can feel better merely by understanding the relationship between when we eat, what we eat, and how we feel.

Why not chart out your energy pattern and correlate it with your eating pattern? You'll find that there is a relation.

The basic governing factor seems to be the level of sugar in your blood at any given time.

You may fool your stomach between meals with celery, sour pickles, and carrot sticks, but you can't fool your bloodstream. If you have a low, or a falling, level of blood sugar, you're going to go right on having the fatigue symptoms until you change your eating pattern.

GETTING OLD DOESN'T HAVE TO MEAN BEING TIRED. "I guess I'm getting old because I'm tired so much of the time." This misconception is one I hear all the time.

I concede that getting older is inevitable. Getting tired is not. I have found in thousands of cases that once an individual is put on this diet he can be rather well along in years and still have energy that he didn't even realize he was capable of experiencing. I know, from having seen it happen so many times, that not only will you feel better on this diet than on any other diet, *but better than you even consider normal for yourself.*

Fatigue isn't necessary. It isn't normal. Whatever your age, if you're tired, if you don't have energy, then you can pretty much assume that it's because something is wrong with you. And if you are significantly overweight as well, the chances are that your problem may well be your carbohydrate metabolism—and that you have hypoglycemia.

DEFINITION AND CAUSES OF HYPOGLYCEMIA. Hypoglycemia is literally translated from the Greek to mean an abnormally low blood sugar level: *hypo* meaning "under," *glykis* "sweet," *emia* "in the blood."

There are several types of organic hypoglycemia, which may spring from a variety of causes. We're *not* going to discuss these here because 90 percent of all low blood sugar is what is called functional hypoglycemia. And 90 percent of *that* is caused by the overreaction to carbohydrates, which we have talked about earlier. This overreaction causes a surplus of insulin to be released into the bloodstream, the prime action of insulin being to lower the blood sugar level.

Contrary to your first thought, hypoglycemia is not due to a lack of sugar in your diet but is a matter of excessive insulin response—or hyperinsulinism. Never forget that sugar in your diet makes it worse in the long run.

SYMPTOMS OF HYPOGLYCEMIA. Depression and fatigue are not the only symptoms. Among the multitude of others, which *may* be due to hypoglycemia, are irritability, nervousness, dizziness, headaches, faintness, cold sweats, cold hands and feet, weak spells, drowsiness, forgetfulness, insomnia, worrying, confusion, anxiety, palpitations of the heart, muscle pains, hostility, belligerence, antisocial behavior, indecisiveness, crying spells, lack of concentration, twitching of muscles, gasping for breath, digestive disturbances, ulcer syndrome, phobias and fears, suicidal intent, convulsions, allergies, blurred vision, addictability to alcohol and drugs, lack of sex drive in women, sexual impotence in men, underachievement at school, terrors and nightmares—even unconsciousness.

Not all hypoglycemics are overweight (two of my prettiest nurses are hypoglycemics and one wears a size 3, the other a size 7), but almost 70 percent of my patients who are overweight have low blood sugar of one type or another when they come to me. And I estimate that three out of four people with low blood sugar are overweight.

A well-known actress who is a patient of mine is one. After even the most modest carbohydrate binge, *down* goes her energy level, *up* goes her weight. "If I eat an apple, it hits me like eating three pieces of candy," she reports. "Before I came to you, I couldn't lose. And I *couldn't* understand why." She lost ten pounds in a month on this diet.

THIS IS THE MOST UNDERDIAGNOSED OF ALL DISEASES. One of my colleagues says, "Hypoglycemia is a symptom of body malfunction so common in our society today that the person who feels good is an oddity." I think of it as the twentieth-century disease because it results from our body's response to the historically unique dietary stress caused by eating mainly refined carbohydrates.

The symptoms are so numerous and diverse that many doctors mistrust and deny the very idea of this disease.

Hypoglycemia is undersuspected and underdiagnosed to an extent without parallel in medicine. Perhaps this is due to the fact that this subject is covered for perhaps an hour in a four-year medical teaching program. Or, to the medical textbooks, where it is described as a relatively rare condition.

In looking back, I realize that I must have missed hundreds of cases as an intern and resident by not suspecting low blood sugar. None of my instructors were thinking that way either. So please don't blame the doctor who doesn't diagnose or understand your low blood sugar; he can't be expected to know more than he has been taught.

I do know this: Whoever first defined hypoglycemia as existing when the blood sugar falls below 45 milligrams percent (these are the units in which blood sugar is measured) or about half what should be circulating in the blood, set back medical progress in this area by a generation. Because of this, the average doctor is afraid to diagnose a patient as suffering from this ailment unless he sees that magic number.

Although the low reading is useful in selecting cases for medical research, most hypoglycemics' blood sugar does not fall that low, even when patients are disabled by their condition to the point of being bedridden.

HOW MUCH "MENTAL" ILLNESS IS WRONGLY DIAGNOSED? One out of every two hospital beds in the United States is occupied by a mental patient. Along with other doctors, I am convinced that what's wrong with a large proportion of these patients is not mental but physical—functional hypoglycemia that could be controlled easily by a carbohydrate-free diet.

Hypoglycemia can mimic almost any neuropsychiatric disorder, and patients with hypoglycemia have been incorrectly or incompletely diagnosed as having schizophrenia, manic-depressive psychosis, and a variety of other ailments.

THE RIGHT DIET COULD RESCUE MANY OF ALL MENTAL PATIENTS. The sad thing is that when patients are institutionalized for mental illness, the diet they get in the institution is low in cost and high in carbohydrates. This is the exact opposite of the treatment that might improve their condition. It is my belief that if we put these mental patients on a zero-carbohydrate diet we could empty a significant number of the beds now occupied by psychiatric patients.

One proof of this is the good results that many of the new breed of nutritionally oriented psychiatrists are getting by treating patients with megavitamin therapy and a low-carbohydrate diet.

LOW BLOOD SUGAR MAY BE TEMPORARY, OR IT MAY BE RECURRENT. Temporary low blood sugar can be caused by an emotional shock or strain. Anxiety increases the output of insulin and this can exacerbate all the low blood sugar tendencies. Many of us may get temporary hypoglycemia as a result of overindulging in carbohydrates or alcohol, the way we do when we let go at holiday time, or on a vacation, for example.

Recurrent low blood sugar is the commonest form I see. If you duplicate the dietary pattern that brings on hypoglycemia, you duplicate the symptoms. The person who feels fatigued every afternoon at 4 P.M. because he eats a high-carbohydrate lunch every noon is a typical example. When your doctor takes your medical history, this can be his most important clue to the diagnosis.

HERE'S HOW ANYONE CAN CONTROL HYPOGLYCEMIA. Whatever the cause, the normalizing process is the same. There is only one way to break the vicious cycle. The overproduction of insulin (which sends your blood's sugar down) must be stopped. And you can accomplish this by removing from your diet whatever *stimulates* its overproduction—alcohol, caffeine, and, of course, most important, any carbohydrate.

To start with, may I repeat that exercise can be a big

help? I recommend sports, fun games, because they are mentally and physically relaxing. And, by increasing your body's demand for glucose, exercise encourages your body to convert more fat into sugar, thereby stabilizing the gyrations in your sugar level. So exercise produces a special euphoria all its own.

But diet is the real key to the treatment.

When you remove the ready fuel of carbohydrate from your diet, your body begins to search for an alternate source of energy, those vast untapped reserves of stored fat. This changeover is governed by the pituitary, which receives a signal to begin putting out its fat mobilizing hormone. FMH releases energy into your bloodstream by causing the stored fat to convert to carbohydrate. *Thus, the fatigue clears, without having to call upon the defective insulin mechanism.*

ON THE DIET YOUR ENERGY IS HIGH. CHEAT—AND FATIGUE RETURNS. The fatigue symptom is a sort of built-in punishment and reward feature of the diet. It motivates one to stay on the diet, because it's so great to have your energy again, while losing weight as well.

If you go off the diet you learn by sad experience that up to seventy-two hours later you're dragging around again the way you did before you started on the diet.

WHY UP TO SEVENTY-TWO HOURS? Suppose you go *off* the diet on Saturday and you go back on Sunday. Why are you exhausted on Monday and Tuesday? After all, you're back on your diet.

Well, the mechanism here has to do with the time it takes to put out FMH again after you've gone back on the diet. When FMH is circulating in your bloodstream, your fat stores supply you with energy, but by going off the diet Saturday night you *stopped* the FMH from circulating. You got a temporary lift from the carbohydrates you binged on, but then came the letdown. Without your FMH you tend to run down temporarily. Then after two or three days on the diet you've got enough FMH circulating once more so that you again may tap all that energy stored in your fat—thus getting rid of the fat as well as the fatigue.

Got it? It's important to understand. Otherwise you'll be blaming your Tuesday fatigue on your Sunday and Monday dieting instead of on the Saturday binge.

SOME PATIENTS ARE MORE TIRED THAN OTHERS. Now not all patients—even though they have low blood sugar—are equally troubled by this fatigue symptom. Not by any means. But to some people getting back their energy is almost more important than getting back their good figures. Natalie Todd is one of those. One of my nurses asked to tell you about this using my tape recorder.

"It isn't so much the weight I've lost," she says, "it's the difference in the way I feel since I went on the diet. I was always exhausted. My legs were tired, especially. Like lead. I had to spend a day a week in bed, and if I hadn't had to be up to run my business, I would have spent more time there.

"After the diet, the change was unbelievable. In a week I felt better."

AFTER THE DIET—A COMPLETE PERSONALITY CHANGE. "Another thing," Natalie said, "I craved sweets, and ate candy nonstop. I was always hungry. I'd get up from the table feeling starved. That's how I gained, of course. I just couldn't get enough to eat. And all that eating did was make me hungrier.

"I was bitchy, too—irritable, as well as tired and hungry. I tell you my family thinks this diet is a miracle, it has changed me so."

Natalie had low blood sugar, was a chubby child, but a slim bride. She started putting on weight with her first pregnancy, but when she came to see me she was still only twenty pounds over her bridal weight.

"I'd get dressed to go out and then cry," she remembers. "It was because of that extra weight, but it was also being so hungry and exhausted. I was desperate when I came to see you."

A SLOW WEIGHT LOSS BROUGHT A CHANGE IN HER TASTES. She lost the twenty pounds slowly. This has its advantages, because in the months that have elapsed, her tastes in food have changed. Now she positively dislikes sweets. "I'm a big cheese-eater," she says. "Brie. Fontina. Any good cheese. I'm perfectly happy with cheese instead of dessert." Her family has potatoes and rolls, but she's not even tempted by now. "The idea of that exhaustion coming back makes them look like poison to me," she says.

ONE PATIENT HAD BEEN DIAGNOSED AS PSYCHOTIC. Our files are full of histories of patients who have been physically disabled or branded as severe psychoneurotics, yet were merely severely hypoglycemic—all because their blood sugar level didn't fall low enough to satisfy the other doctors they had consulted that this was at the root of their problem. When they were placed on this diet, the symptoms of a lifetime cleared up as if by magic.

One such case sticks in my mind because of her exquisite sensitivity to even small amounts of carbohydrates. Originally Grace R. came to me to lose weight, but her real problems were physical (she was literally bedridden due to exhaustion) and mental (even a psychiatrist I know who understands hypoglycemia very well had diagnosed her as psychotic).

Grace R. weighed 132 pounds when she first came in to see me. Her glucose tolerance test curve looked like hypoglycemia to me, even though her lowest reading didn't drop below 68 milligrams percent.

She told me, "I've been starving myself . . . yet struggling with my weight for years. I once weighed 155. I thought how delightful it would be to weigh 122."

NO MORE TRANQUILIZERS NEEDED. Five years later she weighs 108 and has gone from a size 12 to a size 6. "But the big change has been in my whole frame of mind, an enormous change of attitude," she says. "I'd spent a lot of my life on the couch and with child guidance and marriage counselors. I was on tranquilizers and Thorazine. Three weeks after I started on the diet, no more tranquilizers! Didn't need them. I'd been feeling so depressed, so anxious, so weak or weepy or sleepy all the time. I couldn't concentrate. I couldn't make decisions. I couldn't finish a sentence. Everyone, including me, thought I was the hypochondriac, the psychoneurotic of all time. Then I went on the diet and all that trouble went away. Fantastic!

"I am one of those people whose body can't handle anything that converts to sugar. If I have eight scallops, it puts me in bed for a day with exhaustion." (Scallops are one of the few seafoods that contain any significant amount of carbohydrate—about one gram an ounce.)

WHAT TO DO IF YOU ARE HYPOGLYCEMIC. Because your doctor may prefer to ignore its existence, it is good for you to have the proof that hypoglycemia is a disease in irreproachable medical standing. Dr. Seale Harris first described it as a disease entity in 1924, and in 1949, the American Medical Association gave him an achievement award for this work, and had a medal struck in his honor. This honor has been conferred only a dozen times in the association's hundred years of existence.

We've learned a lot about hypoglycemia since then (including better ways to treat it than the Seale Harris diet). For example, in 1924 and for a generation after that, it was thought that most hypoglycemics were underweight. But in recent years, it has been observed that on the contrary, the majority of hypoglycemics are overweight. Certainly we know from our own work, and from a study done at Hahnemann Medical College, in Philadelphia, that most overweight people are hypoglycemic.

This won't surprise specialists because every study ever done in this field shows that every overweight person runs higher-than-normal levels of insulin and as you remember, low blood sugar and hyperinsulinism are almost invariably found together. Insulin not only converts the sugar into either energy or fat, but it prevents the liver and other tissues from replenishing the blood sugar supply when it is too low.

As you read the last chapter, perhaps you began to wonder about your tiredness, or your edginess, or your down-in-the-dumps reactions. Could they just be due to low blood sugar? If you decide you want to know for sure, you are about to embark upon one of the greatest obstacle courses in medicine.

MOST PEOPLE ASK THEIR DOCTORS FIRST. So, what do you do? Well, you could ask your doctor. But suppose he is one of those physicians who believes that functional hypoglycemia is a very rare condition, indeed?

ONE WAY: A FOUR- TO SIX-HOUR GLUCOSE TOLERANCE TEST. I have long felt that this test should be given routinely to every person who consults a physician even for a routine general checkup because low blood sugar is so common, and so many problems turn out to be caused by a disturbed carbohydrate metabolism. I'm confident that more doctors will get around to doing this simple but time-consuming procedure more frequently. But *you* will probably be the one to ask for it, as a rule.

I've done eight thousand glucose tolerance tests on overweight people. Only 25 percent showed the typically normal curve. Out of the 75 percent who showed a problem response, 25 percent revealed varying degrees of diabetes, and 75 percent showed varying indications of low blood sugar. Now here comes a fact worth noting: 80 percent of the diabetic responders showed manifestations of *both* diabetes *and* low blood sugar. Yes, these two seemingly opposite conditions can and do coexist—and quite commonly. (Fortunately, the normalizing treatment—this anticarbohydrate diet—is the same as when the disorders exist singly.)

HOW TO CHOOSE A DOCTOR. For this test you would do well to choose a doctor who has a reputation for understanding carbohydrate metabolism, for this is one area of medicine where great misunderstanding exists.

If you are concerned about your weight or some of the symptoms described here, ask your doctor if he thinks a six-hour glucose tolerance test would be in order. If he seizes upon this as a grand idea, then there is hope. If he turns down the suggestion, you might wonder what he has against your having such a simple series of blood tests. A glucose tolerance test may be a bit of a nuisance because it requires a half-dozen or so needle punctures, but it is relatively inexpensive, as laboratory tests go. All you do is drink down a beverage containing a standard amount of sugar (glucose) after which blood specimens are taken hourly and tested in the medical laboratory for the level of sugar in the blood.

I recommend a thorough checkup ˙in addition to the prolonged glucose tolerance test; for example, tests to evaluate the thyroid function; a good battery of screening tests of heart, liver, and kidney functions; electrocardiogram—the lot. You need to get an idea as to just what kind of shape you're in. Remember, *overweight is an illness.*

It's best to have all these tests before you go on this diet. Two months later, have some lab tests rechecked (your triglycerides and cholesterol, your uric acid level, and anything else that was suspicious). It's good to measure the improvement. Your doctor should check you, at least at the beginning and every few months during the diet.

GETTING A GLUCOSE TOLERANCE TEST. If you've had no luck getting your doctor to perform your four- to six-hour glucose tolerance test (never settle for a two- or three-hour test), perhaps he would allow you to go to a medical laboratory and have them test you. I am amazed at the number of patients who have taken this alternative in recent years.

So you got over the first obstacle—getting the test done. The second obstacle is having it interpreted correctly. There is currently no commonly agreed upon set of standards to interpret the results of a glucose tolerance test for low blood sugar as there is in the case of diabetes.

THE SECOND WAY: SEE WHAT THE DIET DOES FOR YOU. Will you then allow me to pass on to you the benefits of my experience with patients? I have pored over my data on eight thousand glucose tolerance tests and tried to correlate it with the symptoms my patients have had that have cleared up with this profoundly antihypoglycemic diet. In the process of giving these tests and following the cases of thousands of patients over the years, this is what I have noticed—patients *can* suffer from low blood sugar without a very dramatic finding on the glucose tolerance tests (they have showed the typical symptoms I've mentioned: fatigue, emotional volatility, depression, irritability, inability to concentrate). When I have put them on the anti-low-blood-sugar program—the virtually carbohydrate-free diet—they lose weight and the symptoms clear up most of the time. From my own practice I have observed at least a thousand such people.

I have tried to establish criteria to interpret a glucose tolerance test so that it correlates 100 percent with the actual symptoms, but at present there is no cutoff point or boundary line. I have mentioned some of the more useful criteria in chapter 5. But in the final analysis, the best test is the clinical trial.

IT'S A PRACTICAL TEST ON WHICH YOU'LL LOSE FIVE TO TEN POUNDS. Here is a simple way to find out if you're hypoglycemic. Go on the first week's test diet described in chapter 12. You'll lose weight, of course. If you also notice that you have more energy, and feel noticeably happier, you probably also are correcting your carbohydrate disorder.

YOU CAN LITERALLY BE A NEW PERSON. Within four days a whole dramatic personality change can take place if you have a blood sugar disturbance that is being corrected by the diet. But one warning. As I told you before, some people with low blood sugar are in such a delicate balance that literally *two grapes* supplying three grams of carbohydrate can make all the difference in the world in how they feel.

You won't get the right answers unless you follow the first week's eating program *exactly*. The results may not tell you anything if you decide you just can't skip your breakfast fruit or even if you add tomato catsup to your hamburger.

TRY THE DIET FOR A WEEK. Rather than three big meals, give yourself six or seven small feedings a day. Take the recommended megadoses of B complex, C, and E vitamins, as discussed in chapter 14. This is a must. They will help to keep your blood sugar at an even level. If you lose both weight and symptoms, you know you're on the right track for you.

From this vantage point, I have been tempted to develop a new axiom: *The extent to which you feel better on this diet is the extent to which you are suffering from hypoglycemia.*

PITFALLS IN GETTING CORRECT TREATMENT FOR HYPO-GLYCEMIA. Now that you've overcome the first few obstacles, you still face the obstacle of getting correct treatment. Remember, some doctors still treat this condition by telling you to eat something sugary. Although it is clearly incorrect for long-term treatment, sugar has two distinct uses for the hypoglycemic. One, in the diagnosis—when a symptom is dramatically, although temporarily, relieved by eating a sweet, that proves with near certainty that the symptom is due to low blood sugar. Second, in an emergency, when the symptom gets rather severe, taking a sweet could be useful to get prompt relief (such as when a subject feels faint and ready to pass out). However, it would not be wise to repeat this mode of treatment very often, because sugar makes the condition so much worse in the long run.

Sometimes even in comparatively sophisticated hands, the ideal diet for any hypoglycemic is not easy to find. The Seale Harris diet, which has been a standard dietary treatment for nearly half a century, is not truly low enough in carbohydrates for the majority of patients. And the diet in this book is not suitable for the underweight hypoglycemic (for them, it is *too* strict). It requires an experienced doctor to help the stubborn case of hypoglycemia.

But beware the group of "specialists" who treat hypoglycemia with injections.

CAUTION: INJECTIONS OF ADRENAL CORTICAL EXTRACT AREN'T THE ANSWER. While many doctors underestimate hypoglycemia, a tiny segment has made almost a cult of it.

If you happen to find one of these doctors, you will not only get a most sympathetic hearing and a low-carbohydrate diet but also an expensive series of injections of a drug called ACE.

ACE stands for adrenal cortical extract. The drug companies who make adrenal cortical extract do not recommend it as a treatment for hypoglycemia. It came out thirty years ago as a treatment for Addison's disease (for which a cheaper, better treatment has since been found). The American Medical Association's 1971 Drug Evaluations called ACE "an obsolete preparation."

THE DEVELOPMENT OF EARLY DIABETES IS HASTENED. You may be told that you need ACE injections because your low blood sugar is caused by inadequate secretions from your adrenal cortex. I can only say that because most hypoglycemics are probably early diabetics, and because adrenal therapy aggravates diabetes, the development of diabetes could well be hastened when adrenal injections are given in any significant dosage.

Many such people have come to me with overt diabetes, even though in reviewing the pre-ACE glucose tolerance test it could be seen that an early stage of diabetes already had been present.

When used for the treatment of hypoglycemia, ACE is far more than "an obsolete preparation" in my opinion. It is an unnecessary and a potentially harmful one.

I believe that the cloud over the practices of the so-called hypoglycemia doctors has made the legitimate medical profession overreact, sometimes with some justification, and contributed to its reluctance to accept the existence of this complaint and diagnose and treat it properly. I hope that the ideas I've presented represent a happy medium between these two extremes.

THIS DIET IS SAFE, WHETHER OR NOT YOU HAVE LOW BLOOD SUGAR. It's quite true that all of us—fat, thin, or perfect— whether we have low blood sugar or not, have periods of fatigue, depression, irritability.

Obviously neither this nor any other diet can prevent them. These low times are the lot of mankind.

But it is also true that continuing fatigue, depression, irritability, and all those other symptoms you read about earlier, can have a purely physical basis in cell starvation, due to low blood sugar.

So, as this diet brings down your weight without hunger, and your cholesterol and triglycerides, it will also control your symptoms if you have low blood sugar, early diabetes, or both.

8

TO STAY FAT—

KEEP

ON COUNTING

CALORIES

Earlier in this book I talked about how just "eating less" and calorie counting is a trap. It keeps you fat. (Look around you; the world is full of fat calorie counters!) We're frighteningly locked into the idea that in reducing, it's calories—and only calories—that count. We need to talk more about it. I'm not the first doctor to dispute the calorie theory by any means. But in order to free ourselves of this old and deadly over-simplification, we need to examine still more the evidence that the calorie gospel is a hoax.

It's such a reflex to think, "Look, I'm counting calories. I'm a good dieter. I'm bound to lose."

The job of this book is to change that reflex into, "Look, I'm counting carbohydrates—because it's carbohydrates far more than calories that count."

By the time this new reflex is installed in your subconscious, you'll have shed pounds and years and tiredness. Whatever your age, you'll begin to feel like a person reborn.

But changing reflexes takes time, new knowledge and open-mindedness. Are you ready?

First let's review what we know briefly and then look at some of the new evidence.

EVEN THE MEDICAL PROFESSION ADMITS THAT LOW-CALORIE DIETS HAVEN'T WORKED. We've all been exposed to a great number of reducing diets but there are really only two basic categories: those that depend on reducing the total intake of calories, and those that depend on the reduction of carbohydrate intake, where calories needn't be counted.

The balanced low-calorie diet has been the medical fashion for so long that to suggest any alternative invites professional excommunication. Yet even most doctors admit (at least privately!) the ineffectiveness of low-calorie diets—balanced or unbalanced.

It is also admitted in the medical press. In a comprehensive review of thirty years of medical literature, two Philadelphia doctors, A. J. Stunkard and M. McLaren-Hume, observed that most attempts to control overweight have been ineffectual.

The low-calorie "balanced" diet is theoretically a lifetime diet. But only theoretically. The public has been exposed to a barrage of medical and popular propaganda on its virtues for sixty years. The public read, listened, tried it. Again and again and again. With and without medical supervision.

AFTER SIXTY YEARS OF CALORIE-COUNTING 60 PERCENT ARE STILL WORRYING ABOUT OVERWEIGHT. Nevertheless, as numerous studies and polls have shown, 60 percent of our adult population is still—quite rightly—worrying about overweight. *No studies based on a balanced low-calorie diet have ever shown better than a 2 percent long-term success rate.* There's the pragmatic proof that balanced (or unbalanced) low-calorie diets don't work. On imprisoned laboratory rats, yes. On hungry, free-living humans, no.

CAN YOU COUNT THE REASONS WHY LOW-CALORIE DIETS DON'T WORK? We know that low-calorie diets don't touch the primary cause of most overweight—disturbed carbohydrate metabolism.

LOWER ENERGY OUTPUT. Another reason why low-calorie diets fail to work is that the dieter adjusts to the low-calorie intake with a proportionate decrease in total energy output. Dr. George Bray, of Tufts University School of Medicine, has demonstrated that people on low-calorie diets *actually develop lower total body energy requirements* and thus burn fewer calories.

The longer they remain on a low-calorie diet, the lower becomes their basal metabolism and the less they lose until eventually the low-calorie diet may stop working.

THE THIRD REASON: UNLESS YOU TAKE PILLS, YOU'RE ALWAYS HUNGRY. But the main reason low-calorie diets fail in the long run is because you go hungry on them. In order to get your weight down, you must cut your calories to a point where you don't feel comfortable. And while you may tolerate hunger for a short time, you can't tolerate hunger all your life. When your guard is down, perhaps because you're upset or depressed, you're going to seek the oldest, easiest, most reliable of solaces: food. So, naturally, you gain the weight back again.

And if you go to a doctor to be treated for overweight, what do you get? A low-calorie diet! The same old treatment. You may also get with it a box of confetti-colored diet pills —appetite suppressants; amphetamines, basically—sometimes with additions.

NO DOCTOR CAN MAKE STARVING TOLERABLE. The reason the appetite-killing amphetamines have been dispensed with such a lavish hand is that no doctor can make hunger bearable. So the pills are handed out to bridge the gulf between the patient's natural appetite and the inadequate diet prescribed by the doctor. Yet the starvation diet is the only prescription the calorie doctors have had to pass out. You get the diet list, a sheet of calorie counts, a couple of suggested menus, and a peptalk. No matter how effective the peptalk, the message is the same: Eat less than the quantity of food that you've found natural and comfortable all these years.

That is very easy advice to give; but it's like telling your kid sister to swim the English channel. The advice is not at all easy to follow. And I think the fault here lies with the physician in asking his patient to do something that he probably can't do himself. If somebody gave me the project of trying to follow the 1,200 calorie diet, I'd cry.

FROM NOTHING TO EIGHT BILLION DOSES ANNUALLY IN FORTY-FIVE YEARS. In 1930, two significant events occurred.

Drs. Newburgh and Johnston of the University of Michigan published their classical energy balance studies, in which they showed that under the conditions of their experiment, weight loss could be predicted from the calorie deficit of a diet. Their conclusion: "We wish to commit ourselves to the statement that overweight is never directly caused by abnormal metabolism but that it is always due to food habits not adjusted to the metabolic requirements." Despite the fact that only a few patients were studied and that the data in no way supported that conclusion, this statement became the gospel, and is still quoted by more conservative authorities today.

The second event was the discovery that amphetamine, which had been synthesized in 1927, had the remarkable effect of reducing the appetite.

"What a fortunate combination," doctors remarked. "Eating too much is the cause of overweight, but the pharmaceutical industry can provide us with a medicine that will make us eat less."

And so the use of amphetamines grew to the point where a federal ruling cut down its manufacture; it was estimated that eight billion doses a year were manufactured in this country—enough to keep every man, woman, and child among us high on "speed" for six weeks a year.

AS A METHOD OF WEIGHT CONTROL, THEY'RE A FAILURE. Even to this day, the overwhelming majority of patients who consult a physician complaining of serious overweight will walk out with a prescription or a supply of amphetamines or a drug related to it.

And they don't even work! There has never been a long-term study of amphetamines showing any benefit in weight reduction. Dr. Margaret Albrink says, "Appetite-suppressant drugs of the amphetamine group are effective for only a few weeks. Dependence on their stimulatory effect occasionally makes withdrawal a problem."

WHY AMPHETAMINES CAN'T HELP YOU LOSE WEIGHT. Why don't they work? In the main, because there is a tolerance to their effect after a few weeks. This may be because they require a reserve supply of adrenaline in the body in order to be effective and this supply becomes exhausted after a brief interval.

Also, it has recently been demonstrated that amphetamines cause a gradual week-by-week *increase* in the levels of circulating insulin. Now if insulin prevents your fat stores from breaking down, how can that help you lose weight?

At any rate, all human and animal studies alike show that upon discontinuance of amphetamines, the body weight goes back to a point above the starting level. Patients like to explain their weight rebound on psychological factors ("I got upset and started eating compulsively again."). But how do you explain the overgain in laboratory animals, living under controlled conditions, who gained when amphetamines were withdrawn?

Overgain upon withdrawal is the *expected* effect of diet pill usage. It occurs in all mammals. Diet pills are really appetite postponers. *The freedom from hunger they buy will have to be paid back later.* And the longer they are used, the greater will be the repayment.

Yet patients still come to me asking for "something to curb my appetite." (And thousands don't come to me because they know I won't prescribe diet pills.) My reply is, "Why should we curb your appetite? You have a lifelong weight problem and you must learn at some point in your life to work with your own natural biologic urges, such as your appetite. How can you begin to learn if your appetite is suppressed unnaturally by a drug?" A very different story from the *natural* decrease in hunger that goes with the lifelong diet in this book.

Thus, the claim that amphetamines are useful for "re-training eating habits" is shown for what it really is: a gross deception—a deception that has led amphetamines to becoming, in the words of Dr. George R. Edison, writing in the *Annals of Internal Medicine* in 1971, "perhaps the most serious drug of abuse in the United States," and "no less a menace than heroin."

AMPHETAMINE ADDICTION: COST OF THE CALORIE DOGMA. As you have gathered, I don't believe that there is any place for amphetamines in the treatment of overweight. As a side effect they make your heart beat faster, raise your blood pressure, and have been accused of speeding up the aging process. I have personally observed that they leave profound hypoglycemia in their wake. They have been responsible for many cases of serious mental illness, and even death. They recently have been implicated in the epidemic of "strokes" in young people. The depression that follows their use is one of the leading causes of suicide in our culture. The Food and Drug Administration (FDA) should have taken them off the market a long time ago. Never has any drug been allowed to exist with such a high incidence of abuse relative to use. When the International Narcotic Enforcement Officers Association asked me to address their Albany convention in 1971, I recommended to them that the manufacture of amphetamines be totally prohibited.

The calorie dogma got them off to fame, and has kept them there. Most amphetamines get into the hands of the public to be misused because somewhere along the line a doctor has prescribed them to allay the hunger that goes with the low-calorie diet he hands the patient.

WHY ARE THEY STILL PRESCRIBED? Dr. Edison sees many reasons. One is the economic benefits of their sale. Another may be because physicians themselves use these pills more often than the general population. Also he opines, "Because both doctor and patient sense, without verbalizing, that they are dealing with a problem that is nearly untreatable in traditional terms."

By "traditional terms," of course, he means by treatment with a low-calorie diet. But—as I said earlier—even with the pills, low-calorie diets don't take weight off permanently. Beatrice Goodman is typical of hundreds of my patients who are cases in point.

SHE HAS BEEN TAKING PILLS SINCE SHE WAS NINE! Beatrice Goodman is a pretty blond woman who now looks a good ten years younger than her age. She had been taking diet pills since she was a fat nine-year-old, 80 percent of her life. At fourteen, at her present height of 5 feet, 1 inch, she weighed 145 pounds. And in spite of the pills she has weighed within twenty pounds of that (up or down) most of her life since. Never had she succeeded in getting her weight down to what it should be.

She once told me, "The first time I came, Dr. Atkins, I overheard you tell your nurse, 'She won't be back.' You thought I wouldn't stick with a doctor who wouldn't give me pills after so many years of taking them. But I found the diet really very painless right from the beginning."

A TYPICAL YO-YO DIETER. Beatrice's weight has always fluctuated widely. "I would lose thirty pounds on the pills in a couple of months," she says. "Then I'd be put on maintenance, start eating a little more food, and that would be the finish. I could put on ten or fifteen pounds in a week.

"I don't drink. Bread was my worst thing. And I'm a snacker. I'd eat everything in sight if I was upset. And when I saw thin people with good figures, I'd get upset. Now I don't get upset; I'm happy with me."

FROM SIZE 18 TO SIZE 8—WITHOUT PILLS. She came to me in October 1969, weighing 166 pounds and wearing a size 18. Her mother was diabetic, and her glucose tolerance test revealed that she had hypoglycemia. On this metabolic diet program she has lost steadily. Without pause. Beatrice now wears a size 8 and is still losing at the rate of about a pound a month. (Earlier it was around a pound a week.)

"My face was like a moon," she recalls. "I had two chins. And my complexion used to be awfully dry. In the winter especially. My hands would get so cracked they hurt. My skin isn't dry now, and I think it's because I eat plenty of fat, which I couldn't before. If I ate lobster, I couldn't eat the butter sauce."

"I WASN'T HUNGRY FOR A MINUTE." "But on this diet you have so much to eat," Beatrice said. "The first week I lost four and three-fourths pounds—more than I had been losing on the pills. Yet I got so much food I wasn't hungry for a minute. All my eating habits have changed. In fact, I can't imagine eating any other way. I even think my neck has got longer! I suppose it's just because it's thinner. But the best part is I know I'll never have to go hungry again."

Some of you will read this story and believe it and yet, because your own calorie conditioning has gone on for so long you will think, "I know that pills are bad, but after all isn't it absolutely proved that you can only lose weight if you take in fewer calories than you burn up?"

I can only say to you . . . it is anything but proved. The calorie theory has become one colossal hoax with which commercial interests and the nutrition establishment have been successfully victimizing the hungry dieting public for too long.

Why is the idea of calories so much a part of our dietary thinking and how can it be so wrong? We all know someone thin who eats like a horse and someone fat who eats like a bird. Contrary to the popular misconception, it is probable that overweight people actually do eat less than people who have no trouble staying at a normal weight.

Every study on food intake of overweight people compared to normals confirms this. Dr. M. L. Johnson, Dr. B. S. Burke, and Dr. Jean Mayer showed this with overweight adolescent girls in Boston.

FAT GIRLS ATE 25 PERCENT LESS—AND GAINED ON IT! In the Berkeley, California, school system, Ruth L. Hueneman followed the daily calorie intake of 950 teen-agers from the ninth to the twelfth grades. She took body measurements of each. And she took careful dietary histories.

This is what she reported early in 1968: The average calorie intake for all ninth-grade boys who weren't overweight was over 3,000 calories per day. For similar girls it was 2,060 calories per day. But the average calorie intake of *the overweight boys was only 2,360 calories* per day. And the *fat girls only took in an average of 1,530* calories a day.

In the three years the study covered, there were no significant changes in the percentage of overweight and non-overweight students. But there was one very sad and important change. In spite of *eating less* during this three years, both fat boys and fat girls got fatter.

MY OWN EXPERIENCE CONFIRMS THESE STUDIES. I have had thousands of overweight patients who habitually eat as little or *less* than their normal-weight friends. In my experience this group outnumbers the patients who overeat.

So stop believing this calorie gospel. Start asking questions about that sacred cow—the calorie.

WHAT IS A CALORIE? The calorie is a unit of heat (or energy). Just as inches are units of length, calories measure the amount of heat (and therefore energy) a particular food or drink will provide. Specifically it is the amount of energy required to raise the temperature of one gram of water from zero to one degree centigrade. Multiply by a thousand and you have the kilocalorie—or the calorie as we know it today.

CALORIES OUTSIDE THE BODY CAN BE MEASURED ACCURATELY. The calorie theory has held sway for almost two centuries, ever since the renowned French physicist Antoine Lavoisier formulated his laws of thermodynamics. Heat energy cannot be created from nothing, he stated. The medical men from that day on adapted this to read: Calories in equal calories out. Otherwise weight gain or loss must take place.

As early as 1760, Joseph Black had devised a calorimeter, an apparatus for measuring these energy units. So when you read on the label of a bottle of diet soda that it contains one calorie you can believe it.

But what about the other part of the calorie balance sheet? How about the calories your body burns up? Just how are they measured?

They are not measured directly. *They are measured by inference.* The only measurable data are the amount of oxygen the body uses, how much carbon dioxide is expended, changes in body temperature, and so forth. Using a fixed formula, your caloric output—the amount of heat energy you use ordinarily—can be calculated, *provided all other factors are kept constant.* One of the items kept constant is the composition of the diet. *In other words, diets of different composition were never tested.* Yet this is the basis of the calorie dogma.

Well, it may be dogma, but it isn't very accurate. You've just been reading about a few of the many studies that suggest this . . . studies that have shown that contrary to the common medical impression it happens more often than not that overweight people eat *significantly* fewer calories than nonoverweight controls—and yet do not lose and sometimes even gain weight!

IT ISN'T HOW MANY CALORIES, BUT THE KIND OF CALORIES THAT COUNT. It was not until thirty years after the Newburgh and Johnson studies were made that two English researchers, Kekwick and Pawan, demonstrated that while people lost weight on a 1,000 calorie a day diet of protein or fat, *no weight was lost* on a 1,000 calorie a day diet of carbohydrates.

My own observations have been much more dramatic. It has been my clinical experience over the years with patient after patient that *weight will be lost even when the calories taken in far exceed the calories expended, provided the patient stays under his Critical Carbohydrate Level.*

YES, YOU CAN LOSE—AND LOSE A LOT—WHILE OVEREATING. Let's look at just the mathematics in the case of Herb Wolo-witz. (For his whole case history see chapter 9.) In seventeen weeks Herb lost eighty-five pounds—*and all this while he was eating 3,000 calories a day.* That is not a short-term loss.

Now for the mathematics: If Herb loses 5 pounds a week and if 1 pound of fat represents 3,500 calories, then $5 \times 3,500 = 17,500$ calories a week, 2,500 calories a day. In order to explain this phenomenon using the calorie theory, Herb would have to burn up $3,000 + 2,500$ calories or 5,500 calories a day! But Herb has a normal basal metabolism and a sedentary job as a real estate broker. The most liberal estimate of his caloric expenditure could not exceed 3,000 calories a day.

Where are the 2,500 calories a day going? Bear in mind that Herb had gained weight—got up to 367 pounds—*with the same metabolism* and without eating more than 3,000 calories a day. And he received no medications while he lost that eighty-five pounds. Nor was he physically more active while he lost that weight.

THE KEY TO THE CALORIE FALLACY. I have seen similar calorie discrepancies in at least a thousand different patients. So I *know* the calorie theory is wrong. For years I have been trying to find out why. I have been scrutinizing the basic premises of the calorie-in-balances-the-calorie-out misconception. And these are the conclusions to which I have come:

The calculation of calorie outflow is based on the assumption that fat, as it is burned in the body, is completely degraded (biochemically broken down) to yield all the potential heat (energy) that it contains. (The end products are the basic substances, carbon dioxide and water.) If any portion of the fat molecule were to leave the body in another form containing potential energy, the calorie theory would be proved wrong.

We already know about our wonderful friends those ketone bodies and how they are being excreted in the urine. We measure them with our "turning-purple" sticks. Dr. Kekwick and Dr. Pawan, in their pioneering research, were the first to point out that a significant amount of latent energy *is* excreted in this form. On a low-carbohydrate diet *nearly three times as much energy is lost* in the urine and stools, mainly in ketones, as on a high-carbohydrate diet.

And, as you have read, the ketone calories lost in the urine are just a part of the good news. A significant amount of ketone bodies are also excreted by way of the air we breathe. So that even more ketone bodies are excreted in merely breathing than Kekwick and Pawan accounted for in their study.

THE DIET REVOLUTION CALORIE THEORY. No studies have been done to demonstrate the complete reason why one can eat all he wants and still lose weight. These studies should be done now, and when they are, the old calorie theory surely will be dead and the new one will read:

Calories in equal calories used plus *calories excreted unused.*

Then we can go about our business of extending the Diet Revolution right past the protests of the nutrition old guard.

I think the old guard is beginning to weaken now.

Nutrition Reviews, which is sponsored in large part by manufacturers of refined carbohydrates, asked Professor D. A. T. Southgate, of Cambridge, England, and one of the world's foremost authorities on calories, to write an original article for it. His conclusion: "Over the last few years, evidence from a number of sources has accumulated showing that the simple calculation of metabolizable energy of a diet is inadequate to account for observations on energy balances and body weight changes." He states that there is definite evidence that it is the *relative proportions* of protein, fat, and carbohydrate in the diet that determine the calorie outflow.

But most doctors—and most of the public—are still victims of the old calorie hoax.

THE CALORIE HOAX. I think a cruel hoax is being perpetrated on the public by making us believe that we have no alternative but to believe in the calorie theory.

As a result, people are being forced to the conclusion that the wrong diet (the balanced low-calorie diet) is really the best diet for them. Because of motivation and their determination, they can lose weight—temporarily. But biochemically, cutting calories has always been a cruelly inefficient way to lose weight, even temporarily, because the carbohydrates in the balanced low-calorie diet not only keep you from burning your own fat, but they create hunger as well.

Every week five or six people tell me that they've never been able to stay on a low-calorie balanced diet for more than a few days. Well, that's natural. Each of the case histories that follow is typical of a hundred similar stories.

VICTIMS OF THE CALORIE HOAX. Suzy has a pretty face but is very much overweight. She joins a weight-losing club where people are applauded if they lose (and sometimes booed if they gain). Suzy follows the diet that they prescribe —a balanced low-calorie diet. She doesn't like skim milk but she drinks it. She eats more fruit than she is accustomed to.

And because the diet actually insists on more food and carbohydrates than she had cut down to, she gains weight. When she "confesses" this at the club, somebody boos her. Suzy doesn't cry but her heart is heavy with discouragement. Suzy is a victim of the calorie hoax.

THE YO-YO VICTIM. Henry was a fat boy and now he is a fat man. His self-confidence is shot. He knows he must take a stand so he goes on a diet. He cuts his quantities way down. He is hungry all the time but stoically he ignores it. He *must* get rid of this fat. Finally, after weeks of hunger, he can't stand it. He begins to eat like a maniac. Every year he goes through the same shameful, painful ordeal. And every year he gains back more than he lost. Henry is a victim of the calorie hoax.

THE MODEL DIETER. Gladys does everything right. She eats diet bread, diet desserts, diet cottage cheese, diet fruit, diet candy. She drinks only diet drinks. She cuts every corner. She seldom does anything that seems to be wrong. But Gladys is still a size 16 and all her friends a size 8. Gladys is a victim of the calorie hoax.

THE CLASSIC VICTIM. Marty asks his doctor, "Why am I fat? I really don't eat that much." The doctor explains to him very patiently, "If you would only eat less than you burn up, you wouldn't be fat. The fact that you are fat implies that you're not really telling us the truth. Because it's not really possible for you to eat the quantity you say you do and still be so much overweight." Marty is a classic victim of the calorie hoax.

WHAT MISCONCEPTION IS HOAXING THESE PEOPLE? *The misconception that one must just eat less, rather than differently* in order to lose weight. The mistaken belief that the number of calories we take in explains differences in body weight.

If calorie counting was the solution to the overweight problem, we wouldn't have so much of it, because we're a very calorie-wise nation. We know how to count calories and we know how to cut them. Everyone is trying to sell us on a happy way of feeling hungry. But we just don't want to go hungry.

YOU CAN LOSE WITHOUT HUNGER OR PILLS. There are a lot of ways of serving food attractively on a low-calorie diet, but the quantity that feels right inside your belly is something else, because in point of biological fact the foods that produce the sensation of satiety just don't get into the diet or bloodstream.

It isn't necessary to go hungry to lose. Take the case of a well-known New York economist. He is 5 feet, 11 inches and weighed 271 pounds when he came to see me. His blood pressure was high, he had hypoglycemia, and there was a family history of diabetes and overweight. Over a year's time his weight has come down to 194. This is lower than it has been since his college years. And he's still losing.

HE FOUND OUT THE CALORIE BOOKS ARE WRONG. "My own experience proves that the calorie books are wrong," he says. "I'm losing faster on 1,800 calories a day than I was losing on 1,000 calories when I was eating a 'balanced diet.' I know because I've been counting calories for twenty years.

"It's hard work to get down to 1,000 calories a day, but I had to. Some people were losing on 1,500 calories a day but not me. And I had long ago cut out drinking. To lose twenty pounds took months of torture. I felt starved; I'd go to the gym and lift weights, and the only thing on my mind was food.

"But I never would experiment with fad diets. I didn't believe in them. I believed in the calorie books . . . that losing was a matter of less input and more output. But if that was right, I should have been losing four pounds a week, and I was only losing two and feeling lousy.

"When I first heard about your diet, I thought it was a faddy diet. It took me a year to get here—with some sense of despair and a tiny hope. The first two weeks I lost sixteen pounds. Yet in those earliest days I'd eat a pound of meat at a sitting. Then I settled down to losing about two and one-half pounds a week—but pretty much month after month after month."

NOW HE'S EATING MORE AND LOSING MORE. "The point is the diet was a waltz compared to the other diets I've been on. There's no question but that I'm eating more and losing more. And it's the easiest diet to follow that I know of. For instance, fat is the last thing you eat on a conventional diet. Not on this.

"By October I felt better than in I don't know how many years. Last week I even stayed up all night playing poker."

A typical day's meals:

Breakfast:	One egg, four slices of bacon, coffee.
Lunch:	Baked oysters, veal piccata, cooked vegetables, salad.
Dinner:	Fillet of sole (with butter but no breading), asparagus with hollandaise, salad.
Dessert:	Zabaglione made without sugar.
Before Bed:	A slice of Brie (with which he may have some of the sixteen ounces of wine he is allowed per week).

THE ANGUISHED BASIC QUESTION IS NEVER RAISED. Very few patients can bring themselves to embarrass the doctor by asking the anguished basic question, "Why do I get fat when people I eat lunch with do not? We get about the same amount of exercise. We're around the same age. We eat and drink pretty much the same things."

There's very little that a hard-core calorie-counting doctor can say about that stubborn riddle. He knows from his practice that all those patients who make these claims aren't lying, or deluded. He's probably aware that if one parent is overweight, there's a 40 percent chance of overweight in the child. If both parents are overweight, there's an 80 to 90 percent chance the child will be overweight too.

He sees that the calorie theory doesn't fit real life, but he is stuck with it. He needn't be.

ARE SOME BORN FAT PRONE? Doctors who sat in on the round table on overweight at the convention of the American College of Physicians in Philadelphia a couple of years ago heard that some people simply have more fat cells than others, frequently from babyhood. These excess fat cells are lifelong installations. They create hunger—though why and how isn't fully understood. And their presence heralds the metabolic disorder that contributes to making an individual even more overweight prone. On a calorie-counting regime, hunger makes a permanent weight loss virtually impossible.

Only on a hunger-free diet can the fat prone hope to lose.

GRAM COUNTING IS EASIER, BUT DIFFERENT. Because we've been brainwashed for so long you'll have to be on guard all the time. But I know it can be done.

You'll get a lot of static at first as you switch from counting calories to counting grams. You explain to a friend that you're counting *carbohydrates* now, *not* calories, and you explain the new regime. But she is *still* going to say, "Oh, but surely you can have carrot sticks! No calories in *those!*" Or, "What? You can't have grapefruit? (Or catsup or skim milk?)"

So then you explain (or you don't) that because you're eating *differently,* it is not calories that you count, but carbohydrates. And that some *low*-calorie foods are loaded with carbohydrate and some *high*-calorie foods have none. Like butter, and mayonnaise. And pastrami. And spareribs. And roast duckling.

And after you've explained, she is still going to say,

"Here's extra lemon for your lobster, dear. I know you won't take the butter sauce."

Well, she's only trying to help. She can't because she has been brainwashed. So have we all. When she hears the word diet, she is locked into a calorie-count reflex.

I'm writing this book to unbrainwash you. I want to change your mental and emotional reflexes about calories. About carbohydrates, too. If I succeed, your diet troubles are over.

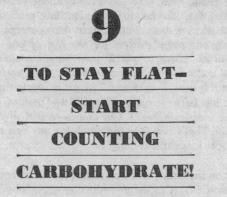

9

TO STAY FLAT—
START
COUNTING
CARBOHYDRATE!

Most patients whom I see regularly, once a week or once a
month, don't have to learn this simple drill. Because I do the
calculating for them. I just ask them what they've missed
most in their diet. I say, for example, "Have you missed
fruits? Vegetables? Wine?" Then each week, as long as the
diet is working correctly, I may add approximately five to
eight grams of that item to the diet. It may be four glasses
of wine a week, extra servings of allowed vegetables, a quarter
of a cantaloupe four times a week. This continues until each
patient's Critical Carbohydrate Level is established—twenty to
forty grams a day usually.

But, since you won't be coming to see me, you're in
charge of your own diet. So it's vital that you learn where
those killing carbohydrates lurk and how to keep book on your
own intake. What we're after is to supply you with what you
may miss but without disturbing the normalizing process that
is going to take off every last unwanted pound, and give you
back your youthful energy and good looks.

WEAR CARBOHYDRATE SPECTACLES FROM NOW ON. Now the way to succeed in losing without really trying is to put on carbohydrate spectacles and look at your world of food through them from now on. Forget about calories. Forget about high fat, low fat, high protein, low protein, balanced diet, unbalanced diets. Forget everything—except one thing.

Only one thing matters for the rest of your life. Does what you are about to put in your mouth contain carbohydrate? If it doesn't contain carbohydrate, feel free! Fill up!

But if it does, how much? Two grams—as in three grapes? That's a lot. Better consider skipping it. (Besides, what good are three measly grapes?) Ten grams—as in a sliver of birthday cake? That's certainly too much for any one mouthful if you want to lose without hunger.

A LOWISH CARBOHYDRATE DIET (THE KIND YOU'VE HEARD ABOUT BEFORE). A moderate reduction of carbohydrate intake doesn't mean much, I have found. Because our carbohydrate intake is so high that a moderate reduction means we're still getting excessive amounts. (Once you start actually counting the grams, you'll see this for yourself!)

The result: you don't lose hunger, you don't lose weight, you don't lose the fatigue, depression, irritability that accompany high insulin and low blood sugar levels. A lowish carbohydrate diet doesn't change your chemistry.

The point I'm trying to bring out is this: Only with drastically reduced carbohydrate intake do we see the benefits of carbohydrate restriction; the sense of well-being, the loss of hunger, and of pounds and inches.

What do I mean by "drastically reduced"? I mean an intake of well below forty grams of carbohydrate per day. And that's the upper limit. That's where most of you will end your diet and start maintenance. Where you start the diet, of course, is with a daily intake of zero grams of carbohydrate. Although we allow salad on the diet from the start, and lettuce has carbohydrate in it, the amount it contains is so minute as to be biologically the equivalent of zero.

The business of discovering where the killer carbo-hydrates lurk is fascinating.

LIFE WILL BE FULL OF SURPRISES. With your carbohydrate spectacles on, you know that a lemon (6 grams) almost equals half an orange (7.5 grams) in carbohydrates. On the other hand, half an avocado (only 5.4 grams) is a good buy for a luncheon salad, even running over with crabmeat (4 ounces equals 1.3 grams) moistened with mayonnaise (1 tablespoon is only .2 of a gram).

You learn to be wary of all commercial tomato products. One tablespoon of catsup contains 4.9 grams—and whoever uses as little as one tablespoon!

Now, some of you are old hands at gram counting, but for those who aren't, let's start at the very beginning.

DEFINITION OF A GRAM. What is a gram anyhow? Well (just as a calorie is a unit of heat), a gram is nothing more than the basic unit of weight in the metric system. To be precise, a gram is 0.035 of an ounce, thus there are about thirty grams to the ounce.

So when we talk about how many grams of carbohydrate there are in a half cup of cooked peas, for example, we are talking about the amount of carbohydrate, by *weight*, which has been determined in a laboratory to be built into that half cup of cooked peas.

YOU CAN LOOK UP THE CARBOHYDRATE CONTENT OF FOOD IN A GRAM COUNTER. Just as you've been accustomed to look up calorie values in a calorie counter, you can check the carbohydrate content of almost any food or drink in a carbo-hydrate gram counter.

You'll find the carbohydrate gram content of the foods that are particularly relevant to this diet in a variety of sources. Calculating carbohydrates in your diet couldn't be easier . . . once you're clued in.

If you want to know the carbohydrate gram count of

practically everything edible, I can recommend several books to you.

Most portable is the little purse-sized *Carbohydrate Gram Counter* put out by Dell Publishing Company.

SEVENTY-FIVE HUNDRED FOODS ARE LISTED IN THE SECOND BOOK. A more comprehensive book is Barbara Kraus's *Calories and Carbohydrates*, published by Grosset and Dunlap, Inc., and constantly being revised so that it is up-to-date. (Make sure you get the very latest edition.) It lists the calorie and carbohydrate content of seventy-five hundred edibles and drinkables. Brand names are given. This can make a big difference.

And most comprehensive of all is a handbook published by the Department of Agriculture. It contains not only the carbohydrate content of 2,483 edibles and drinkables, but also the amount of fat, protein, and food energy they contain, as well as the amounts of five minerals and five vitamins. It's a great buy for $1.50, and should be in every cook's library. Its title is *Composition of Foods, Agriculture Handbook No. 8.* To get it, you write the superintendent of documents, U.S. Government Printing Office, Washington D.C. 20402.

MYTHS THAT NEED TO BE UNLEARNED. To lose weight and all those other nasty signs of premature aging, you have to *un*learn some dearly held beliefs. But these beliefs are myths, not facts. Let me give you some examples:

MYTH: A person needs fruits and vegetables for vitamins, minerals, and bulk. What about orange and grapefruit juice, for instance?

FACT: What you need is the Vitamin C in citrus fruit and the other vitamins and minerals in fruit, all of which you get from other foods on this diet and your vitamin supplement *without* also taking in the fruit sugars that trigger off your hyperinsulinism. You get ample bulk and variety from the green salad and other vegetables on the diet.

MYTH: Everybody needs milk; at least one or two glasses a day. If you want to lose weight, you should drink skim milk.

FACT: Everybody needs the nutrients in milk, and you *get* them on this diet—in a long list of cheeses, including cottage cheese. But for people with a disturbed carbohydrate metabolism, the milk sugar or lactose in milk aggravates the disorder.

MYTH: A person needs sugar for energy and for the functioning of the brain cells.

FACT: What you need is some sugar in your *bloodstream*, not in your *diet*. The surplus fat you are stirring in your body is easily converted into carbohydrate (glycogen) so that it can be used for energy, instead of disfiguring your body and shortening your life by remaining as fat.

YOUR NEAREST AND DEAREST WILL (UNCONSCIOUSLY) DO THEIR BEST TO CROSS YOU UP. It takes a little practice to unscramble the confusion in your head between low calorie and low carbohydrate. And your friends, loved ones, and hostesses won't be any help. Everybody has ideas, instilled in childhood, about certain foods that are just *bound* to be good for you ... the natural foods.

ARE THERE "GOOD" CARBOHYDRATES AND "BAD" CARBOHYDRATES? "Oh, but this is that wonderful *raw* sugar," your hostess croons. "Natural sugar. Full of all kinds of vitamins and things."

Well, it does have a few molecules of iron and other minerals. But it also has all the disadvantages of refined sugar in that it overstimulates insulin flow. Its chief advantage, says one hep nutritionist, is that, "Perhaps it builds mental health by instilling a sense of virtue in its users."

IS HONEY A "GOOD" CARBOHYDRATE? And how many times have you heard about the mystic virtues of honey? Your friend looks at you unbelievingly and says, "No sugar at all? Well, at least you can have some of this honey. That's a *natural* food, very good for you."

Not if you're allergic to carbohydrates. You explain (or you don't!) that one tablespoon of honey contains 17.3 grams of carbohydrate. It's even higher than sugar! (One tablespoon of sugar contains only 12.1 grams.) If twenty-five grams of carbohydrate per day is your CCL, one good drizzle of honey and you've *had* it! Remember that the world's first sugar refiner was the honeybee.

MANY PEOPLE BELIEVE THAT NOT TO DRINK ORANGE JUICE IS DOWNRIGHT SACRILEGE. "Good God, you can't have orange juice?" you'll hear.

Not at over three grams of carbohydrate per ounce. Not when in a few quick swigs you've used up eighteen grams of your day's allowance. Who needs it when a Vitamin C tablet is so handy?

BEING AGAINST MILK IS LIKE BEING AGAINST MOTHERHOOD. When you wear your carbohydrate spectacles, skim milk suddenly looks very different. Your friend says, "It isn't cream —I know that's horribly fattening. This is just milk. Skim milk at that. Full of calcium, you know. *Milk* can't hurt you, for heaven's sake."

Oh, but it can—with twelve grams of carbohydrate in every cupful of it! Forget that old idea that everyone needs a quart of milk a day (and what's more wholesome than a nice piece of homemade cake with it?). Instead of milk, take the heaviest cream you can get in your coffee. Only a trace of carbohydrate in a tablespoonful of *that*. Or take your coffee *mit schlagober* (whipped cream), as they do in middle Europe. Well sweetened and with mountains of cream, it's as satisfying as a murderous dessert—and with this you'll lose instead of gaining.

IF IT'S "NATURAL," HOW CAN IT BE BAD FOR YOU? Your hostess says virtuously, "I never eat rich desserts either, but surely you can just have some of these marvelous *naturally* cured raisins and dates. There's not a grain of sugar on them."

Plenty in them, though. The dates are 78 percent sucrose (table-sugar-type sugar); the raisins 64 percent. In a half cup of raisins, 55.7 grams of carbohydrate. In one date, 5.8 grams of carbohydrate.

Or if there's pie for dessert, this is what you'll hear. "Well, if you can't have pie, then have some fresh fruit. Now come *on*, on *any* diet you can have fresh fruit."

That's yesterday. Today you tote up the carbohydrate count: in an apple, twenty grams; in a banana, twenty-six to thirty grams; in a pear, around twenty-five grams; in a half cup of quick-thaw mixed fruit, over thirty-six grams. Coffee anyone?

Cookies, cakes, and pies are full of "empty" calories, with little or no nutritional value. The menus and meal plans in this book are all based on protein and packed with nutrients.

The conservative Food and Nutrition Council states that for adequate nutrition *every adult should take in sixty grams of protein a day*. Now, it's not easy to get those sixty grams of protein a day on a low-calorie diet. In our culture, there are some of us who don't take in that amount of protein on a high-calorie diet, because so much of our food intake is usually carbohydrate.

NO "EMPTY" CALORIES ON A GRAM-COUNTER'S DIET. On a low-carbohydrate diet, however, it's a breeze to get *more* than an adequate intake of protein.

You'll take in approximately 164 grams of protein in a day if you start it with two slices of bacon and two eggs for breakfast; have a five-ounce cheeseburger and a green salad for lunch; have six big shrimps (maybe scampi?) for a first course at dinner, then two big lamb chops, a green salad, and a four-ounce piece of cheesecake (see recipe section) for dessert.

This is a fairly typical diet revolution day for a big eater—more food than most people actually would consume because of the unhungriness that is a strong feature of the diet. However, suppose you could eat this much? You've taken in around 2,000 calories. But because you've taken in *less than 10 grams of carbohydrate* you'll lose weight and feel great—and one of the reasons is because of the 164 grams of protein you put away so easily.

All because you've switched from being a hungry calorie counter to being an *un*hungry carbohydrate counter.

COUNTING CARBOHYDRATES DOESN'T MEAN YOU HAVE TO GO WITHOUT DESSERTS. Look at the dessert recipe section of this book. You'll see that you can have wonderful desserts on this diet: cheesecake that's sweetly rich and creamy smooth; chocolate mousse; whipped cream, pies, even candy . . . dozens of other sweets that are all very low in carbohydrate.

And I promise you that once you start thinking about desserts while wearing those carbohydrate spectacles of yours, you'll begin having new dessert ideas all your own . . . just as luxuriously sweet and just as low in carbohydrates as those in this book. I know this will happen. It happens with most of my patients. They sit in the waiting room exchanging dessert and other recipe ideas by the hour.

The recipes in this book are largely the work of just two of these patients, and they have developed hundreds of others. Once your mind is focused on the challenge of how to put together low-carbohydrate desserts, you'll find that if you like cooking you have an exciting new outlet for your creativity. If you don't like cooking, stick with the desserts in this book, varying the flavors to your heart's content.

YES, *anyone* CAN LOSE ON HIGH-CALORIE FOODS BY COUNT-ING GRAMS. Take the case of Martin G. He was born hungry.

He was a fat baby and has been fat—and a big eater—all his life.

When he started on my diet, I asked him to write down every day everything he ate—exact quantities. He did this conscientiously.

Ordinarily Martin loves to play ball, but he hurt his ankle so he hasn't had any exercise at all the last six weeks. Nevertheless, he has lost forty-four pounds in four months on this diet program and is still losing.

He has a teen-ager's taste in food (he rarely eats lettuce or vegetables). But what is interesting is the quantity of food he eats while continuing to lose.

His breakfast is always the same: four ounces of a low-carbohydrate fruit-flavored drink, two eggs (usually scrambled in butter), and three slices of bacon. Coffee with heavy cream.

MARTIN G. EATS ENOUGH FOR TWO—BUT NOT CARBOHYDRATES. Here is a fairly standard lunch: two Swiss cheese "sandwiches"—he uses two slices of Swiss cheese for the outside, instead of two slices of bread, and four slices of bologna inside. So lunch is a total of four slices of Swiss cheese, eight slices of bologna. To this he frequently adds two slices of roast beef or two fried eggs and a quarter or half a jar of macadamia nuts. He drinks a lot of diet cola.

A typical *dinner* is two eggs, four slices of bacon, four slices of bologna, two slices of roast beef, half a grapefruit, coffee. *Another dinner:* two frankfurters, three hamburgers, two colas, three light coffees. *Another:* shrimp cocktail, half pound of chopped liver with onions, iced coffee, quarter jar of macadamia nuts. *Another:* beef stew with one pound of meat and onions, two light coffees.

Before bed he sometimes has half a jar of nuts, or a few slices of cheese with a diet cola.

"I used to eat all day long and at night too," he says. "Pizzas were my downfall. I couldn't stop eating them. I felt the same way about ice cream. Now I can pass a pizza without a pang. Take a whiff and just pass by. It's so great to be able to get into good-looking clothes again. And I feel so good. But the reason I'm able to stay on the diet—and was never able to stay on any other—is because I can eat all I want. And as long as I keep the carbohydrates way down, the pounds drop off. I don't feel guilty and I don't feel hungry and I keep on losing."

A BIG-EATING BROKER WHO LOST A POUND A DAY THE FIRST TWELVE WEEKS. Herb Wolowitz came to me one June day weighing 367 pounds. He was a thirty-two-year-old real estate broker who had been a two-hundred-pounder since the age of sixteen. He had tried diet pills and had started and quit Weight Watchers many times. The last hundred pounds were of recent acquisition. I discovered that he had the typical diabetic-hypoglycemic glucose tolerance curve that most over-weight patients show (his blood sugar rose to 292 and three hours later it was 67). He also had high blood pressure and high triglycerides.

Herb told me he didn't eat much at meals, but he did "nosh" a lot on sweets after dinner. I placed him on the diet in this book, and he followed it correctly but he ate large quantities. For breakfast he usually had a cheese omelet and with lunch and dinner he rarely ate less than two and one-half pounds of red meat. By the most conservative of esti-mates, his calorie intake was a minimum of 3,000 calories a day.

HE CUT CARBOHYDRATES BUT NOT CALORIES. But four months later he weighed 282 pounds. In seventeen weeks he had lost eighty-five pounds! His blood sugar and his blood pressure were now normal, his triglycerides had fallen 75 points and his cholesterol, 30 points. He felt great, as if he had been given a new lease on life (which he had!). And, of course, he was never hungry. How could he be eating all that food?

First we added a few more vegetables, then some alcohol,

later some fruit, still later nuts. Herb's weight loss began to slow down to two pounds a week. But he is even happier, because this new way of eating doesn't seem to Herb like a diet. "I'm losing but I'm not on a diet—I'm eating up a storm," he says happily. "It's fantastic!"

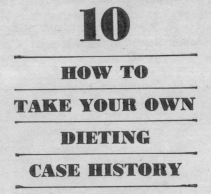

10

HOW TO

TAKE YOUR OWN

DIETING

CASE HISTORY

Let's pretend this is your first visit to my office. At this visit I would give you a physical examination, complete with a glucose tolerance test. But before that I would start out by asking you certain questions. The questions that follow aren't the only ones I ask, but they include three main areas that it is important to explore. The first is your family history, because this gives us the true picture as to your biological tendency to overweight. The second is a history of what has happened to you on previous diets. The third is an analysis of your present eating pattern.

Suppose you get a pen or pencil and prepare to answer in writing the questions I'll be putting to you in this chapter.

YOUR CHILDREN'S HEALTH TOO MAY BENEFIT. This operation will let you climb outside your skin and gather a little about your past, present, and probable future as far as weight control is concerned. You may get some big surprises. This new view of you may add years to your life and undreamed-of vitality to your years. Even your children's health can benefit from what you may learn in this chapter.

You can't read your horoscope without knowing exactly when and where you were born. And it's difficult to treat your overweight successfully without knowing its birthdate. (As you read on, you'll understand why this is so.) Was it before you were conceived? In your babyhood? Adolescence? After your pregnancies? Recently? Or did it come on gradually and insidiously over the years?

GET A DOCTOR'S-EYE VIEW OF YOU. By the time you've finished reading this book, what we're going to find out is to what extent is *your* overweight due to carbohydrate poisoning? How—and to what extent—does your particular heredity, body type, and diet history account for this metabolic disorder? And what is likely to happen to you as a result of this disturbed carbohydrate metabolism if you ignore it?

When you finish answering the questions that follow, you'll see your situation with a new objectivity.

FIRST LET'S TALK ABOUT YOUR FAMILY. Please answer these questions on the pad of paper I have asked you to take up.

Your mother's approximate height?

Your father's approximate height?

What was the most your mother ever weighed?

What was the most your father ever weighed?

(To calculate the approximate degree of their overweight, if any, multiply the number of inches over five feet by five for a woman, seven for a man, then add one hundred. For example, a woman 5 feet, 6 inches should weigh in the neighborhood of 130 pounds: a man of 5 feet, 6 inches should weigh somewhere around 142 pounds. That's very roughly the ideal weight for anyone—including you. For a more exact idea, see the tables on pages 297–298.)

Do you have brothers and sisters who are overweight? How much? (The majority of you whose parents and siblings are overweight have a weight problem yourself.)

Can you think of any member of your family who has had diabetes? Hypertension? Heart disease? (Parents, grandparents, sisters, brothers, uncles, aunts?)

Are your parents living? If not, how old did they live to be? (If they died natural deaths, the answer strongly suggests to what extent longevity runs in your family.)

How long were they in good health? What was the cause of death? Answers to all the questions above give us a hint as to *your* special vulnerabilities.

LIKE FATHER, LIKE SON. I think that when a parent and child have the same body build and the same height, the child could well look to what kind of illness his parent had, and if it was heart disease, he'd better be careful. I feel that if you don't pay attention to these matters at the earliest possible age, which always is *now*, it can be too late. If you just wait until you already have the symptoms of diabetes or heart disease, you've undoubtedly waited too long.

High triglyceride levels, high cholesterol levels, high insulin levels, and high blood sugar levels run in families. These four risk factors are all interrelated, and they all tend to appear where there is a family history of overweight. If this is your background, this is very important. It means that your life expectancy is 80 percent dependent on what you eat (which may govern those levels) and how well you take care of yourself.

NOW LET'S TALK ABOUT YOU AND WHAT HAPPENED TO YOU ON PREVIOUS DIETS. I suggest that you also write down the answers to the following questions. They'll help to externalize your situation, let you see more clearly where you are in life.

Your age? Your height? (This oddly enough is a figure many people exaggerate. Get ready to be both honest and surprised. Measure yourself with a yardstick on a door jamb.)

What is your ideal weight? If you once were at your ideal weight, you'll remember it. Otherwise, use the tables on pages 297–298.

Were you a fat baby? Get out those baby pictures; or

cross-examine your older relatives. If you were a fat baby, you need this diet more than most people. (The earlier you put it on, the harder the struggle to lose it and the sicker your metabolism as a rule. Especially ominous is overweight that began before the age of ten.)

What do you think first caused you to put on weight?

What is the least you ever weighed as an adult or even in your late teens? (If you looked well then, that weight might still be your goal weight.)

What's the most you ever weighed? (If you are not at your all-time high weight, remember that your peak weight is one which you might be expected to level off at if you were not dieting.)

When was that?

NOW IT IS TIME TO LOOK IN THE MIRROR OF YOUR DIETING PAST. What diets have you been on? List them, and after each diet note these seven things.

1. Your age.
2. How much did you lose?
3. How did you feel on the diet. For example, were you hungry? How was your energy level? Were you bored?
4. How long were you on it?
5. Why did you quit?
6. How much did you gain back?
7. How fast did you gain it?

What would be the virtues of an ideal diet for you? Would it have to solve a hunger problem? Or a boredom problem? If it is either of the two, you are in luck, for this diet solves these problems. The hunger would be cured by the diet itself, and the boredom by all the wonderful recipes as well as the variety the diet affords.

LET'S GO BACK TO QUESTION NUMBER 5. Nothing is more important to your success with this diet than to think long and carefully about your answer to question 5: Why have you quit in the past? Take time to go into this a bit.

Did you stop because there was something wrong with the diet (it didn't work, or it left you hungry, bored you)? Or was it just because you loved eating more than being slim? In other words, because you didn't really care enough about your appearance and health to stay on it.

Or did you quit because something upsetting happened in your life about then, so that you were under unusual stress and the stress of going hungry was more than you could handle on top of it?

Pause to tote up just how many times you've started a diet, and then quit. Do you find that you quit different diets for basically *similar* reasons?

Don't be discouraged as a result of reviewing your dieting past. Be objective. Try to see yourself as your doctor might see you.

There's real value in this exercise for you. You're going to be given an easier, more enjoyable, more efficient diet than you've ever experienced. But when it comes to changing your eating habits (even though there's no hunger or boredom involved) it's vital to realize with crystal clearness the role that you and your values play.

To make even the world's best diet work you've got to *care*. No diet, no matter how perfectly conceived, is more than a tool—an instrument that the motivated individual can use—to accomplish a goal he wants. No diet can *make* you lose weight.

PART THREE OF YOUR DIET PROFILE: WHAT IS YOUR EATING PATTERN? Now, let's try to get a picture of your eating habits. That's where we'll be starting from.

What is your usual carbohydrate intake? That's what is important.

I hear many people say, "Well, actually I don't think I take in very many carbohydrates. I don't take sugar in my coffee. I seldom eat gooey desserts. And at dinner I just don't put bread on the table anymore."

Well, that's all to the good. But it isn't good enough, good as it is, *if* (a) you're overweight and (b) you aren't metabolizing carbohydrates properly. Either or both of these conditions indicate that you're still taking in too many carbohydrates for *you*.

Our national eating habits being what they are, it's easy to take in 50 percent of your calories in carbohydrates, even if you *don't* have a mouth full of sweet teeth.

HOW MANY CARBOHYDRATES DO YOU TAKE IN PER DAY? I want you to find out for yourself what your usual carbohydrate quota is. Like this:

1. *For three days minimum (a week would be better) eat and drink just as you usually do.* No virtuous abstainings. Just relax and do what comes naturally.
2. *Write down everything you put in your mouth—liquid or solid. Quantities too, as nearly as you can guess.* Carry a notebook in your purse and just *as soon as you've eaten or drunk, jot it down.* If you wait to do it later, you're all too likely to forget something.
3. Forget calories. Just *write down the item and quantity. Later on you look up and then add up the grams of carbohydrates you're taking in.* To do this, simply look up the item in the carbohydrate gram counter mentioned earlier in chapter 9. Use the gram counter just as you use a calorie counter, only it's carbohydrate grams you count.

This is an important exercise. Why? Because you see your eating habits through new eyes. It makes you carbohydrate conscious, carbohydrate wise as nothing else can.

COULD A SAMPLE DAY'S EATING GO SOMETHING LIKE THIS? Let's take what might be a sample day's eating for most people who think they are eating "carefully" to keep their weight under control. It's not a dieting day. It's just an ordinary cautious eating day.

	CARBOHYDRATE CONTENT IN GRAMS
BREAKFAST	
6 ounces orange juice	19.0
1 cup cornflakes	24.7
1 cup skim milk	13.4
1 tablespoon sugar	12.1
Coffee without sugar	Trace
COFFEE BREAK	
1 cup fruit yogurt	26.0
LUNCH	
4-ounce hamburger	0.0
on a roll	20.7
3 tablespoons catsup	13.5
½ cup coleslaw	8.1
Diet Pepsi (12 ounces)	18.0
BEFORE DINNER	
2 ounces gin	0.0
8 ounce glass tonic	18.4
10 potato chips	10.0
DINNER	
1 cup tomato soup	15.7
6-ounce steak	0.0
Baked potato	20.8
¾ cup peas	17.1
½ honeydew melon	11.0
Coffee without sugar	Trace
BEDTIME	
1 glass skim milk	13.4
1 small banana	21.1
TOTAL	300.0

This is six or seven times as much carbohydrate as you can take in and hope to maintain a weight loss. As for losing on this high an intake of carbohydrate—forget it!

Though a few carbohydrate-sensitive people can maintain a reasonable weight on 60 grams of carbohydrate per day, my experience with thousands of such patients, as I said earlier, is that the majority find their Critical Carbohydrate Level to be 40 grams daily—or less. When they take in more than that, they get hungry—and then gain.

Yet you can see how easy it is to overeat carbohydrate in today's culture—even for people who think that they're on a diet, and who go hungry (and therefore some days go overboard altogether and eat their heads off!).

Take Mary Lou's eating pattern. Mary Lou is secretary to one of my friends. She doesn't eat breakfast. Lunch is usually soup and a sandwich (around ten to twenty grams of carbohydrate in the soup, twenty-four grams in the two slices of sandwich bread and a few more grams for the filling).

Around four or five o'clock she has a medium-sized apple (20.5 grams). If she doesn't go out for dinner, she has a frozen TV dinner (Swanson's Chinese dinner is a favorite). It contains 40.5 grams of carbohydrate and is fairly average for the "light" frozen TV dinners.

While her dinner is heating she munches on carrot strips (5.6 grams of carbohydrate per one-half cup). She skips dessert. Before bed, she has a glass of skim milk (13.4 grams of carbohydrate).

Because she has been so good all day (no Danish at coffee-break time, no dessert for either lunch or dinner, no drink before dinner), she rewards herself with three Nabisco Fig Newtons along with her milk; another 30.3 grams of carbohydrate.

Total for her dieting, hungry day: around 160 grams of carbohydrate. And if she drinks her favorite Diet Seven-Up or Diet Rite or Diet Pepsi during the day, another nine grams of carbohydrate goes down her unwary gullet with every six ounces!

REREAD YOUR OWN BIOGRAPHY. Read over the notes you have made about yourself. Get a clear picture of the person you are, the person whose eating habits are going to be retrained so that you can't possibly go back to eating the killing old ways. Does this sound impossible? Thousands of my patients are evidence that it *is* possible. Not only possible, but painless!

But first you must realize the extent, the seriousness, of your weight problem—just as I do after interviewing a patient. That's where answering those questions will help you.

Let's suppose you're Mrs. A. for example. Your parents were slim, healthy, long-lived. This is the first time you've ever dieted. You're middle-aged, but you never ate desserts, you played tennis, you kept your figure. And it's only recently (since your husband died) that the scales told you you were wavering between ten and fifteen pounds over your lifetime weight. If your case history is anything like Mrs. A.'s, you have no problem at all, comparatively. On this diet, you'll drop that weight without the slightest effort. And you'll keep it off easily with a very comfortable CCL of probably sixty grams of carbohydrate per day. Your spirits will perk up, too, and your interest in men.

DOES YOUR CASE HISTORY READ LIKE THIS? On the other hand, your dieting "profile" may be more like that of Mrs. C. Your parents were overweight and either (or both) were diabetic. You have been on the plump side ever since you were a baby. You have tried a great many diets. You lose but you regain even more than you lost. By now you're veering between being fifty to eighty pounds over your ideal weight. You love sweets. You're a night eater.

Well, Mrs. C., you're like most of my patients. You can become a model size and stay that way. And you will feel wonderful while you're shedding both weight and a disproportionate number of inches. But you're playing for much higher stakes than Mrs. A. You're playing for your life. And your commitment to the project must be total. That doesn't mean that you must suffer privation or hunger or discomfort.

But it does mean that you've got to put away once and for all the naïve idea that you can diet for a while until you've lost the worst and then go energetically back to digging your grave with your teeth. You're not weak willed. You're not a glutton. But you are sick. Very sick. Getting well must be your first concern. You can never look forward to not being on a diet.

OR ARE YOU MR. OR MRS. B.? You're not Mrs. A.? You're not Mrs. C.? Perhaps your case history is more like that of Mr. or Mrs. B. One (or both) of your parents were overweight. But you were slim until your pregnancies (or, Mr. B., until a few years after you got out of the army). You've tried various diets. You lose—but, of course, sooner or later you gain it back. You'd be happy people if you could just drop twenty to thirty pounds.

On the other hand, lots of people you know are in the same boat. And dieting is such a bore. It isn't as if you ate ignorantly. You eat carefully (except during vacations and the holiday seasons, of course). Plenty of fruit. Not much fat. No bread on the table. And you play golf. You swim. You even do the Royal Canadian Air Force (RCAF) exercises most mornings.

Mr. and Mrs. B., you have my sympathy. You don't deserve to be loaded down with those unpleasant extra pounds. But because we're not on guard against the carbohydrates that are the major cause of those creeping pounds, we're innocent victims of carbohydrate-itis, the insidious, invisible, all-pervasive plague of our century.

But once you know what causes this disease, Mr. and Mrs. B., you can lick it—and without a pang.

Take my own history. I didn't have either a doctor or a book like this to help me. I have a big appetite but no one has ever accused me of having willpower. Yet I've been able to train myself so that when I walk into a cocktail party with a smorgasbord, that picture doesn't even reach my brain. The picture I see goes from my eye to my hand. My eye will see protein (which I call *my* food). It will not even see *their* food (the carbohydrates). I just automatically grab the protein. I don't even have to think about it because it's a habit, a habit that by now has become a reflex. At first I *thought* about it. Now I don't have to think about it anymore.

RETRAINED EATING CAN BE AS REFLEX AS BRUSHING YOUR TEETH. And this is what I propose to do for you. I propose to train you to a pattern of eating habits that will hold fast even in the midst of a serious emotional upheaval.

Businessmen who come to me sometimes say on that first visit, "But, doctor, I'm under such pressure!" I tell them, "Under pressure you don't forget to brush your teeth. Even if you're in the midst of a corporate upheaval, you'll still remember that. Why? Because it's so important? Or because it's such a habit?" What I hope this book will do for you is to train you to have good eating habits that are just as built-in as brushing your teeth.

11

BEFORE

YOU START ON

THIS DIET

Before you start on this diet, you'll need to take four simple mechanical preparatory steps.

First, you must stop taking certain common medications, which I will explain. They will negate the diet's effectiveness.

Second, make sure the vitamins I'll tell you about are at hand.

Third, buy a package of Ketostix at your drugstore. They're inexpensive and no prescription is needed for them.

Fourth, you should arrange to have a medical checkup to determine your general state of health.

FIRST: ABOUT THE MEDICATIONS YOU MUST DISCONTINUE. If you were to telephone my office for an appointment to start this diet, the nurse would give you these instructions along with your appointment, *subject to your doctor's approval*. "It is important that you stop taking certain medications well before you start on this diet.

"1. Amphetamines (diet pills) must be stopped at least two weeks before you start on the diet.

"2. Diuretics (water pills and/or injections) must be

discontinued one full week before you start on the diet. This includes certain medications taken for high blood pressure that contain diuretics."

Then she would reassure you, "If discontinuing these medications causes you to gain, don't worry. This weight will come off easily once you start on the diet."

WHY AMPHETAMINES KEEP YOU FROM LOSING. There are any number of reasons why amphetamines must be discontinued before you start on the diet. As I've said earlier, I feel very strongly (as does any conscientious doctor) about their addictiveness, and their aging and enormously destructive effect on both the body and mind.

But more specifically, amphetamines are death to any hopes you may have of losing that extra weight for keeps. This is because they have a rebound effect. *With few exceptions,* people who were once on these pills regain far more weight than they lost while taking them, once they go off them.

There isn't anything psychological or imaginary about this. This chemical rebound effect is totally physical, real, measurable—and invariable.

So while the rebound effects of the amphetamines you may have been taking linger on in your system, you could not expect this (or any other) diet to work. Enough time must elapse for this chemical rebound effect to wear off.

However, even if amphetamines were *good* for you, there would be no need for them, because the diet itself is such a powerful appetite depressant.

WHY THIS DIET AND DIURETICS DON'T COMBINE. Now the reason why diuretics must be discontinued is a little different: The diet itself is a very potent diuretic. (Yes, the seven- to ten-pound losses we frequently see the first week are partly due to the natural diuretic effect of the diet.)

So you see, when a synthetic diuretic is combined with the diet, it leads to uncomfortable and even dangerous symptoms of salt depletion and depletion of such vital minerals as potassium and calcium (to name only two).

YOU MAY WANT A WORD WITH YOUR DOCTOR HERE. Now the situation is a bit different when I am not going to be seeing you soon in person, and getting your full medical history.

Suppose that you are taking a heart medicine or a blood pressure medicine that contains a diuretic. It is not the place of this book to suggest that before going on this diet you stop a medication a doctor has prescribed for you. If you are on such medication, all you can do is ask your doctor if he thinks it would be in your best interest to go on this diet and go off his medication, or to go on a less effective diet and continue taking the medication. I personally never have to worry about this problem with my patients, for I am in a position to discontinue, adjust, or substitute any medication as seems to be warranted.

I repeat: I do not recommend that you go on this diet if you are taking medication containing diuretics, or an amphetamine. This is a situation that calls for consultation with a physician on whose judgment you can rely.

SECOND: HAVE THESE VITAMINS ON HAND WHEN YOU START YOUR DIET. Now, let's talk about vitamins and the diet. I'll start out by saying that approximately 10 percent of the people who begin this diet experience less than the ideal feeling of well-being. There is always a reason.

Surprisingly often I find the reason is malnutrition. Vitamin and mineral reserves are so depleted in some dieters that it requires more than a week of taking high dosage vitamins and minerals to rebuild that reserve. But after a few weeks—between the effect of the diet and the vitamins—there is a wonderful upsurge of energy.

FOR LEG CRAMPS, TAKE CALCIUM. FOR FATIGUE, THE ANSWER MAY BE POTASSIUM. When there are leg cramps, extra calcium is in order, and there is often a kind of fatigue for which potassium supplements are the specific.

About vitamins in general, I don't believe in minimum daily requirements. I believe in optimum dosage. I have used vitamins in megadoses in my practice with great success.

All the big drug companies put out a multivitamin and mineral tablet or capsules in therapeutic strength. Ask your druggist about them. Or you may get them from your health food and vitamin store. (This is not the place to enter into the "natural" versus "synthetic" vitamin controversy.)

If the minimum daily requirement is one capsule or tablet, you would probably be better off taking two a day. And supplement these if necessary with other vitamins—once you've read the vitamin contents on the label.

I like to see my patients taking in not less than eight hundred units of Vitamin E daily, and around one thousand milligrams of Vitamin C. I believe in at least double the therapeutic dosage of the full spectrum of the Vitamin B complex, and much more if hypoglycemia seems to be the problem.

You cannot safely increase the standard dosage of Vitamin A (twenty-five thousand international units) nor of Vitamin D (four hundred international units). But so-called overdoses of the other vitamins are simply flushed away by the kidneys. And the mineral and vitamin needs of individuals vary widely—on or off any diet. What may be an overdose for somebody else may be barely enough for *your* body's needs, depending on various factors: your age, the stress you are under, and your past history of diet and of previous medications.

Don't *wait* for symptoms of these deficiencies to appear. Don't just say "I feel fine, so I don't need them." Now is the time to take protective measures.

THIRD: EXACTLY HOW YOU USE KETOSTIX TO FIND YOUR CCL (CRITICAL CARBOHYDRATE LEVEL). You'll want a package of Ketostix right there in your bathroom medicine chest when you start the diet. If the nearest druggist doesn't happen to carry them (and doesn't want to order so inexpensive an item for you), keep on shopping until you do find them. It shouldn't be any problem.

I want to make it clear that using the urine test sticks are not by any means essential to the success of this diet. I use them with all my patients. But thousands of readers of articles about this diet have lost all the weight they wanted to without knowing anything about the use of these urine test sticks.

David Brown, the motion picture mogul, is one example. He lost forty pounds on this diet just by reading about it in *Cosmopolitan* magazine, which is edited by his wife, Helen Gurley Brown, and following it entirely on his own.

However, using the test sticks and seeing them turn purple, does add interest to the venture from the very beginning. This visible and dramatic proof that your body is burning off its fat gives you somewhat the same kind of psychological bracing that you get from a daily confrontation with your doctor. The test sticks, too, are a big help at those times (which occasionally happen to almost everybody) when you mysteriously seem to have gone over your Critical Carbohydrate Level and have stopped losing. They're a big help in checking your progress with the job of getting under your CCL again. You see, the turning-purple reaction sometimes anticipates what's shortly going to show up on the scales. It should encourage you by demonstrating that you are burning up your fat stores, even when the scale shows you to be on a "plateau."

THE HAPPY "TURNING-PURPLE" TEST: SIGN OF YOUR META-BOLIC BREAKTHROUGH. *Before* you start on the diet I am going to review precisely how I want you to use these Ketostix on this regime. Consider what follows a rehearsal—a kind of preview of what is to happen.

STEP ONE: KEEP A FOOD DIARY FOR TWO DAYS—THEN TEST. I could just say, after two days on the diet, test your urine. But success is doubly sure if you keep a record of exactly what you eat at first. Quantities aren't important. What is important is that what you eat contains no carbohydrate at all, and no alcohol either. In the next chapter you will read what this diet *is*, and later find recipes and menus to help you follow it.

But now the point I want to make is:

Keep a diary of everything you eat. I think it would be a good idea to show this diary to somebody—perhaps a friend or your mate. Who in your life can play this role of doctor/superego? You need a Somebody to check with, perhaps a Somebody who has read this book and lost some weight.

Better yet. How about placing a bet with someone? A bet you can't afford to lose. I've found this can provide compelling motivation to stay on a diet. Just make sure it is a long-term bet, because *staying* thin is your objective. As I like to tell my patients, "Any idiot can *lose* weight—it's staying thin that's the test!"

After you have written down everything you have eaten for two days, begin to test your urine. (You might test from the beginning, but you should be surprised if it were to turn before two days on the diet.) Just hold the strip where the urine will wet it; or collect a sample in a paper cup, and put the tip of the urine test stick in it. The color at the submerged tip may begin to show some shade of purple within the first minute. When it does, you are in luck. You are beginning to break down your fat deposits and excrete acetone—or ketone bodies. This usually begins around the second or third day.

WHAT TO DO IF THE TEST STICK DOESN'T CHANGE COLOR. If the test stick doesn't turn purple, then one of two things is taking place. Either you're not following the diet correctly or you have a rather unusual degree of metabolic resistance. First establish that you are following the diet correctly. And do it for at least five days. If the stick is still not turning even lavender, then cut out your salad for a few days and see if it doesn't turn. Salad is the only significant source of carbohydrate in the diet at this point. As soon as the Ketostix turns purple, put the salad on the diet again. Now you're back on the first week's diet.

Once you have established that you can produce acetone, you have every right to expect that you will do so every day. From then on, you add the foods you have most missed in approximately five-gram units.

WARNING: THE TIME OF DAY YOU TEST MAKES A DIFFERENCE. One day a week test your urine right through the day —morning, midday, evening, night. Find out which hour of the day gives you the deepest reaction. (Usually it's in the evening.) If that's the time that gives you the deepest reaction, then that's the time you should check.

As long as the test stick shows some degree of purple or lavender, you're all right. But any day in which you go from a deep purple to a light shade or to no change of color at all (beige) is a day in which you've had more carbohydrates than you should have.

Go back and look at your eating diary. See if you can pick out what carbohydrates you have had and how many grams you have had. Was your daily total twenty grams? thirty-five? forty-five? Whatever that amount, it was too much.

HOW TO KNOW WHEN YOU'RE NEAR YOUR PERSONAL CCL (CRITICAL CARBOHYDRATE LEVEL). When the Ketostix doesn't change color, you've probably exceeded your Critical Carbohydrate Level. Go back to the basic diet of the first week until the test stick turns purple again. Then start adding in your carbohydrate increments until your test stick turns so pale a purple that you know you're approaching your personal CCL.

As you begin to be familiar with your own reactions, you begin to learn what foods affect your Ketostix tests. You'll have a very good idea as to exactly what is *your* Critical Carbohydrate Level.

I must say that I have treated many people whose urine has stopped showing the purple reaction, yet they continue to lose weight and feel well. This occurs when there is only a moderate increase of acetone in the blood, but not enough to spill over into the urine. It is perfectly all right, providing there has been no increase in appetite or drop in energy compared to the early weeks, and when the *weight loss is continuing*.

PURPLE MEANS YOU'RE LOSING—AND NEVER HUNGRY. There's another way of knowing that your metabolism is being normalized. As I've said before, the diet is working if you notice a decrease in your hunger. It is not working if you notice that you are hungry. So being hungry is neither right, nor desirable, nor necessary.

Usually the deeper the purple shown on the Ketostix, the less the hunger. The paler the color shown on the Ketostix, the more the possibility of hunger. However, you will find which shade of purple correlates best with your own feeling, and this, for you, is the ideal. It's easy to follow your progress. Just be aware of your decreased appetite and note that you are losing at a comfortable pace.

FOURTH: WHAT YOU NEED TO KNOW ABOUT YOURSELF MEDICALLY. When I took on the responsibility of writing this book, I knew that the effect of the book would be to take dietary advice out of the hands of the doctor, where I personally believe it belongs, into the hands of the reader himself. In point of fact, it is self-evident that the selection of one's diet is under the control of the individual dieter. And because you readers *need* the benefits of this diet, I agreed to transfer my medical management into your own hands.

But there are measures I take as a matter of routine, which I feel you should arrange for in order to insure the smooth functioning of the diet.

Before any patient starts with me, I take a comprehensive series of blood tests, which I recommend you have your own physician give you, particularly if you have more than twenty pounds to lose. Get a routine series of blood tests as a base line so that if anything changes, you will know where you stand. The blood counts, sugar level, cholesterol, and triglycerides should improve, but the uric acid level may go up. For my patients, this rarely poses a problem because I routinely prescribe a drug to prevent uric acid formation for my patients if the uric acid level is high to begin with, or if it goes above the normal range after being on the diet.

After all, this diet is not a fad diet, nor is it designed for a quick weight loss, but it's going to be the way you eat for the rest of your life.

So don't you think it would be nice to have your own personal doctor confirm what you are about to experience—that this diet will make you a healthier person than you ever thought you would be again, and that your medical laboratory tests will show this, too?

12

THE REVOLUTIONARY

NEVER-HUNGRY

NO-LIMIT

STEAK-AND-SALAD-

PLUS DIET

PLUS NUMBER 1: STEAK PLUS ALMOST ANY MEAT, FISH, OR FOWL. And now for the diet. A patient christened it the steak-and-salad diet—and that does rather sum up the plot of it.

Of course you aren't confined to steak. You can have almost any kind of meat, fish, or fowl . . . including such usually forbidden goodies as ham, spareribs, bacon, roast pork, corned beef, roast duckling, lobster with butter sauce.

One of the big reasons this diet works so successfully is because you eat protein and fat. And you eat them in just about the sixty to forty proportions in which they usually occur together in nature: in a reasonably lean cut of beef for example. Some people actually don't like fat. They do better on a low-fat diet, but I don't encourage a no-fat diet, ever.

In so many of the low-calorie diets, fat is a no-no. I have seen women on diets so low in fat that they couldn't manufacture enough female hormones to have a regular menstrual cycle. Now if your very function of being a woman can be impaired by going on a low-fat diet, low-fat diets are to be considered with extreme caution.

There are many reasons why fats and oils are desirable in a reducing diet. For one thing, they keep your skin smooth and lubricated. And that isn't all.

WHY FATS AND OILS HELP YOU STAY ON THE DIET. The fat in the diet helps to keep you unhungry. It helps to stabilize your blood sugar level. And, as I've explained earlier, it helps to sneak off calories by the excretion of ketone bodies. Biochemically, remember that fat opposes the desired formation of ketone bodies with an efficiency of only 10 percent, compared to 58 percent in the case of protein and 100 percent in the case of carbohydrate.

A big advantage: it allows for enormous variety in your diet; that's vital.

Almost best of all: it keeps you from feeling deprived.

It's luxurious to slather mayonnaise on your cold salmon, to use it in tuna salad and chicken salad, and to help yourself to butter sauce on your asparagus and lobster. It's fun to crunch away on those delicious fried pork rinds, while your friends who are on calorie-counting diets watch you enviously. It's easy to stay on the diet that allows you to live it up with the slim gourmets.

Both you and I would like to see the weight loss as rapid as possible and this diet does provide rapid weight loss. But it's even more important that it be as effortless as possible. I don't think dieting should be a hardship. I think the whole experience should be a pleasure. If an effortless dietary regime makes you get slimmer and the whole experience is pleasurable, you'll stay with it. And that's the only kind of a diet that's of the slightest use to you—one you can live with and enjoy for the rest of your life. A lot of adjectives have been applied to this diet but the one that best describes it is *livable*.

PLUS NUMBER 2: GREEN SALADS PLUS . . . The second plus is that you're allowed green salad with your lunch and dinner. Yes, even though this first week of the diet is called a carbohydrate-free diet and lettuce contains a tiny bit of carbohydrate. But in biological systems an approximation can do the job. Biology isn't quite like engineering. Given the amount of carbohydrate in these two salads, what happens in the body is approximately the same in 99 percent of dieters as if no salad had been eaten. So why not eat those salads? They are a lifesaver. To eat just protein and fat without the garden-fresh crispness that salad provides is a drudgery. So I thank the Lord that greens contain so little carbohydrate. Those salads make all the difference between a diet that's aesthetic, appetizing, human, and one that's an uncivilized drag.

ROQUEFORT CHEESE DRESSING (OR ALMOST ANY FAVORITE). And the salad greens needn't be dry. You can load your salad greens with a nice oily Roquefort cheese dressing, oil and vinegar, mayonnaise, even a Caesar salad dressing. Leave out the croutons and use crumbled fried pork rinds instead.

PLUS NUMBER 3: FILLING, HIGH-CALORIE SNACK FOODS. Not celery, carrot sticks, and rabbit-food snacks, but have imported cheeses of every description, stuffed olives, crisp fried pork rinds. This last discovery has a hundred uses—a substitute for toast, dinner rolls, or crackers to use with a dip or a spread, or as breading or stuffing or filler. You can use them as a pie crust for a quiche Lorraine or even for matzoh ball soup (see our recipe on p. 190).

You can have other snacks you never dreamed of enjoying on a diet: caviar, crabmeat, deviled eggs, beef jerky (this was a favorite "chew" with Buddy Hackett). And don't forget the leftovers from yesterday's luxurious dinner as snacks.

PLUS NUMBER 4: DESSERTS. The first week you can have carbohydrate-free gelatin desserts. If sweets are what you miss the most, in the following weeks you can have cheesecake (see page 240), macaroons, pudding, fresh strawberries in artificially sweetened whipped cream, mocha pie, chocolate mousse *prepared the way this book recommends*. See the dessert section for these and dozens of other eye-popper meal endings.

And if you don't want to bother making desserts, try heavy cream in your well-sweetened coffee or even topping your coffee with sweetened whipped cream. This meal-ending soothes the savage taste buds and leaves your appetite level calm and undisturbed.

PLUS NUMBER 5: EAT WHEN YOU WANT—BUT START WITH A BIG COZY BREAKFAST. You'll find that starting the day with a fulfilling breakfast gives you a big comforting reserve of energy for the day's activities. People with weight problems often eat no breakfast and very little lunch. Typically, they're nighttime eaters.

Though you're encouraged to eat anytime that you are hungry on this diet and you are also encouraged not to eat unless you are hungry, breakfast is an exception.

A reversal in timing here will hurry along a reversal in your measurements, also in your sleep and energy patterns.

So what will you have? Bacon and eggs? Ham and eggs? Name your omelet. Invent your own. Why not try steak for breakfast? Try heavy cream in your sweetened coffee even if you aren't used to it. It makes you feel spoiled—very luxurious.

Try breakfast on for size . . . whatever size you would like to be instead of the size you are. A big bacon-and-egg breakfast will get you there faster. I've seen so many thousands of fat, depressed people who came in saying, "But I never eat breakfast," finish by being slim, cheerful people who ate big breakfasts every morning of their lives.

THE FIRST LIFE-CHANGING WEEK. Eat nothing that's not on the list.

MEAT

Steaks
Corned beef
Lamb chops
Tongue
Hamburgers
Bacon
Any kind of
      meat in any
      quantity—
except meat with
fillers such as
sausage, hot dogs,
meatballs, most
packaged "cold
cuts"

FOWL

Duckling
Turkey
Chicken
Anything with
      wings
No stuffing

DESSERTS

Gelatin with arti-
ficial sweeteners
(e.g., D-Zerta)

CONDIMENTS

Salt, pepper,
mustard, horse-
radish, vinegar,
vanilla, and other
extracts; artificial
sweeteners; any
dry powdered
spice that con-
tains no sugar

DRINKS

Water, mineral
water, Vichy,
club soda; beef or
chicken broth,
bouillon; sugar-
free diet soda;
coffee,* tea, de-
caffeinated coffee

FISH

All fish, including
canned salmon,
tuna; any kind of
seafood, includ-
ing oil-packed
and smoked, *ex-*
cept oysters,
clams, mussels,
scallops, and
pickled fish

* *Special note on caffeine and Diet Cola.* Because most heavy people have some hypoglycemia, coffee, which contains caffeine, should be limited to six servings a day (cups). If you *know* you have low blood sugar, better limit it to three. As of the date of publication, Diet Rite Cola and Diet Pepsi contain not only caffeine but a significant amount of carbohydrate, so, fair warning, read the labels even on diet drinks carefully and control your intake accordingly.

EGGS

Boiled, fried, scrambled, poached, omelet —any style and with no limitations

SALADS

Two small green salads a day (each less than one cupful, loosely packed) made only of leafy greens, celery, or cucumbers and radishes. Dressings with vinegar, oil, salt, dry spices, herbs, grated cheese, or anchovies. Or else a sour pickle in place of a salad. Plus . . . green olives.

(BUTTER & MAYONNAISE) FATS

Butter, margarine, oils, shortening, lard, mayonnaise. (Fats have no carbohydrates.)

JUICE

Juice of one lemon or lime.

CHEESE

Four ounces a day of any hard, aged cheese. No cream cheese or cheese spreads.

HEAVY CREAM

Four teaspoons a day. (Cream has less carbohydrate than milk—so don't use milk.)

THE DIET REVOLUTION RULES.

1. Don't count calories.
2. Eat as much of the allowed foods as you need to avoid hunger.
3. Don't eat when you're not hungry.
4. Don't feel you must finish everything on your plate just because it's there.
5. Drink as much water or calorie-free beverages as thirst requires. Don't restrict fluids . . . but it is not necessary to force them either.
6. Frequent small meals are preferable.
7. If weakness results from rapid weight loss, you may need salt.
8. Every day take a high-strength multivitamin pill.
9. Read the labels on "low-calorie" drinks, syrups, desserts. Only those with no carbohydrate content are allowed.

THE DIET REVOLUTION VEGETABLES (NOT FOR LEVEL ONE).

Asparagus	Chinese Cabbage	Sauerkraut
Avocado	Eggplant	Snow Pea Pods
Bamboo Shoots	Kale	Spinach
Bean Sprouts	Kohlrabi	String Beans
Beet Greens	Mushrooms	Summer Squash
Broccoli	Okra	Tomatoes
Brussels Sprouts	Onions	Turnips
Cabbage	Peppers	Water Chestnuts
Cauliflower	Pumpkin	Wax Beans
Chard	Rhubarb	Zucchini Squash

THE DIET REVOLUTION SALAD MATERIAL.

Celery	Fennel	Parsley
Chicory	Lettuce	Peppers
Chinese Cabbage	Olives (*Green or Black*)	Radishes
Chives		Scallions
Cucumber	Onions	Watercress
Endive	Pickles (*Sour or Dill*)	
Escarole		

THE DIET REVOLUTION DRINKS: A FEW OF MANY POSSIBILITIES. A sugarless lemonade or limeade made with spring water makes a nice aperitif. Perrier and Saratoga Geyser are delicious sparkling waters. OK diet sodas (to mention a few): No-Cal, Cott, Hoffman, Shasta, Diet Vernors, Fresca, and Tab.

THE DIET REVOLUTION SUBSTITUTES. Heavy cream diluted with water when milk is called for in cooking . . . Bean sprouts for rice . . . Use the listed vegetables for bread stuffing . . . Soya powder (full-fat) for flour (half the amount called for in the recipe).

THE DIET REVOLUTION SANDWICHES. Because bread is a no-no, you dream up "finger food" with ingenuity. Chopped raw onion in smoked salmon. Sour cream and caviar between two cucumber rounds. Ham with mustard between two slices of Swiss cheese. A stick of Cheddar in a lettuce leaf. Lobster mayonnaise cuddled in a whole cucumber, sliced lengthwise in two. Use endive instead of crackers to scoop up dips.

THE DIET REVOLUTION SALAD GARNISHES.

Crumbled Crisp Bacon
Fried Pork Rinds (*Instead of Croutons*)
Grated Cheese

Minced Hard-Boiled Egg Yolk
Minced Sautéed Mushrooms
Sour Cream

THE DIET REVOLUTION APPETIZERS OR SNACKS.

Aspics (*Unsweetened or Artificially Sweetened*)
Baken-ets with Cheese
Cheese (*Any Hard Type in Cubes*)
Chicken Drumsticks
Chicken Wings, Broiled
Eggs, Deviled

Meatballs (no filler)
Pâté
Salmon, Smoked
Sardines
Sausages, Cocktail Type
Shrimps (With Mayonnaise Dip)
Steak Tartare

THE DIET REVOLUTION NO-NO'S. (This is not a complete list, by any means.) For you they're poison—don't forget it.

Bananas	Crackers	Peas
Beans (*Except*	Dates	Pickles, Sweet
Green or	Figs	Potatoes, White
Wax)	Flour	Potatoes, Sweet
Bread	Fruit, Dried	Raisins
Cake	Honey	Relish, Sweet
Candy	Ice Cream	Rice
Cashews	Jam	Spaghetti
Cereal	Catsup	Sugar
Chewing Gum	Macaroni	Syrup
Cookies	Milk	Yams
Corn	Pancakes	Yogurt
Cornstarch		Sweetened

NO "MISTAKES." Sometimes, a single stick of chewing gum or putting milk in your coffee could put you right back to Level One—by upsetting the new chemical balance in your body. Yes, even that much carbohydrate over your tolerance level can turn off your fat-mobilizing hormone. Then you'll need at least two no-carbohydrate days to get it circulating again so that you're unhungry, feeling high, and burning off fat again.

13

HOW TO
FOLLOW THE DIET—
LEVEL BY LEVEL

THE FIRST WEEK: EAT THE MOST, LOSE THE MOST. When you first look at the diet list in the preceding chapter and see that there are no quantitative limitations and that you can eat bacon and eggs, corned beef and pastrami, spareribs, duckling, you may say, "How can I lose weight on this?"

Well, we've already discussed that but it's worth repeating. The reason you can lose weight is that when there are no carbohydrates for fuel the body is forced to burn its own fat. It really doesn't make any difference how rich the zero-carbohydrate foods are, since without carbohydrates very little protein and fat can be stored as fat, so that no caloric deficit is needed. This is why the diet always works. Don't worry about how it may seem to represent more food or richer food than you are accustomed to eat. Don't be afraid to try it.

FOUR BEAUTIFUL THINGS HAPPEN. If the diet is working correctly, you will notice four beautiful phenomena. You will be markedly *freer from hunger* than you usually are. You will notice an increase in well-being. You will notice the *pounds* dropping off. Almost more startling is the decrease in your measurements that the tape measure can tell you about in detail.

WHAT YOU CAN EXPECT TO LOSE ON THIS HIGH-CALORIE DIET. At the end of the first week following this basic zero-carbohydrate diet most men will have lost seven or eight pounds, most women five or six pounds. If you're ahead of that schedule, fine. If you're behind that schedule, it may be that you've always been a slow loser. You would know that from your experiments with other diets. This does not mean that you should be discouraged. You are still going to lose: you can be certain that this diet will work for you.

IF YOU ARE LOSING WEIGHT TOO RAPIDLY . . . If you notice tiredness or feeling washed out at first and this is associated with a rapid weight loss, these symptoms probably come from the rapidity of the weight loss. This can be corrected by increasing your salt intake; also by increasing your intake of potassium, either with potassium pills or liquid or by eating lots of parsley and watercress . . . potassium-rich foods. (Also spinach, chicory, chard, and when allowed: bamboo shoots, mushrooms, and avocado.)

Another corrective action if you feel weakness and are having an overrapid weight loss is to move on to the second level of the diet immediately. The addition of the cottage cheese and the increase of the portion of the salad will slow up the diet's effectiveness a little and let you feel well. You see, a weight loss that is too rapid is more than the body can comfortably adapt to. And it isn't necessary to lose rapidly. It is more important to lose easily; and losing easily means feeling well all the time. I can't emphasize this too much: Quick weight loss is not the primary thing we're after—what we both want for you is an easy and lasting weight loss.

GET READY FOR THE GREAT METABOLIC CHANGEOVER! In any case it is usually only during the first two or three days of the diet (and with only one person in ten) that some such symptoms occur. You see, this is the time during which your old carbohydrate fuel is being used up and the glycogen stores of the liver are being used for energy.

On the second or third or fourth day, as the glycogen is used up, the great metabolic changeover takes place. Now your stored fat begins to be used for energy. It is at this point that the Ketostix will begin to turn purple. You will test your urine and look for this happy sign that your fat depots are under new management! It is at this point you're going to notice the upsurge of well-being and the freedom from hunger that I promised you. (Of course, you weren't hungry earlier, either, because you could eat all you wanted.)

I think the hardest thing about the first week's diet is its unfamiliarity. Rarely are there any of these untoward physical symptoms I've been describing. You may notice a change (a slight diminution) in the bowel pattern because of the lack of roughage. That's no real disaster; it's just a little strange to a person who is used to having a bowel movement every day. This too passes. In the interval, take a *very* mild laxative if you feel you would prefer that. Don't use a laxative that contains sugar however.

NOTICE HOW HAPPILY YOUR BODY RESPONDS. During this first week, pay attention to what happens to your appetite. Are the cravings that caused a lifetime compulsive-eating pattern going away? Are you less obsessed with the need for desserts? Do you have less desire to wander into the kitchen?

Next, take a look at what is happening to your energy level as the week ends. What is happening to your sleep pattern? What about other symptoms from which you may have been suffering? Heartburn, colitis, headaches, shortness of breath or chest pain on exertion? It has been my clinical observation over the years that all of these should get better as the diet progresses.

WHAT HAPPENS AFTER THE FIRST WEEK'S DIET. Most diets are fixed formulas and are therefore short-term and self-limiting. This diet is fixed only for a week. After that—because it must be a lifetime diet, it is as variable as are individual tastes.

I've labeled the additions of carbohydrate that follow "second level," "third level," "fourth level," "fifth level," but in fact the additions are interchangeable and flexible. You can make any of these additions any week that you choose. I could be very arbitrary and specify exactly what you may add each week. It would be simpler, much less confusing, and with much less possibility for error. But I don't impose that rigidity on my private patients, so why should I do that to you? I am so committed to making this a livable lifetime diet that I am letting you select your own variations, within the rules set up by your biological rule book.

PUT BACK WHAT YOU'VE MISSED MOST. The idea is simply to gradually return to your diet first what you missed most. You may not choose to put back any of the small carbohydrate additions I've suggested. You may prefer something quite different that you will pick out of your carbohydrate gram counter. Custom-tailor the diet to suit your life-style.

All that matters is that you add back to your diet a little carbohydrate at a time, and that you stop adding carbohydrate when you've reached your CCL.

Well, allow me to assume that you have been on this zero-carbohydrate diet for a week. Now it is time to evaluate whether or not you may progress to level two. Are you ready to add a few grams of carbohydrate?

HOW TO KNOW WHEN TO PUT BACK A LITTLE CARBOHY-DRATE. Ask yourself: Are the Ketostix still turning purple? Am I still un-hungry? Have I stopped eating at night? Do I have more energy? Am I still losing weight or inches nicely? Remember, your tape measure is a better friend than your scale, not only more accurate, but better able to report on the actual fat (not just temporary water) losses this diet achieves.

In checking thousands of patients' measurements, we

have found that a dramatic loss of inches is *invariable* on this diet. This is true even at times when temporarily no loss of pounds has occurred, so long as the patient has been true to the diet; this is due to the shrinking of fat cells that occurs as they are mobilized to supply the body's energy on the anticarbohydrate regime.

If you are answering yes to all these questions, then you are ready for the second stage of your diet—what I have labeled the second level.

THE SECOND LEVEL: CHEESECAKE FOR DESSERT? At each level, *remember you will add approximately five to eight grams of carbohydrate daily for a week and analyze the results.* Most of my patients agree that the best way to handle the second level is to add cottage cheese . . . if you happen to like it. And if you don't happen to like it just plain, I recommend that you make our delicious cheesecake. It is the mainstay of our diet and one of the recipes that has really made this diet special.

Or perhaps you might like to try some of the other desserts from the recipe section in this book. Either ricotta or cottage cheese contains about one gram of carbohydrate per ounce, and I think the next addition might be as much as eight ounces of ricotta or cottage cheese a day.

You may eat much less cottage cheese and have other goodies instead. There are other things that you might think would be terribly fattening, but they're not very high in carbohydrates. Example: certain kinds of nuts—walnuts, pecans, brazils, and macadamias—are the most suitable. One ounce of these averages under five grams of carbohydrate. Or you may want to have more cream in your coffee. Or use two or three slices of tomato or onion in your cooking. (There is more about the delicious use of vegetables later.)

It is important to many of my younger patients especially to have the comfort of a few sticks of diet chewing gum.

Just keep track of the grams of carbohydrate you're adding to the basic diet per day—keep them under eight—and take your choice.

At the end of a week on the second level, check your progress. If you are still free of hunger, still losing, still "turning purple," you're ready for the third level.

THE THIRD LEVEL: MORE NUTS? OR VEGETABLES? Here we add another five to eight grams more. Some of my patients go for a daily ration of one and one-half ounces of nuts for the third level. But many people want vegetables back on their plates. So alternately, the 5 percent vegetables, the low-carbohydrate ones (see listing chapter 12) can be added to your diet at the rate of one-half cup per day all week long. This means a small serving of one of these vegetables on your luncheon or dinner plate, which represents no more than five or six grams of carbohydrate.

I like to use vegetables to make the meal interesting. This is not the way other diets use vegetables because the low-calorie diets push vegetables to the hilt, to fool the stomach with bulk (at the expense of aggravating colitis or diverticulitis problems, for those who can't tolerate surplus roughage). However, we use vegetables more cleverly. We can sauté meat or fish with onions or add mushrooms broiled in butter. We can serve veal or steak with peppers. We might serve broccoli with hollandaise sauce. We can put a slice of tomato under our cheeseburger and add a couple of slices of bacon to make a tomato-bacon cheeseburger.

It's that kind of thinking with vegetables that gets the greatest mileage out of them. You'll learn—as do all my patients.

After you've been on the third level for a week, you have the option of increasing your allotment of salad, vegetables, hard or fresh cheese; or you may opt for adding some sour cream or fruit to your diet. Or how about having either wine with your dinner or a straight drink before dinner?

THE FOURTH LEVEL: FRUIT? OR ALCOHOL? SOUR CREAM? TOAST? When you begin to add alcohol, be careful that you have no sweet drinks. And don't have drinks that call for mixers, such as Seven-Up or ginger ale or quinine water. You might start with four units of alcohol per week. A unit is one ounce of Scotch or whiskey, or four ounces of dry wine or champagne.

WHAT YOU NEED TO KNOW ABOUT ALCOHOL. Let's talk about alcohol, because for many of my patients this is the number one problem in weight control.

We live in a society where drinking is so much a part of our way of life that it is much harder to turn down a drink than a dessert—even if we like desserts better.

Yet alcohol is a powerful deterrent to a low-carbohydrate diet. If you've read about the Drinking Man's Diet, you know that alcohol is not usually considered a true carbohydrate. And if you enjoy a sociable drink, you will hit upon that fact to justify adding alcohol to your diet.

But this is one diet *where alcohol acts just like a carbohydrate. It makes your body discharge insulin and stops you from putting out FMH.*

There is no hard-and-fast rule about how much alcohol converts into gram-equivalents of carbohydrate, because there is remarkable individual variation in this department.

But this rule of thumb that I use represents the best average value: For every ounce of 100-proof spirits count twenty grams. In other words, one ounce of 84-proof Scotch might be thought of as 16.8 grams. Or four ounces of 24-proof wine might be counted as 19.2 grams.

THE FRUIT YOU'VE BEEN WAITING FOR—BUT BE CAREFUL! If you choose fruit to add to your diet in the fourth level, look at your carbohydrate gram counter to get an idea of what a five-gram portion of fruit is. As you see, melon and berries go the furthest and provide a nice variety because there are many kinds of melons and many kinds of berries. The berries make a wonderful topping for the cheesecake. And small melon balls are very good because you can eat them one at a time every time you feel like a small fruit orgy.

Or would you prefer half a grapefruit two times a week? Or a few small peaches or tangerines for the week? But—a word of caution—*nothing in the diet up to this point is as likely to stop your progress dead as is fruit.*

Now that you're at the fourth level you can consider such additions as sour cream, but watch that gram count when you spoon it out. Or a six-ounce glass of tomato juice, if that's your passion. If your Ketostix are still turning at least a faint lavender, you may want to try adding a half slice of gluten bread or toast per day. The best solution at this point would be to make full use of our more complicated recipes in chapter 15.

THE FIFTH LEVEL: BENDING THE DIET WITHOUT BREAKING IT. If you're one of the lucky people who can even go to the fifth level and still have all the wonderful benefits—no hunger, good chemistry, purple Ketostix . . . you could try using the soya flour recipes that you will find in the recipe section. There are a few grams of carbohydrate in soya powder, but as used in these recipes they are still one of the best carbohydrate bargains that you'll ever find.

Your whole purpose should be to make this diet as easy and congenial as you can. And it is designed for that. You'll find for yourself that there are many ways in which you can bend this diet without breaking it.

If you do break it, voluntarily or accidentally (and you almost certainly will in the years to come), just step back a bit and start over for a few days.

WHAT TO DO WHEN YOU GO OVER YOUR CCL. If you're not too far off, one or two days on the basic diet will bring your chemistry into line. If you're the type of person who has a greater inborn metabolic resistance to losing, do four days on the basic. As long as you have gone back on the basic for four days and your conscience is clear, you're ready to go back to where you left off.

You don't have to go back through levels two, three, and four; but you should go back to where you left off or one stage below where you stopped losing. By first finding the level of carbohydrate intake at which everything seems to be working—and second, the next level where things stopped working—you have found your personal CCL.

This may not run constant through your life because, as I said before, when you lose weight your CCL may change . . . for better or for worse. So always you must look at the end result and ask yourself—how well do I feel? And how well suppressed is my appetite? And how well are my Ketostix checking out?

SUPPOSE YOU ONLY HAVE TEN POUNDS TO LOSE. If your weight problem is a relatively minor one; that is, if you only have ten or fifteen pounds to lose, then you may find you can progress to each new level every four days, the way we recommend to the readers of *Vogue* magazine for their Super Diet.

WHAT TO DO AS YOU APPROACH YOUR IDEAL WEIGHT. Well, now you're a seasoned dieter. You've lost. You've fallen off. You've climbed back on. You're almost home.

When you get to within five or six pounds of your ideal weight, you begin to add items of small carbohydrate content, five grams at a time, until the weight loss slows down to less than a pound a week.

You should lose the last five or six pounds at the rate of no more than a pound a week. You don't worry about your Ketostix changing color at this point, because at that point you're better off to concentrate on what your lifelong diet is going to be, rather than on rushing to get those last five or six pounds off in a hurry. And for advice about that whole happy time, see chapter 15 on how to stay at your best.

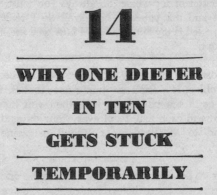

14

WHY ONE DIETER

IN TEN

GETS STUCK

TEMPORARILY

Remember the first sixty-five patients who ever went on this diet? Those AT&T executives I told you about in chapter 3? Remember how every single one of them got down to his diet goal?

When one national magazine wrote about this diet, it called it "The Diet That Works." And it does work.

I have never had a case where the diet could not be made to work. And yet I have had many patients who were sure at some time that the diet was not going to work for them. They were always wrong! There is always an explanation if the patient stops losing. There is always a specific something that is holding up progress. And invariably it can be changed.

I dare say that there will be a percentage of readers who, like my real-life patients, will think when losing slows down that there is something wrong with the diet. Let me assure you that it is only some hidden block that is standing in the way of success. And that can be removed. I'm not guessing about this; I *know* it from seeing the diet take pounds off ten thousand people of all ages and degrees of overweight.

Remember: this temporary hang-up only affects one in ten patients. However, if the time comes when things are not working for you in exactly the beautiful way I've described, let's try to discover what the hidden block may be.

LAST MONTH'S DIET PILLS AND DIURETICS MAY BE SLOWING YOU DOWN. Check over again the list of medications you have been taking. As you read in chapter 11, sometimes it isn't even what medication you ARE taking, but what you WERE taking that blocks the diet's progress. You may have stopped taking diet pills several weeks before you started the diet. Nevertheless, in some individuals the rebound effect can linger on. That may blow the diet off course for a while.

The same thing is true of diuretics and of medicines that contain them.

If either of these shoes fit you, don't waste your emotional energy getting upset about it. Just be patient. It takes some time for aftereffects of the diuretics and diet pills to pass out of your system—but they *will* leave you. You'll be a slow starter but you'll get there!

THE VERY STRONG TRANQUILIZERS SLOW YOU DOWN; SO DO THE SEX HORMONES. While the mild tranquilizers like Librium and Miltown don't affect the diet, the high potency psycho drugs do, as I have mentioned. Those in the phenothiazine category—Thorazine, Sparine, Mellaril, for example; also the long-term antidepressants or so-called psychic energizers—do the same. If these drugs are prescribed by your doctor, just know that they do inhibit weight loss, and that while you'll lose, it must be at your own slower pace.

I've discussed how the sex hormones not only hold up weight loss but stimulate the production of insulin. Estrogen, the female hormone, does this either in the Pill or taken as estrogen replacement therapy during and after the menopause. Testosterone, the male hormone, has the same effect. You may want to consider other methods of birth control, and for the rest, you can check with your doctor about perhaps cutting down on your present dosage of prescriptions that contain estrogen or testosterone.

A THYROID DEFICIENCY IS AT FAULT FAR MORE OFTEN THAN WE USED TO THINK. Let me remind you again that while the old medical dictum was that thyroid deficiency contributed to overweight in less than 2 percent of cases that's another "truth" to be unlearned.

There are now more sophisticated tests for thyroid deficiency. I find that approximately 20 percent of my patients are underproducing or underutilizing thyroid. And when I correct this, everything begins to fall into place. This is where your doctor can intervene. If you're not losing on this diet, it's not because the diet doesn't work, because it does. So if you are stuck, one possibility is to go and have your doctor check your thyroid function again.

Let me call your attention to the significant and quite valid discoveries of Dr. Irving B. Perlstein, of the University of Louisville, who found that 15 percent of his overweight patients demonstrated antibodies against their own thyroid hormone and needed to be treated with synthetic thyroid medication. Standard thyroid tests do not reveal thyroid autoantibodies.

LET'S RULE OUT SOME EASILY CORRECTED PROBLEMS THAT CAN DISCOURAGE DIETERS. You know that 90 percent of my patients feel extraordinarily well on this diet. But you may be one of those special few who give up because you don't have that feeling of well-being. Let's just go through what I find are usually the reasons this happens.

● *You may not be eating enough . . . or luxuriously enough.*

Usually a person who has been on many diets before and learns about a new diet just sees it as more limitation. And he still maintains the custom of eating small portions. He won't eat the skin on the chicken (though he loves it). He won't use mayonnaise. He refuses shrimp salad or tuna fish salad. He doesn't eat the bacon. He is careful not to have the eggs. This is a big mistake. For him this diet is just further restriction. I think everyone should take full advantage of the new opportunities that the diet provides. It offers good eating. It should be enjoyed!

● *Salt deprivation and potassium deprivation are common and cause discomfort.*

This can be corrected by eating a lot of salty foods and either taking potassium supplements by mouth or eating parsley.

● *Constipation* is sometimes a problem.

This can be obviated by using gentle laxatives.

RARELY, LOW BLOOD SUGAR SYMPTOMS CONTINUE. But the most troublesome of these diet discouragers applies to a very few people who are so constituted that they have low blood sugar symptoms even on this ultra-low-carbohydrate diet. This is probably because the mechanism for the conversion of their own fat into fuel is inadequate.

Although we recommend that everyone take vitamin supplements, the person with stubbornly low blood sugar seems to respond very well to what we call megadosages. A megadose is in the range of hundreds of times the minimum daily requirement. I prescribe megadoses of B complex, C, and especially E vitamins. I have found through clinical experience that Vitamin E seems to be very useful in coping with the symptoms of low blood sugar on this diet.

If this does not work, then you should move up to a higher level of carbohydrate intake in dieting. The second week's diet as described contains approximately ten grams of carbohydrate a day. Go to the third or fourth week's level of carbohydrate intake—moving up to about a thirty-gram carbohydrate intake and see if the symptoms pass over. You'll lose more slowly, but it's more important to feel well while losing. Usually the symptoms of low blood sugar will be ameliorated with the passage of time, probably because the deficient vitamins and nutrients are being restored gradually.

A TABLESPOONFUL OF POTATO SALAD CAN SLOW YOU DOWN. Unless you're one of these hard-core unfortunates, you can drop weight fast as well as euphorically on this diet . . . as long as you keep those carbohydrates at arm's length. But if you're off-again-on-again with carbohydrates you'll get nowhere fast. Those who think, "Well it can't do much harm if I go off the diet just for dinner," are due for a nasty surprise on the scales next morning. It is my observation that a patient who takes in seventy-five grams of carbohydrate (the amount in one wedge of pecan pie) will gain back two to three pounds.

As the Ketostix will tell you by refusing to change color, even a tablespoonful of potato salad can throw off the entire new fat-burning chemical balance you have been working to achieve.

But suppose you know better than to eat a tablespoonful of potato salad. You know potatoes are a starchy vegetable and you're not having any of those. But what did you have?

I find that when I ask patients to keep a written record of everything they eat, we often can discover hidden sources of carbohydrates, sufficient to interfere with the diet.

A patient may have used sweet relish or catsup on his hamburger, or a commerical French dressing that contains sugar. Or there may be filler in what he thinks is pure ground meat. Delicatessen coleslaw, which contains sugar, is a common stumbling block. Or he may be drinking the wrong diet soda. Or he may have forgotten that his cough syrup or throat lozenges are big sources of sugar.

KEEP A WRITTEN RECORD OF EVERYTHING YOU EAT—AND COUNT THOSE GRAMS. The first move you make if you're not losing as fast as you'd like to is to write down everything you eat. Don't wait until the end of the day to do this. Write it down practically as you eat it. Keep a little notebook in your purse or pocket for this. Or, if you're home most of the time, keep a memo pad tacked up on the wall in the kitchen.

Calories aren't important. What counts is the amount of carbohydrate you eat or drink. Don't guess how many grams go into your mouth. Calculate the grams minutely. Look up what's in every item, until you know by heart where those killer carbohydrates hide.

The Ketostix will act as a check but sometimes it's a good idea to show your record to a friend who has had experience with the diet. An outside opinion as to where you may be overlooking a hidden source may be helpful. A fresh mind applied to the problem sometimes makes all the difference.

READ ALL LABELS CAREFULLY—INCLUDING THOSE ON DIET FOODS. To stop these leaks it is vital to read all labels carefully. You'll be amazed at how many foods that don't even taste sweet (soups, salad dressings, ready-prepared foods of all kinds) contain sugar. Our major manufacturer of "killer catsup" tries to masquerade his inclusion of loads of deadly sugar with the happy term "natural sweetener." Starch or flour are also everywhere, it sometimes seems.

The labels on some diet foods boast about containing no sugar but say instead that the product contains certain hexitols or sorbitol. The label tells you that these are metabolized as carbohydrates but more slowly. This is probably true, but the important thing is that they are metabolized as a carbohydrate. Therefore they prevent your body from burning up its fat, and throw a complete monkey wrench into an ultra-low carbohydrate diet.

So one must be particularly careful to read the labels on diet foods, because your guard is down then. And when hexitol or sorbitol is on the label just count it in your own mind as a carbohydrate because that's what it is.

IT'S POSSIBLE TO SLOW YOURSELF DOWN BY EATING TOO MUCH SALAD. Because the green salad is the only source of carbohydrate in your first week's diet, those who have a great metabolic resistance to losing have to be careful not to eat too much salad. Rarely, I find that it's necessary for these biologically handicapped people to reduce the size of the salad or even cut it out entirely in order that the metabolic changeover take place. This is necessary in only one case in a hundred. However, it can happen, because there are all degrees of metabolic resistance in this world.

It's very unusual indeed for a new patient to get stuck in this way. It's a little less extraordinary when a patient has lost a great deal of weight, sixty to eighty pounds or so, and then gets stuck.

As you know, the Ketostix will tell you by turning purple just when you're taking in the right amount of carbohydrate. However, if you find you are having trouble after the first week in spite of sticking meticulously to the diet—reading labels, writing down every bite, counting every gram—then I would suggest that you try the first week's diet minus the salad until your body starts burning its own fat. Once the Ketostix are turning purple again you can put back the salad: at first in small quantities, and then add more. Finally add carbohydrates each week in five-gram increments.

USE THE KETOSTIX TO CHECK YOUR PROGRESS. Because you may be losing in inches and not in pounds the sure way to check that you are burning your own fat is with the Ketostix. However, I have to tell you that the urine test of one person in ten doesn't turn purple under any circumstances, though he may be losing beautifully both in pounds and inches. If you are one of these, don't let it worry you. Why should it—as long as you're losing? Just accept the fact that it's normal for you to be exceptional—just as some quite normal individuals' hearts are positioned on the right side of the body. Don't let this unusual reaction (or anything else) discourage you. Because your attitude is all-important.

YOUR ATTITUDE TOWARD YOUR OWN BODY MAKES A DIFFERENCE. Some people think that it's their fate to be overweight. Not so. Nobody needs to be overweight. These pessimists are the victims of a misconception. They think you can be on a diet part of the time and stay slim. They go away to a spa or a diet camp or they go on Metrecal for a while and feel that should take off the weight and solve the problem. That's not how a lifetime problem is solved. I constantly have to remind my patients that *taking* the weight off is not the objective; *keeping* it off is.

My most effective dialogue with a recalcitrant patient goes something like this:

Q: Do you look upon chocolate (or cake, or bread, or desserts—fill in your favorite carbohydrate) as something you *give up* when you're on a diet?

A: *Sure I do.*

Q: Then I suppose you look upon it as something you *do* eat when you're *not* on a diet?

A: *That's right.*

Q: Well, there's your problem. As long as you look upon being off your diet as part of your future plans, you will *never* solve your weight problem. This can only happen when you accept the reality that if you have a weight problem for life, you must stay on a diet for life.

This diet is a very effective tool for weight control. It is proven. It is safe. And, as a lifetime way of eating it is more effective than the calorie-restricted diet because it is pleasant and easy and you are never hungry.

But it still takes two to tango. The diet is one partner. You are the other. The diet is only an instrument; you have to want to use it. Otherwise it's like a lazy housekeeper's broom.

It is necessary for you to have respect for your body for you to use this tool. It's the only body you'll be issued. You've got to spend the rest of your life in it. You must treat it like your greatest possession; you must become a kind of "health nut."

I find that a dieter who goes astray is almost always helped by undertaking a regular exercise or games program of some kind. Join a gym class. Play tennis, golf, handball, badminton. Take up bicycling, hiking, horseback riding, jogging, swimming, rowing, skiing, dancing, yoga, judo, karate, fencing. Get your friends involved with you. Set up a seven-day-a-week exercise program. The awareness of your body that this stimulates automatically makes you aware and more on top of your eating. Sort of, "Hey, look at me. I'm really tightening up my body." This reinforces the desire to stay on the diet. The more you can get with your body the faster your progress toward taking pride in it and enjoying it.

15

MEAL PLANS

AND

RECIPES

A vital part of a Diet Revolution is providing foods that we enjoyed as prerevolutionaries but now made up in such a way that the carbohydrates are left out. This can be done quite nicely by using the recipes that follow, plus the recipes in my cookbook, to be published in the near future.

THE MAIN COURSE IS EASY. For a Diet Revolution meal, main courses provide no problem. In our culture, the main dish usually consists of protein and fat, anyhow. We've presented a few of our favorites, but after working with them, you will soon learn how to modify your own favorite main course recipes to make them perfect for your new way of life.

Vegetable dishes don't present any real problem on a low-carbohydrate diet if you just keep a close eye on your carbohydrate gram counter. You'll get some ideas here that will take vegetable dishes out of the routine category. You'll also learn new ideas for soups, for that filling first course, and for salad dressings, sauces, and desserts.

REPLACING BAKED GOODS AND SWEETS IS HARDER—BUT POSSIBLE. What about starches? How can you replace bread and baked goods? You can! It's all here. This requires a special kind of ingenuity—the kind that challenges professional food technologists. I am sure that these recipes will help you forget that you ever wanted to stuff down starches.

But the real challenge is in providing that one taste that all of us seem to crave—the taste of something sweet. Ironically, this task was much easier several years ago, *before* the Diet Revolution. In those days, we not only had our trustworthy ally, saccharin, but also its most palatable sidekick, the cyclamates.

YOUR WORST ENEMY—THE SUGAR INDUSTRY. The revolution-against sugar has a powerful, entrenched arch-enemy, the sugar industry itself. It is no secret that the sugar industry spent vast sums of money and lobbied tirelessly to discredit cyclamates and remove them from the market, thus destroying the one competing sweetener that not only was its match, tastewise, but was not fattening and did not lead to diabetes, high triglycerides, and premature heart disease. And as I have mentioned, in October 1969, they got the FDA to ban cyclamates when they succeeded in showing federal authorities that a few tumor-susceptible laboratory rats developed bladder cancer when fed the equivalent of two hundred bottles of diet soda a day for a lifetime.

I felt strongly enough that this represented a grievous error on the part of the FDA that I became the spokesman of the Ad Hoc Committee for the Fair Evaluation of Sugar and Sugar Substitutes. Our group placed ads in the *Wall Street Journal*, the *New York Times*, and the *Washington Post*, demanding that the Secretary of Health, Education and Welfare run comparative toxicity studies between equivalent amounts of artificial sweeteners and sugar itself. But our small voice was lost in the roar created by the multibillion-dollar sugar industry.

I would prefer that all my patients use cyclamates if it were possible, for the simple reason that they are far superior in taste to saccharin alone. But it is illegal to manufacture or sell them in this country, even when a doctor is willing to prescribe them.

For the moment, try to find cyclamates, if you can. They are still available in some foreign countries. By pressure of public opinion (that's you!) I hope we all can lobby until *some* more satisfying no-carbohydrate sweetener is put on the market, despite the wishes of the sugar industry to the contrary. (See the last chapter.)

THESE RECIPES USE SUGAR TWIN. My food technologists, Fran Gare and Helen Monica, have tested all the currently available saccharin sweeteners and have settled upon Sugar Twin as the most palatable, despite two unfortunate facts: it *does* contain carbohydrates (dextrins), and in taste it is no match for any cyclamate sweetener. All recipes are calculated in terms of Sugar Twin. When new sweeteners become available, learn the equivalents to Sugar Twin and use them in its place.

When brand names are used, it is because they are especially low in carbohydrate content and taste especially good.

We are proud to point out that no recipe contains more than six grams of carbohydrate per serving.

MEAL PLANS FOR THE FIVE LEVELS

OF THE DIET

I want to make it quite clear that what follows is *not* a rigid schedule of meal plans that you *have* to follow in order to lose on this diet. Nothing of the sort!

What these are instead is a handful of sample menus to give you an idea of the wonderful variety of good meals this diet allows. You'll notice that I have given you a complete set of menus for all seven days of the first week—or the First Level, as I call it. But at subsequent levels (or weeks), I've given you a few days' worth to use as examples. Make your full week's selection from the level you're at—or you can select menus from the preceding levels.

I don't expect that most of you will feel like making this much of a production of meal preparation every day. You may well be quite contented most of the time with meat, chicken, or fish with salad for lunch and dinner. Most days you may crunch on Baken-ets instead of a Diet Revolution Roll with your big breakfast.

But once or twice a week, when you feel like a change or making a splash, showing off a bit (either for the family or because company's coming), I hope these menus will give you inspiration. That's the reason for their presence here.

Note: when quantities are specified that is because the dish contains enough carbohydrate so that the amount you take in must be limited. When no quantities are given, the size of your portion can be as big as your appetite.

If, by now, you are carrying a gram counter with you and religiously checking the carbohydrate content of everything you put in your mouth, you may wonder how the first week's diet given here can be called a "biologically zero" carbohydrate diet, since each meal contains a few grams of carbohydrate.

Well, as I wrote in the chapter on the diet itself, biology isn't quite like engineering. In biological systems, an approximation can do the job. And I know this from the dramatic weight losses of thousands of patients: what happens in the body, given the amount of carbohydrate in this First Level diet, is approximately the same in ninety-nine out of one hundred dieters, as if there were literally no carbohydrate at all in the diet.

So don't worry about eating those fresh green salads; they're what make the diet so pleasant to live with right from the beginning.

Bon appetit!

Meal Plans

LEVEL 1

Day 1

BREAKFAST

* Scrambled Eggs with Spicy Ham
* Diet Revolution Roll and butter
  Bouillon, coffee, or tea

LUNCH

  Cold-cuts sandwich on * Diet Revolution Roll with mayonnaise or mustard
  1 cup of salad (loosely packed), oil and vinegar, or a dressing from the recipe list
* Raspberry gelatin
  Diet soda, coffee, or tea

DINNER

* Chicken soup with Matzoh Balls
  Your favorite cut of steak
* Caesar Salad with * Caesar Salad Dressing
* Gelatin, diet soda
  Coffee or tea

SNACK

  Baken-ets
* Stuffed Celery
  Diet soda

  NOTE: *Read the label on your favorite diet drink. Calorie content will be there. The rule of thumb for translating calories into carbohydrates is this: for every four calories, you take in one gram of carbohydrate. Don't forget to count those grams, too, in your daily total.*

  * When dishes are preceded by an asterisk—*—recipes can be found in the recipe section of this chapter.

LEVEL 1

Day 2

BREAKFAST

* Eggs Benedict with * Hollandaise Sauce on * Diet Revolution buttered Roll, cut in half
Bouillon, coffee, or tea

LUNCH

* Chicken Salad with mayonnaise and celery
* Deviled Eggs Curry
1 cup of tossed green salad, oil and vinegar, or a dressing
from the recipe list
Diet soda, coffee, or tea

DINNER

~ Beef broth with * Noodles
Assorted seafood grilled with * Lemon Butter Sauce
1 cup of lightly tossed salad, including green pepper,
radishes, and celery
* Roquefort Dressing #2
* Gelatin
Diet soda, coffee, or tea

SNACK

Mixed cold cuts with mustard
* Diet Revolution Roll
Diet soda

LEVEL 1

Day 3

BREAKFAST

Cheese omelet with bacon
* Diet Revolution Roll with butter
Bouillon, coffee, or tea

LUNCH

Deviled Ham stuffed into * Ham and Cheese Rolls
1 cup Romaine Lettuce with * Caesar Salad Dressing
* Diet Revolution Roll and butter
* Gelatin
Coffee, tea, or diet soda

DINNER

* Stuffed celery with Gorgonzola
* London Broil in natural gravy or * Diet Revolution Open
Roll
Endive and parsley salad, with oil and vinegar dressing or a
dressing from the recipe list
* Gelatin
Diet soda, coffee, or tea

SNACK

Baken-ets with tuna salad
Diet soda

LEVEL 1

Day 4

BREAKFAST

* Austrian Soufflé served with breakfast sausage
* Diet Revolution Roll and butter
Bouillon, coffee, or tea

LUNCH

* Bacon Cheeseburger on * Diet Revolution Roll
Green salad with oil and vinegar, or a dressing from the
recipe list
* Gelatin
Diet soda, coffee, or tea

DINNER

* Egg Drop Soup
* Scampi
* Caesar Salad with * Caesar Salad Dressing
* Gelatin
  Diet soda, coffee, or tea

SNACK

* Ham and Cheese Rolls stuffed with deviled chicken
  Baken-ets
  Diet soda

LEVEL 1

Day 5

BREAKFAST

Soft-boiled eggs with bacon crumbled in them
* Diet Revolution Roll and butter
  Bouillon, coffee, or tea

LUNCH

* Stuffed Lettuce with hard cooked eggs
  Sliced green peppers, radishes, cucumber, and celery
      (about 1 cup, loosely packed)
* Roquefort Dressing #2
* Gelatin
  Diet soda, coffee, or tea

DINNER

Antipasto (salami, green pepper, anchovies, prosciutto with
    oil, vinegar, and herbs)
Veal breaded in * Diet Revolution bread crumbs
* Lemon Butter Sauce

Tossed green salad with * Roquefort Dressing #2
* Gelatin
Diet soda, coffee, or tea

SNACK

* Bacon and Cheese Balls
Diet soda

LEVEL 1

Day 6

BREAKFAST

Delicatessen omelet with mustard
* Diet Revolution Roll with butter
Bouillon, coffee, or tea

LUNCH

Salmon salad on roll with melted cheese on top
Green pepper rings
* Gelatin
Diet soda, coffee, or tea

DINNER

* Chicken Dijon
Hearts of lettuce salad with * Roquefort Dressing #2
* Gelatin
Diet soda, coffee, or tea

SNACK

Hard cheese and Baken-ets
Diet soda

LEVEL 1

Day 7

BREAKFAST

Poached eggs with Canadian bacon
* Diet Revolution Roll and butter
Bouillon, coffee, or tea

LUNCH

* Hamburger Fondue
1 cup Romaine lettuce with * Caesar Salad Dressing
* Gelatin
Diet soda, coffee, or tea

DINNER

Shrimp Cocktail with * Roquefort Dressing #2
Boiled lobster with melted butter sauce
Mixed vegetable salad with dressing from the recipe list
* Gelatin
Diet soda, coffee, or tea

SNACK

Chicken Broth (or bouillon) with noodles
Green pepper stuffed with your favorite fish salad

LEVEL 2

Day 1

BREAKFAST

Lox and sautéed onion omelet
* Caraway Diet Revolution Roll with cream cheese
Bouillon, coffee, or tea

LUNCH

Avocado stuffed with crabmeat
Tossed green salad with dressing from the recipe list
* Cheesecake (1 slice)
Diet soda, coffee, or tea

DINNER

Mixed grill with * Garlic Butter Sauce or * Béarnaise Sauce
Tossed salad with * French Dressing
* Gelatin Parfait with Whipped Cream
Diet soda, coffee, or tea

SNACK

Assorted smoked fish
Hard cheese
Diet soda

LEVEL 2

Day 2

BREAKFAST

Sunny-side-up eggs with breakfast sausage
* Mustard Sauce
* Diet Revolution Roll and butter
Bouillon, coffee, or tea

LUNCH

* Tomato Delight
Tossed green salad with * Green Goddess Dressing
* Diet Revolution Caraway Roll and butter
* Cheesecake (1 slice)
Diet soda, coffee, or tea

DINNER

Cucumber Balls
* Veal Piccata
* Spinach Salad (1 cup spinach, loosely packed)
* Ice Cream (½ cup)
Diet soda, coffee, or tea

SNACK

12 olives
Cottage cheese
Diet soda

LEVEL 2

Day 3

BREAKFAST

* Spinach omelet with * Steak Sauce
* Diet Revolution Onion Roll
Bouillon, coffee, or tea

LUNCH

Chef's Salad with * Roquefort Dressing #1
* Diet Revolution Roll and butter
* Gelatin Parfait
Diet soda, coffee, or tea

DINNER

* Cream of Chicken Soup
* Chicken Cordon Bleu
Mixed green salad with your favorite dressing from the
recipe list
* Mocha Pie
Diet soda, coffee, or tea

SNACK

* Dried Beef Rolls
  Olives
* Capuccino Cooler

LEVEL 3

Day 1

BREAKFAST

Assorted smoked fish with chive cream cheese
* Diet Revolution Onion Rolls
  Bouillon, tea, or coffee

LUNCH

* Cottage Cheese and Sour Cream
* Tossed Vegetable Salad with your favorite dressing from
  the recipe list
* Ice Cream
  Diet soda, coffee, or tea

DINNER

* Fried Eggplant
* Pot Roast
  Mixed green salad
* Walnut Torte with * Mocha Whipped Cream (one serving)
  1 glass dry white wine from wine and liqueur list, coffee, or
  tea

SNACK

Cottage cheese with Baken-ets
12 Olives
* Quick Peppermint Fizz

LEVEL 3

Day 2

BREAKFAST

* Eggs Benedict with Hollandaise Sauce
* Diet Revolution Roll with butter
  Bouillon, coffee, or tea

LUNCH

* 1 Stuffed Zucchini
  Tomato slices with * Roquefort Dressing #1
* Root Beer Float (1 8-ounce glass)
  Coffee or tea

DINNER

* ½ cup Vichyssoise
* Barbecued Chicken
* Tossed Vegetable Salad with * Creamy French Dressing
* 3 Macaroons
  Diet soda, coffee, or tea

SNACKS

Cold cuts such as Capocollo, Mortadella, Kielbasy, Head-
cheese, Beef Jerky, Vienna-type sausage
12 Olives
1 glass dry red wine from the wine and liqueur list

LEVEL 3

Day 3

BREAKFAST

Salami and Munster cheese omelet

* Diet Revolution Caraway Roll
  Bouillon, coffee, or tea

LUNCH

* Vegetables with a Dip (about 1 cup, loosely packed)
  Choice of cold cuts on * Diet Revolution Roll and mustard
* Cheesecake
  Diet soda, coffee, or tea

DINNER

  Italian olive salad (about ½ cup)
* Stuffed Sole
* Spinach Salad with * Caesar Salad Dressing (1 cup spinach,
    loosely packed)
* Strawberries and Cream
  1 glass dry white wine from wine and liqueur list
  Coffee or tea

SNACK

* Tangy Meat Balls with sour cream or cottage cheese
  Pickled mushrooms
  Diet soda

LEVEL 4

Day 1

BREAKFAST

  Steak and eggs with * Steak Sauce
  Bouillon, coffee, or tea

LUNCH

* Potato Pancakes (6) with sour cream
* Tongue sandwich on Diet Revolution Bread

* Chocolate Egg Cream
  Coffee or tea

DINNER

½ small cantaloupe
* Tempura with a variety of sauces (* Cold Horseradish,
  * Mustard, * Garlic Butter)
* Pudding with a Punch
  Diet soda, coffee, or tea

SNACK

* Cheese Crackers
  Olive and cottage cheese dip
  Baken-ets
  Glass of white wine from wine and liqueur list

LEVEL 4

Day 2

BREAKFAST

* French Toast, Slim-ette Maple Syrup or * Strawberry Jam
  Canadian bacon
  Bouillon, coffee, or tea

LUNCH

* Quiche Lorraine (about ¼ recipe made in a tart shell)
* Caesar Salad with * Caesar Salad Dressing (about 1 cup,
  loosely packed)
* Chocolate Mousse
  Diet soda, coffee, or tea

DINNER

* Chicken Salad on a lettuce leaf
* Veal Rolls with sautéed mushrooms

Mixed green salad (1 cup, loosely packed) with * Creamy
   French dressing
1 glass of dry white wine from wine and liqueur list
* Strawberry Cantaloupe Pie
Coffee or tea

SNACKS

* Cheese Ball
  12 Olives

LEVEL 4

Day 3

BREAKFAST

Mushroom and sautéed onion omelet
Bacon
Slices of Diet Revolution Bread or a Diet Revolution Roll
Bouillon, coffee, or tea

LUNCH

Assorted cold cuts
* Cole Slaw with * Sour Cream Dressing
* Strawberries and Cream
  Diet soda, coffee, or tea

DINNER

½ avocado Vinaigrette (oil, vinegar, and spices)
Sliced steak with a variety of sauces (* Steak Sauce,
      * Béarnaise, * Garlic Butter)
* Savory Broccoli (½ cup)
* Pumpkin Pie with * Mocha Whipped Cream
  Diet soda, coffee, or tea

SNACK

> ½ cup of mixed nuts (walnuts, pecans, Brazil nuts, al-
> monds, filberts, or Macadamia)
* Peppermint Fizz

LEVEL 5

Day 1

BREAKFAST

> ½ grapefruit
> Scrambled eggs with bacon
* Diet Revolution Roll or bread
> Bouillon, coffee, or tea

LUNCH

> Knockwurst and sauerkraut
* Cottage Cheese with * French Dressing
* Cherry Mold
> Diet soda, coffee, or tea

DINNER

* Egg Drop Soup
* Lobster Cantonese (1 serving)
> ½ cup snow pea pods in * Butter Sauce
* Key Lime Pie
> Chinese tea and wine, if desired, from wine and liqueur list

SNACK

> Tuna fish with * Cream Sauce
> Olives
> Sour pickle
> Diet soda

LEVEL 5

Day 2

BREAKFAST

* Strawberry Jam Omelet with sour cream
* Diet Revolution Roll and cream cheese
  Bouillon, coffee, or tea

LUNCH

* Spinach salad with a can of tuna fish mixed in
* Caesar Salad Dressing
  6 strawberries with ½ tablespoon Kirsch
  Diet soda, coffee, or tea

DINNER

Chopped liver on a lettuce leaf
Corned beef and cabbage
Hearts of lettuce with * Creamy French Dressing
Cherry tomatoes
* Chocolate Cheesecake (1 portion)
Diet soda, coffee, tea, and dry red wine, if desired, from
    wine and liqueur list

SNACK

Melon and Prosciutto
* Capuccino Cooler

LEVEL 5

Day 3

BREAKFAST

Cream cheese, lox, onion, and tomato on * Diet Revolution
Rolls

Scrambled eggs
Bouillon, coffee, or tea

LUNCH

¼ cantaloupe
* Chicken Salad plate with * Deviled Eggs Curry
* Tossed Vegetable Salad with * Creamy French Dressing
* Diet Revolution Bread and butter
* Ice Cream
Diet soda, coffee, or tea

DINNER

Avocado with * Roquefort Dressing #1
* Spareribs
* Creamed Spinach (about ½ cup)
1 glass dry red wine from wine and liqueur list
* Coffee Walnut Chocolate Roll
Coffee or tea

SNACK

* 3 Chocolate Balls or 5 * Peppermint Squares
½ cup nuts (walnuts, pecans, Brazil nuts, filberts, or
Macadamias)

For those who prefer eating out, we are including some dishes
you may order after you have reached the fourth level of our
diet plan. These are only suggestions. You may find other
foods on the menus that conform to our plan.

Chinese Food

APPETIZERS

Seafood balls
Shrimp wrapped in bacon
Barbecued pork

Chicken in tin foil
Barbecued spareribs
Seafood brochette

SOUP

Egg drop (*without the starch*)

Clear chicken broth

Chicken with Chinese vegetables

ENTREES

Shrimp with garlic sauce

Seafood Go Ba (*no rice*)

Pepper steak (*without starch*)

Lung Tong Gai Kew (*without starch*)

Steak Kew (*without starch*)

Kowloon Steak (*without starch*)

Fung Corn Lung Har (*without starch*)

Mandarin Chicken Lub (*without starch*)

Woo Hip Har (*without starch*)

Egg Foo Young dishes

Chinese Tea

Italian Food

APPETIZERS

Antipasto

Clams Casino

Cheese-stuffed celery

Prosciutto and Melon

SOUPS

Stracciatella soup

Zuppa di Lunghi (*mushroom soup*)

Zuppa di Aglio alla Napolitano (*garlic soup*)

ENTREES

Veal Piccata

Scampi

Saltimbocca

Lobster Fra Diavolo

Filetto alla Chateaubriand

Fegalo al Vino (*calves' liver with wine sauce*)

SALAD

Caesar salad   Escarole salad

DESSERT

Cheese, melon in season, strawberries

Espresso   Capuccino

French Food

APPETIZERS

Pâté maison   Avocado Vinaigrette
Escargots   Frogs legs Provençal

SOUPS

Onion soup   Consommé

ENTREES

Coq au vin   Seafood Meuniere
Steak Béarnaise   Sole Amandine
Rack of Lamb with Mustard   Veal Cordon Bleu

DESSERT

Fromage   Strawberries and fresh
                                              cream

Menu for Entertaining

CARBOHYDRATE GRAMS ARE ON A PER SERVING BASIS

HORS D'OEUVRES	GRAMS
Deviled Curry Eggs	.5
Cheese Balls	2.0
SOUP	
Vichyssoise	3.1
WINE	
Dry Chablis (2 ounces)	.4
ENTREE	
Chicken Dijon	.8
Caesar Salad	4.1
DESSERT	
Chocolate Mousse	4.1
BEVERAGE	
Coffee with Cream	.8
	15.8

RECIPES

LIST OF RECIPES

HORS D'OEUVRES

DEVILED EGGS CURRY

VEGETABLES WITH DIP

CHEESE BALL

TANGY MEAT BALLS

SCAMPI

QUICHE LORRAINE

SOUPS

CHICKEN SOUP

CREAM OF CHICKEN SOUP

EGG DROP SOUP

MATZOH BALL SOUP

VICHYSSOISE

NOODLES FOR SOUPS

EGG DISHES

OMELET
SPINACH OMELET
BACON AND CHEESE SOUFFLÉ

SCRAMBLED EGGS WITH
    SPICY HAM
EGGS BENEDICT
AUSTRIAN SOUFFLÉ

Main Courses: Poultry, Meat, and Seafood

BARBECUED CHICKEN
CHICKEN CORDON BLEU
CHICKEN DIJON
BREADED CHICKEN, PORK,
    VEAL, OR FISH

BACON CHEESEBURGER
HAMBURGER FONDUE

LONDON BROIL
POT ROAST

VEAL PICCATA
VEAL ROLLS IN WINE

SHRIMP AND LOBSTER CAN-
    TONESE
TEMPURA
STUFFED SOLE
BARBECUED SPARERIBS

Sauces

BASIC CREAM SAUCE
LEMON BUTTER SAUCE
COLD HORSERADISH SAUCE
GARLIC BUTTER SAUCE

STEAK SAUCE
BÉARNAISE SAUCE
MUSTARD SAUCE
HOLLANDAISE SAUCE

Luncheon Dishes

CHICKEN SALAD
TOMATO DELIGHT
STUFFED ZUCCHINI

COTTAGE CHEESE AND SOUR
    CREAM SALAD
CHEF'S SALAD

Vegetable Salads

COLE SLAW

SPINACH SALAD

CAESAR SALAD

TOSSED VEGETABLE SALAD

Salad Dressings

FRENCH DRESSING

CREAMY FRENCH DRESSING

CAESAR SALAD DRESSING

GREEN GODDESS DRESSING

ROQUEFORT DRESSING #1

ROQUEFORT DRESSING #2

SOUR CREAM DRESSING

Vegetables

FRIED EGGPLANT

SAVORY BROCCOLI

CABBAGE SOUTHERN STYLE

CREAMED SPINACH

MOCK POTATO PANCAKES

Bread, Rolls, Crackers, and Pie Crust

DIET REVOLUTION ROLLS

CARAWAY ROLLS

ONION ROLLS

BREAD CRUMBS

DIET REVOLUTION BREAD

FRENCH TOAST

YELLOW PIE SHELL

Desserts

RED GELATIN

CITRUS GELATIN

STRAWBERRY GELATIN

    PARFAIT

CHERRY MOLD

WALNUT TORTE

WHIPPED CREAM

CHOCOLATE WHIPPED

    CREAM

LEMON WHIPPED CREAM

MOCHA WHIPPED CREAM
COFFEE WALNUT CHOCOLATE
    ROLL
STRAWBERRY CANTALOUPE
    PIE
KEY LIME PIE
MOCHA PIE
PUMPKIN PIE
CHEESECAKE

CHOCOLATE CHEESECAKE
MACAROONS
PUDDING WITH A PUNCH
STRAWBERRIES AND CREAM
STRAWBERRY WHIPPED
    CREAM
CHOCOLATE MOUSSE
VANILLA ICE CREAM
STRAWBERRY JAM

Special Category

ILLEGAL, BUT NOT IMMORAL OR FATTENING CHEESE CAKE

Candy

CHOCOLATE BALLS

PEPPERMINT SQUARES

Beverages

PEPPERMINT FIZZ
QUICK PEPPERMINT FIZZ
CAPUCCINO COOLER

ROOT BEER FLOAT
CHOCOLATE EGG CREAM

Snacks

BACON AND CHEESE BALLS
LOX AND CREAM CHEESE
DRIED BEEF ROLLS
STUFFED LETTUCE
TUNA-CHEESE SANDWICH
STUFFED CELERY CAVIAR

STUFFED CELERY WITH
    GORGONZOLA FILLING
COTTAGE CHEESE AND SOUR
    CREAM
CUCUMBER BALLS
MELON AND PROSCIUTTO
HAM AND CHEESE ROLLS

Hors D'Oeuvres

DEVILED EGGS CURRY

SERVES 6

6   hard-cooked eggs
2   tablespoons of mayonnaise
½   teaspoon chopped chives
⅛   teaspoon curry powder
½   teaspoon salt
¼   teaspoon pepper

Cut eggs in half lengthwise and remove yolks to a small bowl.

Add the mayonnaise, chives, curry powder, salt, and pepper to the yolks.

Mash with a fork until well blended.

Fill egg whites with yolk mixture.

TOTAL GRAMS   3.1
GRAMS PER SERVING   .5

VEGETABLES WITH DIP

SERVES 8

GRAMS PER ½ CUP	
Raw cauliflowerettes	5.9
Raw broccoli cut into small pieces	6.6
Radishes	.8
Raw string beans cut up	8.0
Raw mushrooms, sliced	5.0
Cucumber sticks	3.6

2   tablespoons creamed cottage cheese
1   tablespoon white horseradish
1   tablespoon Salad Supreme
1   pint of sour cream
1   teaspoon Krazy Mixed-Up Salt
1   teaspoon minced chives
1½   teaspoons tarragon

Cut vegetables into bite-sized pieces, wrap tightly in foil, or put in cold water in refrigerator until serving time.

Combine cottage cheese, horseradish, Salad Supreme, sour cream, Krazy Mixed-Up Salt, chives, and tarragon.

Refrigerate for at least 2 hours, then put dip into chilled bowl in center of a platter.

Arrange vegetables around dip and serve.

TOTAL GRAMS   28.8
GRAMS PER ¼ CUP SERVING   3.6

CHEESE BALL

SERVES 8

¾   pound aged Cheddar cheese
2   ounces crumbled blue cheese
4   ounces cream cheese
¼   cup chopped walnuts

Bring cheese to room temperature.
Beat with electric mixer for 3 minutes at a medium speed.
Roll into a ball.
Roll ball in chopped nuts and refrigerate until serving time.

TOTAL GRAMS   16.0
GRAMS PER SERVING   2.0

TANGY MEAT BALLS

SERVES 8

6 tablespoons butter
pound ground sirloin
tablespoon sour cream
½ pound Roquefort cheese
teaspoon Krazy Mixed-Up Salt

Melt butter.
Combine meat, sour cream, cheese, and salt.
Blend well and roll into small balls.
Brown in butter.
Serve with toothpicks.

TOTAL GRAMS   4.0
GRAMS PER SERVING   .5

SCAMPI

Makes about 16 shrimp

SERVES 8

pound shrimp, cleaned and deveined
teaspoon vinegar
recipes Garlic Butter Sauce (page 208)
tablespoons grated Parmesan cheese
lemon slices, cut up

Cook shrimp in boiling water with 1 teaspoon vinegar for
minutes.

Combine Garlic Butter Sauce and Parmesan cheese in a
saucepan.

Heat until cheese melts.

Put shrimp in a baking dish and pour sauce over them.
Bake at 300° for 5 minutes.

Garnish with lemon slices.
Serve with toothpicks.

TOTAL GRAMS   20.4
GRAMS PER SHRIMP   1.3

QUICHE LORRAINE

(Serves 12 for Hors d'Oeuvre)

SERVES 8

1 9-inch pie plate
1 pound of crisp bacon
2 eggs
2 egg yolks
1 teaspoon Dijon mustard
½ teaspoon dry mustard
⅛ teaspoon cayenne pepper
⅓ cup bacon fat
½ cup grated Parmesan cheese
2 cups heavy cream
1 teaspoon chopped parsley

Break up crisp bacon and sprinkle half of it into bottom of the pie plate.

Make following custard: Put into a bowl and mix well 2 whole eggs plus 2 yolks, Dijon mustard, dry mustard, cayenne pepper, bacon fat, and ⅓ cup Parmesan cheese.

Scald the cream by heating just to the boiling point (do not boil!).

Pour scalded cream into custard mixture.

Bake at 300° for 35 minutes. Remove.

When set, sprinkle with remaining cheese, bacon, and the parsley.

Serve warm.

TOTAL GRAMS   26.0
GRAMS PER SERVING   3.2

Soups

CHICKEN SOUP

Makes 2½ quarts

SERVES 10

4 or 5 pound chicken, cleaned and washed
3 quarts cold water
1 teaspoon salt
2 stalks celery (or 1 cup)
1 tablespoon parsley
2 tablespoons chopped onion

Place cleaned chicken in cold water. Bring to a boil. Remove foam that forms on the top of the water.

Add remaining ingredients.

Cover and *simmer* the chicken until it is tender (about 3 hours).

The chicken must cool in this broth. It then can be removed and used later in a salad or soup.

After removing chicken, strain soup, and *chill* the broth in a covered container in refrigerator.

Remove the layer of fat that will come to the top when thoroughly chilled.

Heat broth for soup and sauces. Or use it cold to make an aspic or jellied soup.

TOTAL GRAMS   7.2
GRAMS PER SERVING   .7

CREAM OF CHICKEN SOUP

ADD TO EACH CUP OF CHICKEN SOUP:
2 tablespoons heavy cream
1 egg yolk (for thickening)

Simmer (do not boil) for 3 minutes.

TOTAL GRAMS   8.4
GRAMS PER SERVING   .8

EGG DROP SOUP

1   *quart chicken soup*
4   *eggs*

Heat clear soup to boiling. Beat eggs well and drop into
broth by the tablespoonful.
Stir well with a fork.
Simmer 3 minutes.
Serve hot.

TOTAL GRAM   8.4
GRAMS PER SERVING (CUP)   .8

MATZOH BALL SOUP

SERVES 8

1   *egg, separated*
1½   *tablespoons chicken fat*
¼   *cup hot water or soup*
¼   *teaspoon salt*
¾   *cup crushed Baken-ets*
2   *quarts chicken soup*

Beat yolk of egg with softened chicken fat until thick
and well blended.
Pour into hot liquid and beat well.
Fold in salt and Baken-ets.

Beat egg white until stiff but not dry, and fold into mixture.

Chill for about 1 hour.

Heat 2 quarts chicken soup to boiling (recipe page 189).

Wet hands with cold water, and shape mixture into medium-size balls, about the diameter of a quarter.

Reduce heat, cover, simmer gently for 20 to 25 minutes, and serve.

TOTAL GRAMS   Trace

VICHYSSOISE

SERVES 8

4 *leeks, sliced*
2 *tablespoons butter*
1 *cup chicken broth (or 3 chicken bouillon cubes in 1 cup water)*
1 *cup cooked cauliflower*
1 *cup heavy cream*
   Salt and pepper to taste
1 *tablespoon minced chives*

Sauté leeks in butter until soft and golden yellow.

Place leeks and chicken broth in blender and blend until smooth.

Combine leek mixture, cauliflower, cream, salt, and pepper in a pot and cook over a low flame for 10 to 15 minutes.

Run all ingredients again through blender until smooth.

Serve hot or cold garnished with minced chives.

This is truly quite special!

TOTAL GRAMS   24.8
GRAMS PER SERVING   3.1

NOODLES FOR SOUPS

SERVES 2

2   *eggs at room temperature, separated*
¼   *teaspoon Krazy Mixed-Up Salt*
3   *tablespoons butter*

Melt butter in a cookie sheet that has sides.

Beat whites with salt until stiff.

Beat yolks with a fork and fold them into the whites.

Spread egg mixture on the cookie sheet and bake at 350° for 10 minutes, or until slightly browned. When cool, slice in strips and use in soups.

TOTAL GRAMS   1.2
GRAMS PER SERVING   .6

Egg Dishes

OMELET

The how-to for omelets:

Gather all equipment and ingredients. Use a heavy aluminum or iron pan about 2 inches deep. Use 6- or 7-inch pan for 2 or 3 eggs. A 10-inch pan for 6 or 8 eggs.

Use ½ tablespoon butter for cooking a 2- or 3-egg omelet, 1 tablespoon butter for a 6- or 8-egg omelet.

Heat pan over moderate heat or as recipe calls for. Pan should be hot enough to sizzle and foam butter without turning it brown.

Break eggs into bowl and whip until fluffy.

Pour egg mixture into pan. Slide pan back and forth slowly over heat during cooking. Lift the edges of eggs with a spatula or fork, tilting the skillet as you do so, to permit the uncooked mixture to run to the bottom.

Cook eggs until they set lightly, fold omelet over, and serve.

If a filling is desired, the filling should be added *before* the omelet is folded.

Omelets may be filled with many things. Try 2 tablespoons of our Strawberry Jam, or 2 slices of cooked bacon with 1 slice of American cheese, or ¼ cup delicatessen meat. Lox and sautéed onions are favorite fillings for many people.

The spinach omelet that follows is one of our favorite luncheon omelets.

It may be topped with our Basic Cream Sauce (recipe p. 207).

SPINACH OMELET

SERVES 2

½	cup spinach, washed and chopped
3	tablespoons olive oil
1	clove of garlic, minced
4	eggs, well beaten
	Dash of pepper
¼	teaspoon salt
3	tablespoons Parmesan cheese

Make sure spinach is well washed, then drain and dry.

Place olive oil in a skillet and heat.

Add garlic and cook slowly until light brown.

Add spinach and stir.

Cover and simmer for 15 minutes.

In another skillet prepare omelet (eggs, salt, and pepper) for filling.

After eggs have cooked about 1 minute, spread spinach mixture on eggs, sprinkle the Parmesan cheese on top, fold over, and serve.

TOTAL GRAMS	8.9
GRAMS PER SERVING	4.5

SCRAMBLED EGGS WITH SPICY HAM

SERVES 2

4 *thin slices boiled ham*
   Mustard sauce
2 *tablespoons butter*
4 *eggs*
   Salt
   Pepper
1 *tablespoon heavy cream*

Cut ham in half to make squares.
Spread with Mustard Sauce.
Melt butter in skillet.
Beat eggs with cream, salt, and pepper, and scramble in the butter until lightly cooked.
Spoon out some scrambled egg in center of each square, roll up, fasten with toothpicks, and serve hot.

TOTAL GRAMS	4.0
GRAMS PER SERVING	2.0

BACON AND CHEESE SOUFFLÉ

SERVES 6

½   *cup butter*
1   *teaspoon Krazy Mixed-Up Salt, or salt and pepper*
1½ *cups heavy cream*
2   *cups shredded sharp Cheddar cheese (about ½ pound)*
8   *eggs, separated (at room temperature)*
½   *cup crisp bacon, crumbled*
    Prepared soufflé dish (2½ quarts)

Preheat oven to 475°.
Prepare 2½-quart soufflé dish by doubling over piece waxed paper 1½ times diameter of dish and wrapping

around outside diameter of the top. Secure with cord or a rubber band. Butter inside of soufflé dish *and* waxed paper (melted butter is best).

Melt butter, stir in salt and pepper.

Add cream, stirring constantly until smooth (do not boil).

Add cheese, continue stirring until it melts, then remove from heat and cool.

Beat egg yolks until light and add to sauce, beating constantly. (Wire whisks are best for beating soufflés.)

Beat egg whites until stiff, and fold sauce mixture into egg whites, being careful not to break down whites.

Gently sprinkle crumbled bacon on top.

Pour mixture into soufflé dish.

Bake for 10 minutes, lower heat to 400°, and bake 30 minutes more.

Soufflé is done when top is brown and firm to touch.

TOTAL GRAMS	26.3
GRAMS PER SERVING	4.4

EGGS BENEDICT

SERVES 1

1 Diet Revolution Roll, cut in half
2 *slices of ham*
1 *tablespoon of butter*
2 *eggs*
   Pinch of salt
1 *teaspoon vinegar*
1 *tablespoon warm Hollandaise Sauce (page 211)*

Cut the roll in half lengthwise.

Sauté ham in butter about 2 minutes on each side, and place on roll.

Poach the eggs by the following method: Fill small

skillet ⅔ full of water, add pinch of salt and 1 teaspoon vinegar.

Bring water to boiling point and reduce to simmer.

Break egg in a small flat dish.

Slip it (very carefully) into the simmering water. Repeat process.

Dip water from sides of pan and baste eggs as they cook.

When the whites are firm and yolks cloudy, remove eggs with a skimmer and place on cut roll.

Top with Hollandaise Sauce and serve immediately.

TOTAL GRAMS   1.7

AUSTRIAN SOUFFLÉ

2 eggs per person

   Eggs separated (at room temperature)
   Pinch of cream of tartar
1 *teaspoon Sugar Twin per egg*
1 *tablespoon melted butter*

Preheat oven to 375°.

Place shallow baking pan half filled with water on bottom rack of oven.

Prepare soufflé dish by wrapping a cuff of waxed paper around the rim, as described on pages 194–195; grease dish and waxed paper with melted butter.

Beat egg whites with pinch of cream of tartar and Sugar Twin.

Beat egg yolks with fork until smooth, fold into whites, blend for no more than 1 minute, and pour into soufflé dish.

Place in center of baking pan, and cook for about 30 minutes or until firm on the top, and serve immediately.

TOTAL GRAMS FOR 2 EGGS   1.3

Main Courses:
Poultry, Meat, and Seafood

BARBECUED CHICKEN

SERVES 6

¼ cup Steak Sauce
1 tablespoon Slim-ette maple syrup
1 teaspoon dry mustard
1 clove crushed garlic
1 tablespoon white horseradish
4 pounds chicken parts

Combine maple syrup, mustard, garlic, horseradish, and Steak Sauce, and mix until well blended.

Put chicken in sauce and marinate in refrigerator overnight.

Bring to room temperature next day.

Broil as far away from heat source as possible.

Baste and turn often until browned.

This Barbecue Sauce is good on lamb and pork, too.

TOTAL GRAMS   8.3
GRAMS PER SERVING   1.4

CHICKEN CORDON BLEU

SERVES 6

4 chicken breasts cut in half and boned
¼ teaspoon Krazy Mixed-Up Salt or seasoned salt
2 eggs slightly beaten
½ cup Baken-ets
8 slices of ham
8 slices of Swiss cheese
   String
⅛ pound butter
⅓ cup Sauterne (see wine list)

Preheat oven to 350°.

Pound chicken with meat mallet to break down membranes.

Sprinkle Krazy Mixed-Up Salt on chicken breasts.

Dip breasts in egg and then into the Baken-ets.

Place one piece of ham and one piece of cheese on top of *each* chicken breast, then roll each breast with ham and cheese inside, and tie with string.

Brown chicken rolls in skillet in butter.

Remove and put into baking dish.

Pour butter from skillet over breasts, add wine, and bake for 1 hour. Serve one to each person.

(You can also use these as hors d'oeuvres by slicing breasts to size of half-dollars after removing from oven.)

TOTAL GRAMS   5.7
GRAMS PER SERVING   1.0

CHICKEN DIJON

SERVES 4

2   tablespoons butter
1   3-pound broiler, cut up
½   cup Chablis (check wine list)
¼   teaspoon tarragon
     Pinch of thyme
1   small bay leaf
½   teaspoon salt
¼   teaspoon pepper
2   egg yolks
2   teaspoons sour cream
3   teaspoons Dijon mustard
     Pinch of cayenne pepper

Melt butter in pan, add chicken, and cook until browned on both sides, turning once.

Add wine, tarragon, thyme, bay leaf, salt, and pepper.
Bring to boil, cover and simmer 45 minutes.

Discard bay leaf, remove meat and keep warm.

Beat egg yolks into sauce with egg beater, then add sour
cream, mustard, and cayenne.

Heat, stirring constantly, but don't boil.

Put meat into sauce, simmer for 5 minutes, and serve hot.

TOTAL GRAMS   3.2
GRAMS PER SERVING   .8

BREADED CHICKEN, PORK, VEAL, OR FISH

SERVES 4

Make the roll recipe on page 225 and crush the cool
rolls in a blender.

Beat 2 eggs. Dip pieces of chicken, meat, or fish first
into egg and then into the crumbs. Repeat.

For *chicken,* fry in a heavy skillet filled ¼-inch full of
hot vegetable oil (or butter if desired). Allow to brown
well on one side and turn. Brown other side. Cover pan and
cook at a low heat 20 to 30 minutes, depending on the size
of the chicken.

For *pork* or *veal,* fry in the same manner as above, adjusting cooking time to thickness of meat. Cook until tender.

For *fish,* fry in the same manner as above but cook only
5 to 10 minutes, once covered.

Our Mustard or Béarnaise Sauces are quite good with
these fried foods.

TOTAL GRAMS   3.9
GRAMS PER SERVING   1.0

BACON CHEESEBURGER

SERVES 4

1½   *pounds ground beef (preferably round)*
4   *slices crisp bacon*
½   *cup Cheddar cheese*
1   *teaspoon Krazy Mixed-Up Salt or seasoned salt*
    Pepper
1   *teaspoon parsley*
    Bacon drippings

Mix ground beef with bacon, cheese, salt, and pepper. Shape into 4 patties, about 1 inch thick.

Pan-fry over medium heat in bacon drippings, 8 minutes on each side for medium well done, more for well done, slightly less for rare.

TOTAL GRAMS   2.8
GRAMS PER SERVING   .7

Good for first week.

HAMBURGER FONDUE

SERVES 4

1   *pound ground round*
½   *teaspoon onion powder*
    Salt and pepper to taste
2   *tablespoons melted butter*

Combine meat, onion powder, and salt, and roll into small balls.

Dip in melted butter, put in foil-lined broiler pan, and broil until brown.

Serve with any of the following heated sauces for dipping at the table:

Steak Sauce   GRAMS PER SERVING   1.2   (page 209)
Horseradish
Sauce   GRAMS PER SERVING   .9   (page 208)
Garlic Sauce   GRAMS PER SERVING   .1   (page 208)

TOTAL GRAMS   .4
GRAMS PER SERVING   Trace

For the first week of the diet, make the hamburgers as above and serve with the following:

BLUE CHEESE TOPPING

Combine ¼ cup crumbled blue cheese and 4 tablespoons salted butter or margarine.
Spread on broiled hamburgers.

LONDON BROIL

SERVES 4

2 *tablespoons grated Parmesan cheese*
2 *tablespoons olive oil*
2 *tablespoons vegetable oil*
2 *tablespoons tarragon vinegar*
1 *teaspoon Krazy Mixed-Up Salt or seasoned salt*
3 *pounds London Broil*

Mix Parmesan cheese, oil, vinegar, and salt together.
Place meat in mixture and spoon mixture over it.
Refrigerate overnight, then broil as you would steak.

TOTAL GRAMS   2.2
GRAMS PER SERVING   .6

POT ROAST

SERVES 4

3 packages MBT beef broth mixture (dry)
1 medium onion, chopped
   Garlic powder to taste
3 pounds rump roast

Preheat oven to 300°
Sauté onions in well-greased skillet.
Lay 2 large pieces of aluminum foil crisscross in heavy covered casserole so bottom and sides are fully covered.
Place 1½ packages dry MBT mixture and half of sautéed onions on foil.
Rub meat with garlic powder and place meat on foil.
Sprinkle remaining bouillon and onions on top of meat, wrap foil tightly around meat, and cover the casserole.
Bake for 2 hours, then lower to 275° for 1 hour.
Cool slightly before slicing.

TOTAL GRAMS	7.0
GRAMS PER SERVING	1.8

VEAL PICCATA

SERVES 4

1   package of Baken-ets, crushed
1   tablespoon Parmesan cheese
2   eggs, beaten
    Salt and pepper
6   veal cutlets
¼   pound butter
8   tablespoons olive oil
    Grated rind of 1 lemon
1   tablespoon lemon juice
6   lemon slices

Combine Baken-ets and cheese on a flat plate.

Beat eggs, pepper, and salt with fork.

Dip veal first into egg and then into Baken-ets mixture.

Melt butter with olive oil in heavy frying pan.

Fry veal in oil until well browned on both sides (you must keep turning veal).

Place 1 slice of lemon on each piece of veal and sprinkle on grated lemon rind and lemon juice.

Cover and simmer gently for 10 minutes, turning once.

TOTAL GRAMS	10.2
GRAMS PER SERVING	2.6

VEAL ROLLS IN WINE

SERVES 6

6   *chicken livers, cut in half*
3   *tablespoons butter*
8   *slices prosciutto (or cooked lean bacon)*
½   *teaspoon sage*
½   *teaspoon basil*
    Salt and pepper
1½ *pounds thinly sliced veal cutlets, cut in 12 pieces*
24 *toothpicks or string*
1   *cup Chablis (check wine list)*
2   *tablespoons beef stock or water*

Sauté chicken livers in 1 tablespoon butter.

When cooked, chop fine with prosciutto, sage, and basil, add salt and pepper to taste.

Spread mixture on veal slices.

Roll and fasten each slice (use toothpicks or string to hold closed).

Put 2 tablespoons of butter in large frying pan and brown veal in it, turning to cook evenly.

Add wine and cook until nearly evaporated.

Remove rolls from pan, place on a serving platter, and keep warm.

Add water or stock to pan gravy, mix well, and pour over veal rolls.

TOTAL GRAMS   9.38
GRAMS PER SERVING   1.6

SHRIMP AND LOBSTER CANTONESE

SERVES 6

1   cup Basic Cream Sauce (recipe on page 207)
3   tablespoons oil
3   tablespoons onion, chopped
½   pound pork, ground
1   clove garlic, minced
1   can lobster meat
1½   pounds raw shrimp, shelled and deveined
2   tablespoons water chestnuts, chopped
2   tablespoons bamboo shoots, chopped
1   teaspoon salt
⅛   teaspoon pepper
1   cup Chicken Soup (recipe on page 189)
2   tablespoons scallions, finely chopped

Make Basic Cream Sauce. Set aside in double boiler to keep warm.

Heat oil in large skillet, and brown onions lightly.

Add pork and garlic. Stir pork to brown evenly.

Add lobster, shrimp, water chestnuts, bamboo shoots, salt, and pepper.

Sauté 2 minutes.

Meanwhile, heat Chicken Soup to boiling and add to shrimp.

Cover and cook over low heat 8 minutes. Remove and stir Cream Sauce into mixture, blending well. Taste for seasoning, sprinkle with scallions, and serve.

TOTAL GRAMS   29.5
GRAMS PER SERVING   5.0

TEMPURA

SERVES 4

3   *tablespoons sesame seeds, crushed in blender*
3   *eggs*
2   *tablespoons cottage cheese*
10 *shakes Krazy Mixed-Up Salt, or seasoned salt*

TEMPURA—TOTAL GRAMS   9.2

Place all ingredients in blender and run for 3 minutes.
Dip ¼ cup of any two of the following ingredients in
batter and deep fry until brown:

	GRAMS PER ¼ CUP
Shrimp	.9
Scallops	2.0
Fish fillets	0
Cauliflower	3.0
Mushrooms	2.5
Broccoli	3.3
Green beans	3.1

Serve with our Mustard Sauce, Horseradish Sauce, and
Lemon Butter Sauce.

STUFFED SOLE

SERVES 2

2   *tablespoons butter*
½   *teaspoon Krazy Mixed-Up Salt, or seasoned salt*
1   *teaspoon lemon juice*
¼   *teaspoon white horseradish*
5   *drops Tabasco sauce*
⅓   *cup heavy cream*
1   *can crabmeat*
4   *fillets of sole*
2   *tablespoons melted butter*
2   *teaspoons lemon juice*
     Chopped parsley

Melt butter.

Add salt, 1 teaspoon lemon juice, horseradish, and Tabasco.

Blend in cream.

Cook, stirring constantly, until it comes to a boil (but do not let it boil).

Remove from heat, add crabmeat.

Grease a shallow casserole; place 2 fillets in the bottom.

Pour crabmeat mixture on the top, cover with remaining fillets, and spoon 2 tablespoons of melted butter mixed with lemon juice over fish.

Sprinkle with parsley and bake at 350° for 30 minutes.

TOTAL GRAMS	6.0
GRAMS PER SERVING	3.0

BARBECUED SPARERIBS

SERVES 6

3   pounds spareribs
¼   cup chopped onions
1   tablespoon bacon drippings
¼   teaspoon garlic powder
½   cup of water
⅛   cup of lemon juice
2   tablespoons tarragon vinegar
1   tablespoon Lee & Perrins Worcestershire Sauce
3   tablespoons brown Sugar Twin
1   cup Hunt's tomato juice
3   tablespoons of soy sauce (bought in health food store)
¼   teaspoon paprika
1   tablespoon Gold Seal cocktail sherry (optional)

Preheat oven to 450°.

Cut spareribs into rib pieces, place in large pan, cover with waxed paper, and bake for 15 minutes.

Sauté onion in bacon drippings until brown, add garlic powder, and cook for 1 minute.

Add remaining ingredients, and simmer for 25 minutes. Set aside.

Remove waxed paper from ribs.

Pour sauce over ribs, reduce oven to 350°, and bake for 1 hour, basting frequently.

TOTAL GRAMS   27.3
GRAMS PER SERVING   4.6

Sauces

BASIC CREAM SAUCE

Makes 18 tablespoons

½ cup butter
3 egg yolks
¼ cup water
¼ cup heavy cream
    Dash of salt

Melt butter in the top of a double boiler over hot (not boiling) water.

Add egg yolks one at a time, beating with a rotary beater.

Combine cream, salt and water, and add a little at a time, beating constantly.

Continue beating until thick and creamy (4 or 5 minutes).

TOTAL GRAMS   4.8
GRAMS PER TABLESPOON   .3

LEMON BUTTER SAUCE

SERVES 6

3 tablespoons soft butter or margarine
1 tablespoon lemon juice
1 tablespoon minced parsley
½ teaspoon salt
   Dash of pepper
   Grated rind of ½ lemon

Mix all ingredients together, and warm over low fire.

TOTAL GRAMS   4.2
GRAMS PER SERVING   .7

COLD HORSERADISH SAUCE

10 TABLESPOONS

½ cup sour cream
2 tablespoons white horseradish
2 scallions chopped
   Seasoned salt
   Paprika

Combine all ingredients except paprika and put into serving dish.

Garnish with paprika, and refrigerate until serving time.

TOTAL GRAMS   8.7
GRAMS PER TABLESPOON SERVING   .9

GARLIC BUTTER SAUCE

MAKES 5 TABLESPOONS

¼ cup melted butter
2 cloves of garlic put through a garlic crusher
   Krazy Mixed-Up Salt, or seasoned salt to taste
⅛ teaspoon minced chives

Combine all ingredients in saucepan, cook for 1 minute, and serve hot.

TOTAL GRAMS   4.9
GRAMS PER TABLESPOON SERVING   1.0

STEAK SAUCE

11 TABLESPOONS

½   cup Hunt's Tomato Puree
¼   cup water
5   teaspoons distilled vinegar
¼   teaspoon orange extract
⅛   teaspoon salt
1   small clove garlic crushed
1   teaspoon grated onion
½   teaspoon Maggi Seasoning
20   drops of Tabasco sauce

Blend together well, and refrigerate until serving time.

TOTAL GRAMS   13.2
GRAM PER TABLESPOON SERVING   1.2

BÉARNAISE SAUCE

16 TABLESPOONS

BLEND UNTIL SMOOTH:
½   cup butter melted
2   tablespoons lemon juice
3   egg yolks
¼   teaspoon parsley
¼   teaspoon Krazy Mixed-Up Salt, or seasoned salt
½   teaspoon prepared mustard

COOK TOGETHER:

2   tablespoons White Chablis (check wine list)
2   teaspoons dried tarragon
1   tablespoon tarragon vinegar
2   teaspoons chopped scallions
2   pkgs. of Sugar Twin

Gently simmer wine, tarragon, vinegar, scallions, and Sugar Twin in saucepan until volume is reduced in half.

Add to other ingredients in blender, blend until smooth, then reheat over low fire and serve.

TOTAL GRAMS   7.3
GRAMS PER TABLESPOON SERVING   .5

MUSTARD SAUCE

1 CUP (16 TABLESPOONS)

3   tablespoons onion, chopped
1   tablespoon butter
8   tablespoons Dijon mustard
¼   cup heavy cream
½   teaspoon Worcestershire Sauce (Lea & Perrins)
½   tablespoon chopped chives

Sauté onions in butter until soft.
Stir in mustard and cream until well heated (do not boil).
Blend in Worcestershire Sauce.
Sprinkle with chives.
Serve hot.

TOTAL GRAMS   7.0
GRAMS PER TABLESPOON SERVING   .4

HOLLANDAISE SAUCE

MAKES 16 TABLESPOONS

½ cup butter or margarine
¼ teaspoon salt
   Dash of cayenne pepper
2 tablespoons lemon juice
⅔ cup boiling water
4 egg yolks

Melt butter in top part of double boiler over hot (not boiling) water, stirring constantly until creamy.

Add salt, cayenne, lemon juice, and water. Beat constantly with a rotary beater.

Remove top part of double boiler from hot water, add egg yolks, one at a time, still beating, until mixture is light and fluffy.

Replace pot in hot water and continue beating until mixture turns glossy and is slightly thickened.

Cover and keep hot until serving time.

If the sauce should curdle, remix with rotary beater until smooth.

TOTAL GRAMS   5.6
GRAMS PER TABLESPOON SERVING   0.4

Luncheon Dishes

CHICKEN SALAD

5 SERVINGS

1 cup cooked chicken, diced
½ cup diced celery
¼ cup mayonnaise
¼ cup sour cream
¼ cup walnuts
   Salad Supreme to taste
1 hard-cooked egg chopped (as garnish)

Combine ingredients, chill.

Heap in lettuce leaf-lined serving dish, garnish with eggs, and serve.

For a really special treat, add wedges of avocado to this salad.

TOTAL GRAMS   17.3
GRAMS PER SERVING 3.5

TOMATO DELIGHT

SERVES 2 FOR LUNCH

1 medium tomato sliced (6 slices)
   Oregano
   Mayonnaise
4 slices crumbled bacon
2 ozs. sliced natural Muenster cheese

Place tomatoes on a baking sheet.

Sprinkle with oregano, and put a small amount of mayonnaise on each tomato slice.

Sprinkle with bacon, cover with cheese.

Broil in a hot oven for about 3 minutes or until cheese browns.

Serve for lunch or as a side dish.

TOTAL GRAMS   6.7
GRAMS PER SERVING 3.4

STUFFED ZUCCHINI

SERVES 8

8   medium zucchini
½   lb. chopped beef
1   egg
2   tablespoons Parmesan cheese (Romano may also be used)
½   teaspoon salt
½   teaspoon pepper
6   slices prosciutto (or boiled ham)
3   tablespoons Progresso olive oil
1   tablespoon chopped parsley
1   slice lean bacon, chopped
2   tablespoons chopped onion
8   oz. tomato juice (Hunt's)
¾   cup water

Preheat oven to 375°.

Meanwhile, boil zucchini 8 minutes.

Cut it into halves lengthwise, scoop out pulp and save. Do *not* break the skin.

Dice pulp and mix it with chopped beef, egg, Parmesan, prosciutto, salt and pepper.

Stuff zucchini with the mixture.

Heat olive oil in a large skillet.

Add parsley, bacon, onion, and heat together over low fire until well browned.

Stir in tomato juice and water.

Cook for 5 minutes.

Place zucchini in a baking pan just large enough to fit the squash. (The pan must not be too large or you will not have enough sauce.)

Pour over sauce and bake for 30 minutes.

TOTAL GRAMS   39.2
GRAMS PER SERVING   4.9

This is a filling luncheon meal all by itself.

COTTAGE CHEESE AND SOUR CREAM SALAD

SERVES 8

2   cups lettuce or tender raw spinach
1⅓   cups sliced, pared, cucumbers
½   cup sliced radishes
½   cup scallions
        Salt and pepper
2   cups cottage cheese
1   cup commercial sour cream

Wash greens, dry thoroughly, and tear into bite-size pieces (never cut greens). If you use spinach for a green, tear leaves off tough spine and discard spine, using only the leaves.

Add cucumbers, radishes, scallions, salt, pepper, and cottage cheese.

Toss lightly (just enough to mix), spoon sour cream on top, and serve.

TOTAL GRAMS   44.2
GRAMS PER SERVING   5.5

CHEF'S SALAD

SERVES 6 AS A COMPLETE LUNCH

2   cups greens—lettuce, spinach, romaine, escarole, or endive
1   medium tomato, diced
1   cucumber, peeled and cubed
3   scallions, minced
1   can anchovies, drained
½   cup radishes, sliced
¾   cup French dressing (recipe on page 219)
1   cup julienne strips of cooked chicken
1   cup julienne strips of baked ham
1   cup julienne strips of Swiss or cheddar cheese
6   deviled eggs curry (recipe on page 185)

Wash greens and dry well.

Tear into bite-size pieces, put in a large shallow salad bowl.

Add tomatoes, cucumber, scallions, anchovies, and radishes.

Pour half the dressing on mixture and toss.

Alternate a few strips at a time of chicken, ham, and cheese around the edge of bowl.

Place four halves of deviled eggs in the center, remaining halves around the edge of bowl.

Pour the rest of the dressing over all, and serve, making sure when you serve individual plates that each person gets a bit of everything.

TOTAL GRAMS	33.2
GRAMS PER SERVING	5.5

Vegetable Salads

COLE SLAW WITH COTTAGE CHEESE DRESSING

SERVES 8

¼ cup mayonnaise
¼ cup cream-style cottage cheese
½ individual package of Sugar Twin (or 1 teaspoon from box)
1 tablespoon vinegar
½ teaspoon grated onion
¼ teaspoon caraway seed
1 teaspoon celery seed or ½ teaspoon celery salt
2 cups finely shredded cabbage

DRESSING: Combine all the ingredients except cabbage, and refrigerate (flavor is improved when thoroughly chilled).

Shred cabbage as thin as possible and place in a lettuce-lined salad bowl. Pour dressing over, mix well, and serve.

TOTAL GRAMS   23.8
GRAMS PER SERVING   3.0

SOUR CREAM DRESSING FOR COLE SLAW

SERVES 8

1   cup sour cream
1   tablespoon vinegar
1   package of Sugar Twin
½   teaspoon caraway seed
1   teaspoon celery seed or ½ teaspoon celery salt
1   teaspoon salt
4   tablespoons of heavy cream (optional)

Mix all ingredients, and chill.

TOTAL GRAMS   38.2
GRAMS PER SERVING   4.8

SPINACH SALAD

(To be served in place of a vegetable and a salad.)

SERVES 6

1   lb. fresh spinach
½   lb. raw mushrooms, sliced
1   lb. crisp bacon
¼   cup Parmesan cheese (grated)
1   recipe Caesar Salad Dressing (page 220)
4   hard-cooked eggs, chilled and quartered

Wash spinach several times to remove all sand

Dry thoroughly and tear into bite-size pieces, removing stems.

Wash and slice mushrooms.

Combine spinach, mushrooms, and bacon in a salad bowl, sprinkle cheese on top, pour on Caesar Salad Dressing, and toss.

Garnish with eggs.

TOTAL GRAMS   33.9
GRAMS PER SERVING   5.7

A can of tuna fish added to this recipe makes a *delicious* luncheon meal. It will *not* add to the gram count.

CAESAR SALAD

SERVES 8

2   *heads of romaine lettuce*
1   *clove of garlic, cut in half*
   Caesar Salad Dressing (page 220)
1   *lb. of bacon, cooked crisp*
⅓   *cup grated Parmesan cheese*
2   *tablespoons minced parsley*
1   *can anchovies (optional)*
4   *eggs hard-boiled, chilled and chopped*

Wash and dry lettuce well.

Tear into bite-size pieces.

Rub wooden salad bowl with garlic, place lettuce in bowl, add half the dressing, and toss well.

Top with bacon, cheese, parsley, and anchovies.

Pour on remaining dressing, garnish with chopped egg, and serve.

TOTAL GRAMS   32.7
GRAMS PER SERVING   4.1

TOSSED VEGETABLE SALAD

SERVES 6

Wash any combination of greens, lettuce, romaine, raw spinach, escarole, endive, bibb, or watercress. Pat dry on a towel before using. (Dressing won't cling to wet greens.)

Tear greens into bite-size pieces.

Refrigerate.

French dressing is usually used, but try some of its variations.

For 6 people, toss about 2 cups chilled salad greens and about 2 cups of two or more of the following vegetables: (Total grams of 2 cups lettuce = 14.4 grams.)

RAW VEGETABLES	GRAMS PER $\frac{1}{2}$ CUP
Broccoli—*thinly sliced flowerettes*	6.5
Cauliflower—*thinly sliced flowerettes*	5.9
Celery—*slices, cut on bias, or cubed*	4.4
Cucumbers—*sliced or cubed*	3.6
Green pepper—*ringed or cubed*	5.4
Leek or scallions—*sliced*	11.8
Mushrooms—*sliced or cubed*	5.0
Radishes—*sliced or grated*	4.5
Tomatoes—*cubed*	5.3
Zucchini—*thinly sliced or grated*	3.5
Green olives—*pitted or whole*	1.5
Black olives—*pitted*	2.9

COOKED AND CHILLED VEGETABLES	GRAMS PER $\frac{1}{2}$ CUP
Asparagus—*or asparagus tips*	4.1
Cauliflower—*small flowerettes or chopped*	4.6
Green beans—*1 inch long*	6.1

For extra flavor—one or more of the following may be added:

	GRAMS PER ½ CUP
Anchovies—*few fillets, chopped up*	0.0
Bacon bits—*crumbled and crisp*	3.6
Blue cheese—*crumbled*	2.3
Cheddar cheese—*grated or cubed*	2.4
Eggs (hard cooked) chopped, sliced, or quartered	1.0
Lemon rind—*no more than one tablespoon grated*	18.0
Garlic—*crushed*	34.7
Parmesan cheese—*grated*	3.3
Walnuts, Pecans, or Brazil nuts (*chopped*)	17.8

Salad Dressings

FRENCH DRESSING

9 TABLESPOONS

2 *tablespoons tarragon vinegar*
½ *teaspoon Krazy Mixed-Up Salt, or seasoned salt*
3 *tablespoons Progresso olive oil*
3 *tablespoons vegetable oil*
1 *teaspoon finely chopped scallions*
½ *teaspoon chives*
½ *teaspoon parsley*
½ *teaspoon tarragon*

Place all ingredients in a screw-top jar and shake vigorously 30 times.

TOTAL GRAMS   16.2
GRAMS PER TABLESPOON   1.8

CREAMY FRENCH DRESSING

SERVES 10

MAKES 30 TABLESPOONS

    Container with a screw-on top
3   teaspoons Krazy Mixed-Up Salt, or seasoned salt
½   teaspoon dry mustard
½   individual package of Sugar Twin
1   teaspoon Dijon mustard
1½   teaspoons lemon juice
1   teaspoon garlic powder
5   tablespoons tarragon vinegar
6   tablespoons Progresso or Old Monk olive oil
6   tablespoons vegetable oil
1   raw egg, beaten
½   cup heavy cream

Combine all ingredients in screw-top jar, shake well, and refrigerate for at least 1 hour before serving.

    TOTAL GRAMS   9.3
    GRAMS PER TABLESPOON SERVING   .3

CAESAR SALAD DRESSING

SERVES 8 FOR 2 HEADS OF LETTUCE

1   teaspoon Krazy Mixed-Up Salt, or salt and pepper to taste
¼   teaspoon dry mustard
1   teaspoon Dijon mustard
½   individual package of Sugar Twin
    Juice from ½ lemon (about 1 teaspoon)
2   tablespoons tarragon vinegar
2   tablespoons Progresso olive oil
4   tablespoons vegetable oil
1   egg
1   teaspoon garlic powder

Mix all ingredients well, and pour over salad.

TOTAL GRAMS   3.2
GRAMS PER SERVING   .4

GREEN GODDESS DRESSING

16 TABLESPOONS

½   medium avocado
½   cup mayonnaise
1   clove minced garlic
2   chopped anchovies
⅛   cup finely chopped scallions
1   tablespoon parsley
½   tablespoon lemon juice
½   tablespoon tarragon vinegar
½   teaspoon Krazy Mixed-Up Salt, or seasoned salt
¼   cup sour cream

Peel and pit avocado, force through a sieve or mix in a blender for ½ minute.

Put pulp in a bowl with remaining ingredients except the sour cream. Mix well.

Whip the sour cream and fold it in with the other ingredients.

TOTAL GRAMS   18.0
GRAMS PER TABLESPOON SERVING   1.1

ROQUEFORT DRESSING NO. 1

MAKES 14 TABLESPOONS

½   cup sour cream
2   tablespoons tarragon vinegar
1   tablespoon Sugar Twin
¾   teaspoon Krazy Mixed-Up Salt
½   teaspoon celery seed
¼   cup crumbled Roquefort cheese

Place the sour cream, vinegar, Sugar Twin, salt, celery seed, and half the cheese in blender and mix until smooth.

Mix remaining cheese with blended dressing, refrigerate, and serve.

TOTAL GRAMS   **9.4**

GRAMS PER TABLESPOON   **.7**

ROQUEFORT DRESSING NO. 2

SINGLE SERVING

2   *tablespoons oil*
1   *tablespoon cider vinegar*
1   *tablespoon crumbled Roquefort or Blue cheese*
½ *teaspoon of Salad Supreme*

Mix all ingredients and serve.

TOTAL GRAMS   **1.2**

Vegetables

FRIED EGGPLANT

SERVES 4

½ *medium eggplant (about 1 cup)*
¼ *cup grated Swiss cheese*
¼ *teaspoon garlic powder*
¼ *teaspoon lemon juice*
½ *teaspoon Krazy Mixed-Up Salt or salt and pepper*
½ *package crushed Baken-ets*
    Cooking oil

Boil eggplant until tender.

Peel eggplant, chop, put in blender, and run at high speed for ½ minute.

Remove from blender and add cheese, garlic, lemon juice and salt, mixing well.

Shape into small balls, about 1 inch in diameter, refrigerate for at least 1 hour.

Roll cold balls in Baken-ets, and fry in hot deep fat until crisp.

TOTAL GRAMS   10.4
GRAMS PER SERVING   2.6

SAVORY BROCCOLI

SERVES 3

1 package frozen broccoli (1 cup cooked)
1 clove of garlic, sliced
3 tablespoons Progresso olive oil
1 tablespoon Parmesan cheese, grated
½ teaspoon Krazy Mixed-Up Salt

Cook broccoli slightly less than recommended on the package.

Sauté garlic in olive oil until brown. Remove garlic.

Add broccoli, Parmesan cheese and salt, and cook over low heat 5 to 7 minutes stirring occasionally. Serve.

TOTAL GRAMS   11.6
GRAMS PER SERVING   3.9

CABBAGE SOUTHERN STYLE

SERVES 6

1 medium cabbage
½ cup diced salt pork or 4 tablespoons bacon fat
1 individual package of Sugar Twin (or 1 teaspoon from box)

Remove tough or discolored leaves from cabbage and shred the rest.

Heat one inch of water to boiling point in medium-sized pot.

Add cabbage, cover, and cook for about 10 minutes or until translucent.

Sauté salt pork until brown, or heat bacon fat very hot.

Drain cabbage, add salt pork (or bacon fat) and Sugar Twin, cover and cook together for 3 or 4 minutes until hot.

TOTAL GRAMS 19.7
GRAMS PER SERVING 3.3

CREAMED SPINACH

SERVES 8

2   *packages frozen chopped spinach (2 cups cooked)*
4   *tablespoons butter*
1   *clove garlic, crushed*
1   *teaspoon onion powder*
½   *cup sour cream*
⅓   *cup grated Parmesan cheese*
2   *tablespoons minced parsley*
1   *tablespoon sesame seeds*

Cook spinach slightly, less than time recommended on package.

Melt butter in skillet, add spinach, garlic, onion powder, and cook together 5 minutes.

Add sour cream, cheese, sesame seeds, and parsley.

Heat, stirring (but do not boil), until well mixed and hot.

Serve.

TOTAL GRAMS 32.4
GRAMS PER SERVING 4.0

MOCK POTATO PANCAKES

MAKES 15

1¼ *cups cauliflower, cut into small pieces*
½   *tablespoon soya powder*
1   *large egg*
½   *teaspoon salt*
2   *teaspoons grated onion*
½   *teaspoon baking powder*
    Fat to cover fry pan ½ inch deep

Blend all ingredients in blender until smooth.
Drop by tablespoon into deep fat.
Allow to brown on one side, turn and brown on other side.
Remove when firm (do not touch until then).

TOTAL GRAMS   15.4
GRAMS PER SERVING   1.0

Bread, Rolls, Crackers, and Pie Crust

DIET REVOLUTION ROLLS

MAKES 6 ROLLS

    Pam spray
3   *eggs separated*
¼   *teaspoon cream of tartar*
3   *tablespoons cottage cheese*
1   *package of Sugar Twin*

Preheat oven to 300°.
Separate eggs *very carefully* (make sure that *none* of the yolk gets into the whites).

Spray Pam on a teflon cookie sheet.

Beat egg whites with cream of tartar until whites are stiff but not dry.

Fold in yolks, cottage cheese, and Sugar Twin. (Be extremely careful not to break down the egg whites. Mix for no more than a minute.)

Place the mixture carefully on the teflon cookie sheet, gently putting one tablespoon full on top of another until each "roll" is about 2 inches high. Repeat this until you have 6 piles.

Place the cookie sheet in the oven and bake for about 1 hour.

Rolls should resemble delicatessen rolls.

TOTAL GRAMS   3.1
GRAMS PER SERVING   .5

VARIATIONS:

CARAWAY ROLLS

Fold 1 tablespoon of caraway seed into mixture when other ingredients are added.

TOTAL GRAMS   9.4
GRAMS PER SERVING   1.6

ONION ROLLS

2 *tablespoons minced onion*
1 *tablespoon butter*

Mince onions very fine and sauté in the butter.

Dry them well in a paper towel—there should not be *any* grease left on them!

Fold into egg mixture when other ingredients are added.

TOTAL GRAMS   5.6
GRAMS PER SERVING   .9

BREAD CRUMBS

Put the six cooked and cooled rolls in a blender until they form crumbs.

TOTAL GRAMS   3.1

CHEESE CRACKERS

MAKES 20 CRACKERS

Pam spray
4   tablespoons Parmesan cheese or Romano cheese
2   eggs
2   tablespoons butter
¼   cup sesame seed crushed in the blender
1   tablespoon heavy cream
Pinch of salt

Beat all ingredients together until well blended.
Spray Pam on a 10-inch square baking dish.
Spread mixture thinly on pan.
Bake at 300° for ½ hour or until light brown. Cool and slice into twenty 1-inch squares.
Use as a snack or with a dip.

TOTAL GRAMS   14.2
GRAMS PER SERVING 1 SQUARE   .7

DIET REVOLUTION BREAD

12 SLICES

2   eggs separated at room temperature
¾   teaspoon Sugar Twin
¼   teaspoon cream of tartar
2   tablespoons cottage cheese
2   tablespoons soya powder
Pam spray

Preheat oven to 325°.

Spray Pam on a small loaf pan, 6 x 3½ x 2".

Separate the eggs *very* carefully. If one drop of the yolk falls into the whites, you must put them aside and begin again.

Beat the egg yolks with a fork.

Beat the egg whites with the Sugar Twin and cream of tartar, using a wire whisk or hand electric beater so they are very evenly beaten. Beat steadily until whites are stiff, then fold in cottage cheese and egg yolks.

Place the soya powder in a strainer and sift it over the egg mixture.

Fold it in carefully, being careful not to break down the egg white.

Pile the mixture into the loaf pan and bake at 325° (using oven thermometer) for 30 minutes, then turn oven down to 300°, and bake 30 minutes more. You may have to adjust the length of time according to your oven.

Cool. Slice into 12 pieces.

TOTAL GRAMS   10.5
GRAMS PER SERVING   .9

FRENCH TOAST

MAKES 12 SLICES

2   *eggs*
½   *tablespoon cinnamon*
1   *package of Sugar Twin*
1   *loaf of our bread, sliced (12 slices)*
2   *tablespoons butter*

Beat eggs with cinnamon and Sugar Twin.

Dip slices of our bread into egg mixture, covering both sides well.

Melt butter in a skillet.

Put bread into melted butter and sauté until brown, turn and brown on other side.

Remove from the pan and serve with our strawberry jam.

TOTAL GRAMS   18.5
GRAMS PER SERVING 2 SLICES   3.1

YELLOW PIE SHELL

3   egg whites
½   teaspoon cream of tartar
1   package Sugar Twin
2   egg yolks
2   tablespoons cottage cheese
     Pam spray

Preheat oven to 300°.
Separate eggs.
Beat whites with cream of tartar and Sugar Twin.
Beat yolks lightly.
Fold cottage cheese and yolks into stiff whites.
Spray Pam on a teflon pie plate, pour in mixture, and shape to conform to the plate.
Bake at 300° for ½ hour.

TOTAL GRAMS   3.8
TOTAL GRAMS WITH CARBOHYDRATE-FREE SWEETENER   3.0

Desserts

RED GELATIN

(*Raspberry, Strawberry, or Cherry*)

SERVES 8

2 *packages of D-Zerta or Shimmer*
2 *tablespoons of No-Cal raspberry or strawberry syrup*
9 *individual packages of Sugar Twin*

TOTAL GRAMS 11.2
GRAMS PER SERVING 1.4

CITRUS GELATIN

(*Orange, Lemon, or Lime*)

2 *packages of D-Zerta or Shimmer*
1 *teaspoon of orange, lemon, or lime extract*
9 *packages of Sugar Twin*

TOTAL GRAMS 14.4
GRAMS PER SERVING 1.8

Prepare as package directs, adding Sugar Twin. Cool.
Add extract or syrup, stir well, and pour into sherbet glasses or molds.

Refrigerate until firm. The extract or syrup gives this dessert a delicious flavor.

Use strawberry or raspberry syrup in berry gelatins.

Use extracts in orange, lemon, and lime gelatin.

These desserts may be garnished with a tablespoon of whipped cream (1 tablespoon = .4 grams) or chopped nuts (1 tablespoon = 2.2 grams).

STRAWBERRY GELATIN PARFAIT

SERVES 8

Make Strawberry Gelatin according to the recipe. Place gelatin in a parfait dish, alternating with a mixture of 2 tablespoons whipped cream and 1 tablespoon Diet Strawberry Jam.

Top with 1 tablespoon Diet Whipped Cream.

TOTAL GRAMS   39.2
GRAMS PER SERVING 4.9

CHERRY MOLD

SERVES 10

2   packages of D-Zerta cherry gelatin
2   tablespoons No-Cal raspberry syrup
9   individual packages of Sugar Twin
3   tablespoons of lemon juice
6   ozs. cream cheese
1   cup canteloupe balls
½   cup pecans, halved
6½   cup mold, sprayed with Pam

Prepare gelatin as package directs, with Sugar Twin. Cool.

Add syrup and lemon juice.

Chill half of gelatin mixture.

Cover bottom of a 6½ cup mold with the other half of the gelatin mixture.

Shape cream cheese into balls about size of melon balls.

Place half of the cream cheese balls and half of the melon balls into mold.

Trim edge of mold with a circle of pecans.

Chill until firm.

Remove partially-chilled plain gelatin from the refrigerator.

Add remaining cheese and melon balls and the nuts to it.
Pour over jelled mixture in the mold and chill until firm.
If you use Pam, mold should shake out onto serving dish very easily.

TOTAL GRAMS	49
TOTAL GRAMS WITH CARBOHYDRATE-FREE SWEETENER	42
GRAMS PER SERVING	5
GRAMS PER SERVING WITH CARBOHYDRATE-FREE SWEETENER	4

This is a delightful recipe for entertaining. Make half of the recipe and keep it in the refrigerator for a bedtime snack.

WALNUT TORTE

SERVES 12

1   tablespoon Slim-ette maple syrup
7   eggs separated
5   pkgs. of Sugar Twin
1   cup walnuts finely chopped
1½ teaspoons almond extract
    Pam spray

Preheat oven to 325°.
Beat in the small bowl of an electric mixer Slim-ette, almond extract, yolks of eggs, and Sugar Twin. This must be 10 minutes at a medium speed.
Fold nuts into mixture.
Beat egg whites until stiff. Fold ⅓ stiff whites into yolk mixture.
Fold yolk mixture into remaining whites.

Fold walnuts into mixture.

Carefully spoon into a 10-inch ring mold which has been prayed with Pam.

Bake at 325° for 45 minutes for electric, 50 minutes for as oven.

Cool 10 minutes.

Turn onto plate or wire rack and finish cooling.

If you do not eat this immediately, wrap it well to tore it. Keep refrigerated.

This torte is delicious sliced in half lengthwise, filled ith any of the whipped creams (below and pages 234–235), nd put back together again.

TOTAL GRAMS	25.5
TOTAL GRAMS WITH CARBOHYDRATE-FREE SWEETENER	21.5
GRAMS PER SERVING	2.1
GRAMS PER SERVING WITH CARBOHYDRATE-FREE SWEETENER	1.8

WHIPPED CREAM ·

SERVES 12

cup heavy cream
teaspoons vanilla
packages of Sugar Twin

Combine ingredients.
Beat until cream is whipped.

TOTAL GRAMS	9.1
GRAMS PER SERVING	.8
TOTAL GRAMS WITH CARBOHYDRATE-FREE SWEETENER	7.5
GRAMS WITH CARBOHYDRATE-FREE SWEETENER PER SERVING	.7

VARIATIONS:

CHOCOLATE WHIPPED CREAM

Add 2 tablespoons sugar-free cocoa and 3 additional packages of Sugar Twin to cream and whip.

TOTAL GRAMS	23
GRAMS PER SERVING	2.
TOTAL GRAMS WITH CARBOHYDRATE-FREE SWEETENER	21.
GRAMS WITH CARBOHYDRATE-FREE SWEETENER PER SERVING	1.

LEMON WHIPPED CREAM

Add 1 tablespoon of lemon juice, a pinch of grated lemon rind, and 3 additional packages of Sugar Twin and whip.

TOTAL GRAMS	12
GRAMS PER SERVING	1
TOTAL GRAMS WITH CARBOHYDRATE-FREE SWEETENER	10
GRAMS WITH CARBOHYDRATE-FREE SWEETENER PER SERVING	

MOCHA WHIPPED CREAM

1   *cup heavy cream*
2   *teaspoons vanilla*
5   *packages of Sugar Twin*
½   *tablespoon powdered instant coffee*

Combine ingredients and beat together until cream whipped.

TOTAL GRAMS	17.0
GRAMS PER TABLESPOON SERVING	1.1
TOTAL GRAMS WITH CARBOHYDRATE-FREE SWEETENER	13.0
GRAMS PER SERVING WITH CARBOHYDRATE-FREE SWEETENER	0.8

COFFEE WALNUT CHOCOLATE ROLL

SERVES 10

3 eggs separated
   pinch of cream of tartar
3 tablespoons instant coffee
2 teaspoons vanilla
3 tablespoons brown Sugar Twin
¼ cup chopped walnuts
   Pam spray
2 cups of heavy cream
2 teaspoons vanilla
1 tablespoon Sugar Twin

Preheat oven to 375°.

Separate eggs.

Beat egg whites with cream of tartar until stiff.

Dissolve instant coffee in vanilla.

Add to egg yolks instant coffee, vanilla, brown Sugar Twin and walnuts.

Fold yolk mixture into whites.

Spray a 10 x 15 inch jelly roll pan with Pam.

Spread mixture in pan evenly and bake 17 minutes in a gas oven at 375°, 13 minutes in an electric oven at 375° (use thermometer).

Remove from oven, cool enough to handle.

Roll lengthwise, cover with damp cloth, and allow to cool.

Whip cream with vanilla and Sugar Twin.

Unroll cake when it is completely cool. Spread wit
whipped cream and roll up again gently, chill. Slice to serve

TOTAL GRAMS   52.2
GRAMS PER SERVING   5.2

STRAWBERRY CANTALOUPE PIE

SERVES 10

1   yellow pie shell baked (page 229)
1   tablespoon cream
1   3-ounce pkg. cream cheese, soft
1   cup strawberries, cleaned and hulled
¼   cup Slim-ette maple syrup
¼   cup water
1   tablespoon No-Cal strawberry syrup
5   drops red food coloring
1   teaspoon grated orange peel
1   tablespoon butter
½   cantaloupe melon, cut into balls and drained (honeyde
    or casaba may be substituted)

Mix cream with cream cheese and spread evenly on p
shell.

Combine ¾ cup strawberries, maple syrup, and water
saucepan.

Simmer 5 minutes.

Force through a strainer, discard pulp, and seed. Put strained mixture back in saucepan and boil for 5 minutes.

Add strawberry syrup, red food color, orange peel, and butter.

Stir well.

Put melon balls on top of cream cheese.

Spoon strawberry mixture on top.

Garnish with remaining fresh strawberries.

Refrigerate until set.

TOTAL GRAMS	29.5
GRAMS PER SERVING	2.95

KEY LIME PIE

SERVES 10

1   *package D-Zerta lemon gelatin*
¼   *teaspoon salt*
20 *individual packages or 13 tablespoons of Sugar Twin*
4   *eggs separated (4 yolks, 3 whites)*
    Juice of 1 lime
¼   *cup water*
1   *teaspoon lime peel*
1   *cup heavy cream*
1   *tablespoon vanilla extract*
1   *9-inch coconut pie shell (yellow pie shell with 1 table-spoon coconut folded in) (page 229)*

Mix the gelatin, salt, and 4 packages of Sugar Twin.

Beat the egg yolks, lime juice, and water for 2 minutes at a high speed.

Add egg yolk mixture to gelatin.

Cook mixture at medium heat until it begins to boil, stirring constantly.

Remove from heat, add lime peel.

Chill until mixture begins to thicken, stirring occasionally.

Beat 3 egg whites and eight packages Sugar Twin until stiff.

Whip cream with rest of Sugar Twin (8 packages) and vanilla extract.

Fold gelatin into egg whites, then fold whipped cream into mixture, and chill before serving.

Blend well, being careful not to break down the mixture.

Turn into pie shell.

Refrigerate 2 hours before serving.

TOTAL GRAMS	35.9
GRAMS PER SERVING	3.6
TOTAL GRAMS WITH CARBOHYDRATE-FREE SWEETENER	27.9
GRAMS PER SERVING WITH CARBOHYDRATE-FREE SWEETENER	2.6

MOCHA PIE

SERVES 10

2   cups heavy cream
6   packages Sugar Twin
1   tablespoon instant coffee
2   tablespoons Slim-ette maple syrup (no sugar)
1   teaspoon vanilla
1   envelope unflavored gelatin
1   9-inch baked yellow pie shell (page 229)
½   cup toasted coconut

Combine heavy cream, Sugar Twin, coffee, Slim-ette, and vanilla in large bowl of electric mixer, and beat until thick.

Soften gelatin in cold water, put into top of a double boiler, and stir until it dissolves. Cool.

Fold gelatin thoroughly into cream mixture, and pour into pie shell.

Sprinkle coconut on the top, and chill at least 1 hour.

TOTAL GRAMS	38.4
GRAMS PER SERVING	3.8
TOTAL GRAMS WITH CARBOHYDRATE-FREE SWEETENER	33.6
GRAMS PER SERVING WITH CARBOHYDRATE-FREE SWEETENER	3.4

PUMPKIN PIE

SERVES 10

1   shallow baking pan, ½ filled with water
1   baked yellow pie shell (page 229)
5   packages of Sugar Twin
1   teaspoon ginger
1   teaspoon cinnamon
⅛   teaspoon salt
¼   teaspoon nutmeg
¼   teaspoon mace
2   cups canned or fresh pumpkin (fresh is best)
2   whole eggs
1   cup heavy cream
1   teaspoon brandy flavoring

Preheat oven to 375° and set baking pan with water in oven.

Mix Sugar Twin, ginger, cinnamon, salt, nutmeg, and mace.

Add pumpkin and combine well.

Beat the eggs and add the heavy cream and brandy flavoring in a slow, steady stream.

Thoroughly combine egg and pumpkin mixture.

Pour mixture into pie shell and bake in a moderate oven for 40 to 45 minutes, or until a knife inserted in the center comes out clean.

Top with Mocha Whipped Cream (page 234).

TOTAL GRAMS	33.6
GRAMS PER SERVING	3.4
TOTAL GRAMS WITH CARBOHYDRATE-FREE SWEETENER	29.6
GRAMS PER SERVING WITH CARBOHYDRATE-FREE SWEETENER	3.0

CHEESECAKE

SERVES 12

¼ cup heavy cream
8 oz. Tem-Tee whipped cream cheese
1½ envelopes unflavored gelatin
¼ cup cold water
2 eggs at room temperature, separated
3 tablespoons of vanilla
¼ lemon—juice and grated rind
6 teaspoons of Sugar Twin
¾ cup of heavy cream
Cinnamon
Pam spray

Combine the ¼ cup cream and cream cheese in a sauce-pan. Cook over a low heat until the cheese is melted. Sprinkle the gelatin over cold water. Add to cheese mixture.

Stir with a wire wisk until it begins to boil, remove from heat, cool.

Add egg yolks, vanilla, lemon and rind, and 4 teaspoons of Sugar Twin.

Whip ¾ cup of cream with 1 teaspoon of Sugar Twin. Beat the egg whites with 1 teaspoon of Sugar Twin. Fold whipped cream and egg whites into the cool cheese mixture. Sprinkle with cinnamon.

Spray a loaf pan with Pam. Pour mixture into loaf pan and refrigerate.

TOTAL GRAMS	35.3
GRAMS PER SERVING	3.0

LEMON SHERBET

SERVES 6

2 cups heavy cream
5 tablespoons Sugar Twin
1 tablespoon lemon rind, grated
4 tablespoons lemon juice

Stir cream and Sugar Twin until Twin dissolves.
Freeze until mushy.
Remove from freezer and add lemon rind and juice.
Beat until smooth.
Freeze again for about 2 hours.
Beat cream once more and put back in the freezer until frozen.

Tart and delicious.

TOTAL GRAMS	22.6
GRAMS PER SERVING	3.8

MACAROONS

MAKES 25

½ cup almonds
1 cup coconut (unsweetened)
1 tablespoon vanilla extract
1½ teaspoons almond extract
3 tablespoons maple syrup Slim-ette
½ teaspoon salt
2 egg whites

Preheat oven to 350°.

Place almonds in blender for about 1 minute, until they are the consistency of flour (but no longer or they will become a paste).

Place coconut in medium-sized bowl and sprinkle vanilla and almond extract over it.

Add almonds. Mix.

Add maple syrup and salt.

Beat egg whites until stiff but not dry, and fold into coconut mixture.

Drop by teaspoonful onto lightly greased baking sheet. Allow space for spreading.

Bake in 350° oven about 20 minutes or until golden brown.

These cookies freeze well. You may double the recipe. Some night when you're looking for something sweet, you will love to have them!

TOTAL GRAMS   51.9
GRAMS PER SERVING   2.0

PUDDING WITH A PUNCH

SERVES 6

1 *envelope unflavored gelatin*
2 *tablespoons cold water*
4 *egg yolks*
4 *teaspoons of Sugar Twin (or to taste)*
2 *cups heavy cream*
1 *oz. (2 tablespoons) Old Mr. Boston Crême de Cacao*

Soften gelatin in cold water (do *not* let it jell).

Combine yolks and Sugar Twin in a mixing bowl and beat until smooth and creamy.

Scald 1 cup of cream (do not boil), and pour gradually over yolk mixture, stirring constantly.

Put into top of double boiler and cook until smooth and thick, stirring constantly.

Add gelatin, and stir until dissolved.

Cool, stirring occasionally.

Add liqueur. Fold in 1 cup of cream, whipped. Pour into custard cups and refrigerate until firm.

TOTAL GRAMS   16.4
GRAMS PER SERVING   2.7

STRAWBERRIES AND CREAM

SERVES 4

2   packages Sugar Twin
¼   cup heavy cream, whipped (as below)
½   tablespoon Strawberry Jam (page 245)
1   cup of strawberries, washed and hulled

STRAWBERRY WHIPPED CREAM

Combine Sugar Twin, whipped cream, and Strawberry Jam (page 245) in the small mixing bowl of your electric mixer.

Whip until firm.

Serve over strawberries.

TOTAL GRAMS   17.1
GRAMS PER SERVING   4.3
TOTAL GRAMS WITH CARBOHYDRATE-FREE
   SWEETENER   15.5
GRAMS PER SERVING WITH CARBOHYDRATE-FREE
   SWEETENER   4.0

CHOCOLATE MOUSSE

SERVES 8

1   tablespoon cocoa (unsweetened)
1   pint heavy cream (2 cups)
½   package unflavored gelatin in 1 tablespoon cold water
8   teaspoons brown Sugar Twin
¼   cup chopped walnuts
1   teaspoon vanilla
2   egg whites at room temperature

Combine cocoa with ½ cup heavy cream. Heat until cocoa dissolves.

Add gelatin in water.

Heat just to boiling point.

Remove from heat, and cool.

Add walnuts and 4 teaspoons Sugar Twin.

Whip remaining cream with vanilla and 2 teaspoons of Sugar Twin.

Beat egg whites until stiff with 2 teaspoons of Sugar Twin.

Fold cool chocolate mixture into cream and then fold combination into egg whites. Pour into a pretty dish and refrigerate 4 hours before serving.

TOTAL GRAMS	34.0
GRAMS PER SERVING	4.3

VANILLA ICE CREAM

SERVES 7

1   package unflavored gelatin
1⅓ cups + 2 tablespoons cold water
2⅓ cups heavy cream
2   tablespoons Sugar Twin
⅛   teaspoon salt
1   tablespoon vanilla or 2 inches of a vanilla bean scraped

Soften gelatin in 2 tablespoons cold water.

Combine 1⅓ cups heavy cream and ⅔ cups water. Scald (do not boil).

Stir softened gelatin into cream mixture and add Sugar Twin and salt.

Stir until the gelatin is dissolved.

Cool, then add 1⅛ cups heavy cream, ⅔ cups water, and vanilla.

Freeze.

Makes 1½ quarts.

TOTAL GRAMS	27.8
GRAMS PER SERVING	3.0

STRAWBERRY JAM

23 TABLESPOONS

1   *package frozen, unsweetened strawberries*
1   *cup water*
1   *tablespoon strawberry sugar-free gelatin*
1   *teaspoon Wagner's Strawberry Extract*

Bring strawberries to room temperature.

Boil water and add gelatin to it.

Stir until gelatin is dissolved.

Cool in the refrigerator until it becomes the consistency of egg whites.

Bring strawberries to a boil and cook at a high heat for 6 minutes.

Skim off the foam that rises to the top of the berries.

Remove from heat.

Stir for 2 minutes.

Cool.

Add extract and blend.

Fold strawberries into thickened gelatin. Mix well and refrigerate until jelled.

TOTAL GRAMS   23.0
GRAMS PER TABLESPOON   1.0

Special Category

ILLEGAL, BUT NOT IMMORAL OR FATTENING CHEESE CAKE *

6 *eggs*
2 *tablespoons lemon juice*
2 *teaspoons vanilla*
4 *teaspoons soft margarine or vegetable oil*
   artificial sweetener containing cyclamates *equivalent to 30 teaspoons of sugar*

Preheat oven to 350°.
Have ingredients at room temperature.
Put ingredients into blender; blend thoroughly, then gradually add:
32 oz. (1 quart) cottage or pot cheese
Blend until very smooth.
Pour into narrow long pan such as a loaf pan to insure cake against falling.
Top with pure cinnamon if desired.
Bake for about 45 minutes, or until cake is firm.
Turn off oven and leave cheese cake there with door open for about one hour, then chill. Overnight refrigeration will add to flavor.
No-Cal brand syrups can be added for variety in flavors.

* For those of you who have been foresighted or fortunate enough to have kept a supply of cyclamate sweetener on hand, we are including the recipe which throughout the years has been our most successful. Unfortunately, without cyclamates, it just doesn't taste as well.

Candy

CHOCOLATE BALLS

MAKES 26 BALLS

1   cup heavy cream
1   tablespoon cocoa
1   tablespoon unflavored gelatin in 1 tablespoon cold water
2   tablespoons Skippy Chunky Peanut Butter
1   tablespoon créme de cocoa
2   teaspoons Wagner's Chocolate Extract
2   teaspoons brown Sugar Twin
¼   cup chopped walnuts or ¼ cup unsweetened coconut

Combine heavy cream and cocoa in the top of a double
boiler. Heat until the cocoa melts.
Add the gelatin that has been softened in cold water. Add
peanut butter. Heat until it begins to boil, remove from heat.
Add créme de cocoa, extract, and Sugar Twin. Blend well.
Freeze until it can be handled. Shape into balls, roll in
walnuts or coconut. Freeze.

TOTAL GRAMS	44.0
GRAMS PER SERVING	1.7

PEPPERMINT SQUARES

MAKES 16 CANDIES

4   oz. cream cheese
3   tablespoons Old Mr. Boston Crême de Menthe, 42 proof
½   teaspoon vanilla
2   oz. or ¼ cup butter
2   individual packages Sugar Twin
½   teaspoon of peppermint extract Pam spray

Mix all ingredients in a bowl and cream together thoroughly with a fork.

Place in 8-inch-square pan sprayed with Pam.

Put in freezer for at least 1 hour.

The squares must be kept in freezer compartment as they will melt at room temperature.

Cut into 2-inch squares.

TOTAL GRAMS 14.5
GRAMS PER SERVING .5

Beverages

PEPPERMINT FIZZ

SERVES 6

2   cups whipping cream (page 233)
½   teaspoon peppermint extract
1   quart diet ginger ale
1   mint leaf (for garnish)

Beat heavy cream to custard-like consistency.

Add peppermint extract and place in ice tray to freeze.

To serve, place scoop of frozen peppermint cream in tall glass.

Fill with cold ginger ale.

Stir slightly with spoon to make it fizz.

Garnish with mint leaf and serve immediately.

TOTAL GRAMS 8.0
GRAMS PER SERVING 1.3

QUICK PEPPERMINT FIZZ

1 glass diet ginger ale, chilled
Top with scoop of Diet Revolution
  Vanilla Ice Cream or 1 tablespoon of cream
Dash of peppermint extract

TOTAL GRAMS   2.0

CAPUCCINO COOLER

1 8-oz. glass of No-Cal coffee soda
½ teaspoon cinnamon
1 tablespoon heavy cream

Mix the cinnamon with the soda.
Add the cream and stir well.

TOTAL GRAMS   2.5

ROOT BEER FLOAT

1 tablespoon heavy cream
⅓ glass diet root beer
Scoops Diet Revolution Vanilla Ice Cream

TOTAL GRAMS   2.7

CHOCOLATE EGG CREAM

oz. diet chocolate soda
egg
oz. heavy cream

Combine ingredients in the blender and blend till smooth.

TOTAL GRAMS   1.2

Snacks

BACON AND CHEESE BALLS

2   tablespoons grated American cheese
½   tablespoon mayonnaise or mild mustard
3   crisp slices of bacon, crumbled

Blend grated cheese well with the mayonnaise o
mustard.

Shape into balls, and roll in the crushed bacon.

TOTAL GRAMS   1.4

LOX AND CREAM CHEESE

Spread cream cheese with chives on a slice of lox, fold i
half, and eat like a sandwich.

Happy eating!

TOTAL GRAMS   .5

DRIED BEEF ROLLS

SERVES 6

½   cup cottage cheese
1   teaspoon minced parsley
1   teaspoon white horseradish
2   stuffed green olives, chopped
    Dash of paprika
6   slices of dried beef or roast beef
12 toothpicks

Combine all ingredients except beef, and spread on beef slices.

Roll up the slices, fasten with toothpicks, and chill before serving.

TOTAL GRAMS   3.5
GRAMS PER SERVING   .6

STUFFED LETTUCE

2   *lettuce leaves*
¼   *cup of tuna, chicken, or egg salad* *
4   *toothpicks*

Put salad on each lettuce leaf, roll up the leaf, fasten with two toothpicks, chill, and serve.

TOTAL GRAMS   2.0

TUNA-CHEESE SANDWICH

7-ounce can tuna fish
tablespoon mayonnaise
Salt and pepper
Onion powder

Mix tuna with mayonnaise, salt, pepper, and onion powder.

Put mixture between 2 slices of American cheese and eat as a sandwich.

TOTAL GRAMS   1.8

* This amount of salad will supply too few grams to count.

STUFFED CELERY CAVIAR

SERVES 3

1 *bunch of celery*
3 *oz. cream cheese with chives*
1 *small jar red or black caviar*
1 *tablespoon lemon juice*

Stuff celery stalks with cream cheese, cut into bite-size pieces.

Top with caviar and lemon juice, and serve.

TOTAL GRAMS	8.6
GRAMS PER SERVING	2.8

STUFFED CELERY WITH GORGONZOLA FILLING

SERVES 2

1 *bunch of celery*
2 *oz. gorgonzola cheese*
2 *tablespoons butter*
2 *tablespoons cream cheese*

Cream both cheeses and butter together well. Stuff celery with mixture.

TOTAL GRAMS	6.7
GRAMS PER SERVING	3.4

COTTAGE CHEESE AND SOUR CREAM

1 *scoop cottage cheese*
1 *tablespoon sour cream*
½ *teaspoon cinnamon*

Top cottage cheese with sour cream, sprinkle with cinnamon, and serve.

TOTAL GRAMS   3.4

CUCUMBER BALLS

SERVES 2

1 cucumber
French Dressing (see page 219)

With a melon baller, scoop out a pared cucumber.
Marinate in our Diet French Dressing for at least 1 hour.
Drain and serve.

TOTAL GRAMS   5.6
GRAMS PER SERVING   2.8

MELON AND PROSCIUTTO

SERVES 6

1 medium-size cantaloupe
½ lb. Prosciutto

Cut melon into wedges (1 to 1½ inches thick).
Wrap a slice of prosciutto around each wedge, secure
with toothpick. Chill and serve.

TOTAL GRAMS   16.8
GRAMS PER SERVING   2.8

HAM AND CHEESE ROLLS

Swiss cheese slices
Ham slices

Place 1 slice of Swiss cheese on top of 1 slice of ham and roll up ham side out.

Fasten with toothpicks, chill and eat.

TOTAL GRAMS   0.5

Wine and Liqueur List *

WHITE WINES—3 ounces

Chablis—3 ounces	GRAMS
Barton & Guestier—12% *alcohol*	.1
Italian Swiss Colony—Private Stock—12% *alcohol*	.1
Louis M. Martini—12½% *alcohol*	.2
Gold Seal—12% *alcohol*	.4
Italian Swiss Colony Gold Medal—11.6% *alcohol*	.6

Sauternes—3 ounces	
Gold Seal dry—12% *alcohol*	.4
Italian Swiss Colony Gold Medal—11.6% *alcohol*	.6
Louis M. Martini dry—12.5% *alcohol*	.29

White Burgundy	
Pouilly-Fuissé (Barton & Guestier)—12% *alcohol*	.3

RED WINES—3 ounces

Red Burgundies	
Gold Seal—12% *alcohol*	.4
Italian Swiss Colony Private Stock—12% *alcohol*	.2

* N.B. Remember, however, to add the carbohydrate equivalent of alcohol as mentioned on page 147. Where alcohol is heated, some or all of it may be lost through evaporation. Therefore, when using alcoholic beverages in recipes, the carbohydrate equivalent may be quite variable.

Louis M. Martini—*12% alcohol*	.2
Taylor—*12.5% alcohol*	Trace
Châteauneuf-du-Pape (Barton & Guestier)—*13.5% alcohol*	.5

Chianti

Chianti Wine (Louis M. Martini)—*12% alcohol*	.2

LIQUEURS

Creme de Menthe—1 ounce

Old Mr. Boston—*42 proof*	6.0
Old Mr. Boston—*60 proof*	8.5

Creme de Cacao—1 ounce

Old Mr. Boston—*42 proof*	7.0
Old Mr. Boston—*54 proof*	7.0

Products Used in This Book

Baken-ets: *Distributed by Frito Lay, 1261 Zrega Ave., Bronx, N.Y. 10462*

D-Zerta: *Distributed by General Foods Corp., 250 North St., White Plains, N.Y. 10602*

Hunt's: *Tomato products are packed by Hunt Wesson, Fullerton, Calif. 92634*

Krazy Mixed-Up Salt: *Distributed by Haddon House Foods, Marlton Pike, Medford, N.J. 08055*

Lea & Perrins Worcestershire Sauce: *Manufactured by Lea & Perrins, 1501 Pollitt Dr., Fairlawn, N.J. 07410*

Maggi's Seasoning: *Distributed by The Nestlé Co., Inc., 100 Bloomingdale Rd., White Plains, N.Y. 10605*

M.B.T. Broth: Distributed by Romanoff Caviar Co., 605 Third Ave., New York, N.Y. 10016

No-Cal Syrup: Distributed by No-Cal Corp., 921 Flushing Ave., Brooklyn, N.Y. 11206

Pam: Distributed by Boyle-Midway, Inc., 685 Third Ave., New York, N.Y. 10017. Pam may be purchased in the cooking oil department of your supermarket

Progresso Olive Oil: Distributed by Progresso Foods Corp., 100 Caven Pt. Rd., Jersey City, N.J. 07305

Salad Supreme: Distributed by McCormick & Co., 414 Light St., Baltimore, Md. 21202

Skippy Peanut Butter: Distributed by Best Foods, a Division of Corn Products Corporation International, Englewood Cliffs, N.J. 07632

Slim-ette: Distributed by Chelton House Products, Inc., Pennsauken, N.J. 08110. Slim-ette has two dietetic maple syrups. Use the one with "No Sugar" marked on the collar

Sugar Twin: Distributed by Alberto-Culver, Melrose Park, Ill. 60160

Wagner's Extracts: Distributed by John Wagner & Sons, Inc., Soyland, Pa., 18974

Tem-Tee Cream Cheese: Distributed by Breakstone Sugar Creek Foods Div. of Craftee Corp., 810 Seventh Ave., New York, N.Y. 10019

Salad Dressings Available in Stores and Supermarkets

PRODUCT	QUANTITY	GRAM COUNT
Dia-Mel French Dressing (Diet.)	1 tablespoon	.2
Hellman's True Dressing	1 tablespoon	.8
Kraft Blue Cheese Dressing (Diet.)	1 tablespoon	.2

Salad Dressings Available in Stores and Supermarkets (cont.)

PRODUCT	QUANTITY	GRAM COUNT
Kraft Green Goddess Dressing	1 tablespoon	.8
Kraft Herb and Garlic Dressing	1 tablespoon	.5
Kraft Italian Dressing	1 tablespoon	.7
Kraft Roka Dressing	1 tablespoon	.8
Kraft Salad Bowl Dressing	1 tablespoon	.7
Lawry's Caesar Salad Dressing	1 tablespoon	.5
Lawry's Canadian Dressing	1 tablespoon	.6
Lawry's Green Goddess Dressing	1 tablespoon	.7
Lawry's Salad Dressing	1 tablespoon	.8
Lawry's San Francisco Dressing	1 tablespoon	.8
Tillie Lewis Blue Cheese Salad Dressing (Diet.)	1 tablespoon	.2
Tillie Lewis Caesar Salad Dressing (Diet.)	1 tablespoon	.2
Tillie Lewis Whipped Thousand Island Dressing (Diet.)	1 tablespoon	.2
Wish-Bone Low-Calorie Italian Dressing	1 tablespoon	1.1

16

MAINTENANCE:

STAYING

AT YOUR BEST

You DID it! You're the gratified possessor of a trim new figure. You like what you see when you catch a passing glimpse of yourself in a mirror (even though you may find it hard for a while to believe that the slim person you see there is really you).

Like ebullient William Miller, 6 feet, 1 inch, who went from 351 pounds to 190 on this diet, you may be saying, "My life is changed completely. I'm one of the happiest people in the world. People who knew me before don't believe it's me."

Or like Janet Macdonald, whose weight fell from 212 pounds to 120 pounds, "I'm so excited that I've done it. I can't believe it. I go around with a grin on my face all the time."

Or like Sharon Weeks, who came in weighing 179 and now wears a size 10. "Out of it has come a totally new way of looking at things . . . a psychological turnaround. It's hard to get depressed when you see yourself looking the way I do now."

Or like Laurie Meyer, who went from size 24½ to a size

12 on this diet, "I'm on a permanent high. My whole self-perception is different."

Or like Joan Farber, who used to wear size 18 slacks and now buys them in size 9. She says, "My husband is swinging from the chandelier. He says he has a new wife. Well, I AM a different person. Not self-conscious. Now I'm anxious to get out and see people."

Or like Alice Lawrence (she came in weighing 161½ pounds and now wears a size 6) you may be saying, "I'm not a freak anymore. I feel I belong."

ALICE LAWRENCE HAS BEEN A SIZE 6 FOR ALMOST FOUR YEARS NOW. I call Alice Lawrence my ex-problem patient. She is 5 feet, 2 inches and a beautiful woman, but she weighed 161½ and wore a size 16 when she came to see me on the 10 January 1968.

By 1 August 1968 she was wearing a size 6. Almost four years later she still wears a size 6.

There were periods during those months when she didn't lose. "But I never got discouraged because I felt sure I could make it," she says. "It's a way of eating I could live with and enjoy. There's plenty of variety, and always new foods are being added."

Even in her teens Alice weighed between 135 and 150. So naturally she had always been on a diet, losing and gaining, losing and gaining, usually on pills.

"I used to cry myself to sleep at night," she says. "This diet has just made a new life for me."

Both her parents were very much overweight. Her grandmother was a diabetic, and with each of Alice's pregnancies she would gain forty to fifty pounds. She was a night eater. She was a sweets eater. She had low blood sugar. In fact, she had just about every problem a dieter could have; and she has licked them all.

HOW ALICE MAINTAINED HER FORTY-POUND WEIGHT LOSS. During the years of maintenance the overeating of fruit would sometimes raise her weight about the five-pound range

—top. Even without the scale she would know it because she would begin to feel tired again. Also the long-gone craving for sweets would return—a sign that her hyperinsulinism and, consequently, a lowered blood sugar was returning.

So back Alice Lawrence goes on the basic first week's diet until her energy level rises and those few extra pounds disappear along with the craving for sweets. During these recovery times Alice doesn't eat breakfast, but she has two big hamburgers plus a salad for lunch. She'll eat a whole lobster for dinner, and sometimes a Caesar salad too, using Baken-ets in it instead of croutons. Desserts? My cheesecake recipe, page 246, is her favorite but she frequently satisfies that desire for a sweet finish to the meal with sweetenered coffee topped with whipped cream.

MAINTAINING YOUR WEIGHT LOSS IS EASIER ON THIS DIET THAN ON ANY OTHER. I'm not telling you any news when I say that most diet plans fail miserably at keeping your weight down. On low calorie diets you can't get back to your ideal weight without starving yourself. It's hard to decide in cold blood to go hungry. It's even harder to do it; to undergo semistarvation for weeks on end.

But on this diet you can shed those few extra pounds that may have crept up on you with never a hunger pang. It's no trick at all to slip back into that first week's biologically carbohydrate-free diet.

The big myth you have to unlearn: "Now that I weigh what I want I can go back to eating the way other people do."

If you've lost by pills, shots, and/or starvation, your poor hungry body as well as your mind are hell bent for a return to the "normal" eating that made you fat before and will make you even fatter this time.

But if you've lost by keeping the carbohydrates you take in below your CCL, you aren't feeling in the least deprived. So it's only your *head* that needs attention—to be sure that you've got your priorities straight. And priority number one is to understand the scope of the problem.

THE MAIN CHANGE THAT HAS TO BE MADE IS IN YOUR HEAD. Success in maintaining your trim figure and your zest for living is guaranteed if you can achieve this radical change in your thinking.

If you have a chronic weight problem it is essential to totally accept, fully understand that your fat is one symptom of a lifetime disease. Your metabolizing processes are and always will tend to be abnormal. Yes, even if you get slim and stay slim.

Many medical studies have shown that the biochemical responses of a formerly overweight person, such as the excessive insulin release when carbohydrates are eaten, are still quite different from a never-overweight person. In other words, *you cannot eat what normal people eat and expect to stay thin.*

So say this to yourself over and over until you've got it through your rebellious head: "My tendency to overweight is one sign of a chronic metabolic disorder. My physiology doesn't handle certain kinds of food as slim physiologies do. I mustn't try to compare my eating habits to those of a person who has never had a weight problem. Not now. Not ever.

"I have an illness, a lifelong illness. I can't cure it, but I can control it."

Basic to controlling it is to understand that it is a permanent condition . . . about which you can do a great deal. Controlling it isn't all that difficult. Thousands of successfully slimmed patients are evidence of that.

NOW FOR THE MECHANICS OF MAINTENANCE. Once you are down to your ideal weight (and I hope that you lost those last five or six pounds quite slowly) here's what concerns you: how to continue to break even.

Hundreds of my patients never seem to have problems in this area; their weight has stabilized at the ideal level and never changes. Skipping carbohydrates has become second nature to them.

But it's possible to put on a few pounds almost accidentally. Here's how! Any one person's Critical Carbohydrate Level may vary at different times in life, depending on any number of factors. Yours may drop and how could you know it? But you'll gain unless your carbohydrate intake drops as well.

What usually happens: oh, so gradually you unwittingly add too many carbohydrates to your diet. Suddenly, you find that your appetite is stimulated by them. Bread, fruit, dessert, potatoes—suddenly you want more, more, more! Those cravings disappear as soon as you go back to the basic diet for a few days and start stoking yourself with protein and fat exclusively—but instant action is called for.

FIRST, WHAT IS YOUR GOAL? The first rule: decide exactly what you want to weigh *the rest of your life*. Don't be easy on yourself about this. Don't settle for anything less than the weight at which you look and feel your youngest and best.

If you were slim at twenty, perhaps that's your best weight.

If you weren't slim then, see the table of desirable weights on pages 297–298 to get a rough estimate of what your best weight is. Don't assume that you have a large frame and pick the highest weight.

I have found that most people look at themselves through rose-colored glasses when it comes to deciding how much weight they need to lose. My estimate of what they need to lose is usually far more than theirs.

RULES 2 AND 3: GIVE YOURSELF A FIVE-POUND RANGE; AND WEIGH YOURSELF DAILY. Now the next thing is to make up your mind that you'll stay within five pounds of your best weight. With a clear conscience you can allow yourself this five-pound range. And remember: the *upper* limit is the vital figure.

You must make up your mind to get on the scale every morning, as regularly as you brush your teeth. As you look at what your scale tells you, you make your decision. Is your weight at the upper limit? Then you must go on a stricter level of dieting that very day. For most people this means the second diet level.

You must stay on the diet at that level until you have lost that five pounds and reached the *low* range of your ideal weight.

Then and only then are you entitled to put more carbohydrate back in your diet—gradually, gradually. And if it should happen that in a few months the five pounds have reaccumulated, you repeat the cycle.

So you see how vital it is to get on the scale every day and to make it an absolutely inviolable rule to go back to the first or second diet levels when you have reached the top of your five-pound range. This way you can keep your weight within five pounds of your ideal, and without deprivation—since the basic diet takes away hunger and allows you so many goodies.

THE FOURTH RULE: PICK YOUR LIFELONG CARBOHYDRATES. Once you're ready to start your maintenance diet, decide definitely what the carbohydrates are going to be that you will include in your lifelong diet, because that's what your maintenance diet is after all—your lifelong way of eating.

Because of your built-in lifelong metabolic disturbance, your eating and drinking can never become randomized and careless. If it does, back will come those ugly pounds, the fatigue, the premature aging, the nagging hunger and cravings for sweets, the high triglycerides and cholesterol—all your seven deadly horsemen.

The best decision is probably to stay pretty much on the very low carbohydrate diet on which you lost; only now you can feel free to deviate in small ways. So that if you like wine or a drink before dinner, you might let the bars down there a bit.

The second-best decision is to add a few starches; a slice of melba toast, some of the starchy vegetables. But, *the worst decision is to add sweets.*

Some very interesting findings were reported recently by the Brookhaven National Laboratory about the comparative "fattening power" of starches and sweets.

These findings are the result of a series of tests conducted over the past two years by a team of doctors headed by Dr. Walton W. Shreeve.

ONE CALORIE OF SUGAR APPARENTLY PRODUCES MORE FAT THAN ONE CALORIE OF STARCH. Feeding patients diets of alternately high sugar content and high starch content, the Brookhaven doctors found that the percentage of sugar converted to blood fat as a result of the sugar diet was two to five times greater than the percentage converted after the starch diet.

Incidentally, the fat-producing effects of sugar in this experiment were further exaggerated in women who were taking the Pill, which bears out my observation that women taking oral contraceptives are peculiarly vulnerable to the fattening power of sugar.

What the Brookhaven research clearly suggests is startling: it means that a one-ounce piece of fudge (113 calories) is two to five times as fattening as one hamburger roll (116 calories). It also means that a piece of fruit, which is a simple carbohydrate (sugar), is less desirable for your diet than a baked potato, which is a starch.

Whether or not further research bears out the two to five ratio of the Brookhaven research, the underlying facts suggested here are corroborated by experimental observations that on a sugar-free diet there is almost a uniform fall in the level of triglycerides (a blood fat), and in 90 percent of the cases I have treated, the fall in the triglyceride level is dramatically significant.

THE ADDICTION FACTOR: ANOTHER REASON NOT TO ADD SWEETS OTHER THAN THE KIND YOU'LL FIND IN THIS BOOK. I really cannot recommend adding sugar sweets at any point in your regime. I'm not talking about adding a little fresh fruit—berries, melons, particularly. I'm talking about not adding ordinary candies, cookies, cakes, pies, rich desserts. The reason is that such sweets are to people with a disturbed carbohydrate metabolism what alcohol is to an alcoholic, heroin to a drug addict, a pack of cigarettes to an ex-smoker, Vegas to a gambler. The safest move is to stay away from such sweets entirely. It may be that you can't take just a little; your illness doesn't permit it.

Almost all our failures are addicted cake and candy eaters. These are people who have exactly the same problems incurable alcoholics have, a biochemical make-up of which they are the fatalities.

A BINGE EATER IS AN ADDICT. Michael S. used to go on a cake and ice cream binge regularly. He would eat half a gallon of ice cream and a cake between four o'clock and dinner. All this sugar would naturally trigger the pancreas to release a flood of insulin into the bloodstream. And the insulin would shortly and sharply lower his blood sugar to below fasting level. Result: Michael would begin to feel restless, irritable, exhausted, depressed—and *hungry*. More than ever he felt the need of more sugar. He had to have his fix. Sugar could not be addictive if it were not for its result: low blood sugar or hypoglycemia, the withdrawal state of a sugar addict.

Because sugar is cheap, Michael doesn't have to rob or steal to feed his habit, but the habit is just as deadly.

Eventually Michael would get so revolted with his behavior that he would "reform." But a birthday party with a cake, a candy bar to console himself at a time of stress—almost anything would set him helplessly off on another binge.

TO A SUGARHOLIC EVEN A TASTE CAN START A BINGE. The important thing is to avoid the beginning of a binge. An alcoholic is warned against that first drink—even vanilla extract because it contains alcohol. A sugarholic should be told that he cannot afford to have anything—even salad dressings and soups—containing sugar. This can trigger off a binge. Most overweight people wouldn't be thus affected, but a significant number will.

Addictive people seem to have one thing in common: an underlying hypoglycemia. We certainly see hypoglycemia in sugar addicts, in alcoholics, in coffee addicts. People who have studied hard-drug addicts report to me that hypoglycemia is common among them. Cola beverages have long been addictive for many people.

THE STARCHES CAN BE ADDICTIVE TOO. Many forms of the starches can be addictive, though this is somewhat less common. Potato chips. Bread. Crackers. Pizzas. Spaghetti. And when refined flour is combined with refined sugar, as in cakes, pies, cookies, desserts, only a tiny bit is required to set the whole vicious cycle in motion again.

ON THIS DIET EVEN BINGE-EATERS LOSE. A patient will say, "Honestly, doctor, I never stopped eating all weekend! Why? Because I was just plain *bored*." (Or, "I was upset.")

I will ask, "Did you stay on the diet?"

"Yes, but I ate so *much*. It was a real binge. I even got up at four in the morning to have an extra meal. I feel so guilty."

Then comes the big anticlimax. The scales show he or she has lost three pounds!

A few pounds can be gained if this kind of binging goes on long enough of course. But I've never yet seen anybody suffer a significant setback by binging on protein.

You see, binging on protein is self-limiting. The absence of carbohydrate is what limits it. The more protein and fat you eat in combination, the more satiety value the food provides. In the end these binges don't really amount to much. They're *mini*-binges. It's hard to believe, I know, but having treated thousands of binge eaters, I can assure you that it is true.

That's why I am able to say to you, "Do you eat at all the wrong times? Don't worry about it. Keep right on binging. As long as you binge on protein and fat and keep away from carbohydrate, you will not gain any important amount of weight."

WARNING: THE MORE YOU'VE LOST, THE EASIER IT IS TO GAIN IT BACK. If you only had ten pounds to lose when you started on this diet, you'll find it easier to maintain that weight loss than if you had fifty to one hundred pounds to lose when you started. Once the body has filled its fat depots to a certain overweight level, this is the weight that careless eating will quickly return you to.

On the other hand, the person who has lost fifty to a hundred pounds might be more *motivated* to keep off the weight by watching his maintenance diet carefully. His life has been so transformed. It's so wonderful to be able to enjoy trying and buying smart new clothes, to hear compliments, to look like other people, to feel a part of the group. And it isn't as if the maintenance diet left him hungry, left him out of things. It's not a diet, it's just a different, discriminatory way of eating.

It's the way you're going to eat the rest of your life. You can dine in any restaurant in any country and no one needs to know you're being different or choosy about what you eat, while maintaining that *bella figura*.

IN ANY COUNTRY, IN ANY RESTAURANT, YOU GET WHAT YOU ASK FOR. Whether you're eating to lose or just to maintain your present weight, you're always going to be fighting off carbohydrates. They saturate all cuisines.

But it is easy to de-carbohydrate food. All you have to do is say what you want. Ask for de-carbohydrated food and you'll get it. As I have said elsewhere, most restaurateurs are happy to oblige their patrons. It's all in the day's work. They're used to people with mysterious ailments. So you ask, "Is there any sugar in this salad dressing? I'm not allowed to have sugar." Or you say, "I'm allergic to flour. Is there any flour used in preparing the meat this way? I'd like it done without being floured. Or what else could I have instead?"

ITALIAN COOKING CAN BE LOW CARBOHYDRATE IF—I do this in every restaurant I visit. Because I am a bachelor, I eat out a lot so I have quite a nice selection of restaurants trained to take the carbohydrate out of the food I eat.

I think the best place to follow the diet is in an Italian restaurant. I can eat most of the antipasto—the tuna, the sardines, the prosciutto, the Genoa salami, the hard-boiled eggs, the olives, anchovies, pimiento, celery, greens. About all I leave are the fava beans.

For soup I have stracciatella, a clear amber broth with green chopped spinach leaves, chopped eggs, and a liberal sprinkling of Parmesan on top.

For an entrée I can have scampi or rollatini with the sensational triple taste of veal, ham, and cheese, or saltim-bocca, or veal piccata. "No flour," I say, so it comes to me thin and tender, sautéed and fragrant with lemon and a whisper of garlic. My favorite is chicken scarpariello, bite-sized, pan-fried, garlic-scented chunks of chicken.

When everyone else is having pasta, I'm dipping contentedly into a dish of spinach or escarole sautéed liberally with garlic and olive oil. I enjoy watching the linguine eaters eyeing me enviously.

After that I have no room for dessert. Now and then, though, the headwaiter makes a dish of zabaglione in front of me over the spirit lamp, using the sweetener I bring for the purpose.

CHINESE COOKING IS JUST NATURALLY LOW CARBOHYDRATE. It's pretty hard to get in trouble in a Japanese or Chinese restaurant once those carbohydrate spectacles are firmly on your nose. For one thing, they don't serve bread. All you have to skip is rice.

In a Chinese restaurant I have spareribs (though they've been marinated in sweet stuff, it has been broiled away in the barbecuing). One must be careful to stick with the hot mustard sauce and skip the sweet duck sauce.

One course might be soup—egg drop, birds' nest, or sharks' fin soup. Chinese vegetables are uniformly low in carbohydrate, so they combine well with lobster, shrimp, chicken, duck, beef, and pork. But you must say loud and clear that you don't want any cornstarch in the sauce. You can order egg foo yung, too, but *without* the gravy. Fortune cookies are for reading, *not* for eating—on this diet.

In a Japanese restaurant I have just as many choices, such as sushi (marinated raw fish) and sukiyaki. (See recipe in this book for tempura.)

I love to find myself in an Armenian restaurant. I ask for a double order of shish kabob and forget everything else, eating two big skewers full of meat, peppers, mushrooms, onions, tomatoes.

A FRENCH OR JEWISH RESTAURANT IS EASY. I often start with escargots in a French restaurant. Great diet food! Or, the pâté or coquilles St. Jacques.

I love to order anything on the menu that says, "Sauté meunière." And unless you're on the first week of your diet, you can also have any kind of seafood that's "amandine." I may order paillard of veal or coq au vin or duck—"but without the sauce, please." I like the fatness and crispness of duck. (If I'm in a Czechoslovakian, Hungarian, or German restaurant, I'm likely to order duck. They do it extremely well.) I also order quiche Lorraine and treat the crust as if it were cardboard.

Of course salad in a French restaurant is usually great.

A word about salad dressings. Some French dressings have sugar—the commercial orange-colored kind especially. Some Roquefort dressings are low in carbohydrate, but some are thickened, so better ask. Russian dressing always contains sugar. Better ask too about the vinaigrette sauce, as some contain sugar. Well, sugar has a very distinctive taste, remember? It's easy to spot. Starch, flour, cornstarch don't; the taste can get lost in the mixture of food flavors. So when in doubt —ask.

For dessert I enjoy those good French cheeses.

In a Jewish delicatessen I can choose lox and eggs. I can have cold cuts galore—brisket, tongue, corned beef, pastrami, turkey. I avoid the coleslaw; it's made with sugar. But I make free with those crisp, fragrant new dill pickles.

In a Russian restaurant I like to order chicken Kiev. I'll have beef Stroganoff, too, but I ask them to serve it on spinach instead of noodles.

Try using your influence with the restaurants in your neighborhood. What have you got to lose?

ONE EMOTION THAT MUST BE GUARDED AGAINST WHILE MAINTAINING YOUR IDEAL WEIGHT. Even if there were no other reasons for sometimes going over your five-pound range, just the fact that we are so surrounded by carbohydrates makes occasional lapses likely. So don't let it throw you. That's the big hazard.

In my own experience the commonest cause of failure in weight control is a very specific response that goes something like this: "I went off my diet. I gained a little weight. And I was ashamed." There's something about being ashamed that prevents one from making a new start.

If in reflecting about your past efforts to control your weight you remember going through a thought process like this, then you know exactly what I'm talking about.

This is the one emotion that must be guarded against at all cost. There is no room ever to be ashamed over your past actions.

Just put the past away. All we can do is deal with the present; we can't change the past, can we? Remember that. Let the past be valuable to teach you what mental blocks are likely to hold you up—so that you can profit from your mistakes.

Remember that it's easy and a pleasure to lose those few extra pounds by reenacting your first week's diet. So put your mind to planning what zero-carbohydrate goodies you can eat the rest of today and tomorrow. Have something *especially* luxurious—smoked salmon or caviar to start with; medallion of veal on grilled ham with melted cheese as an entrée or a big beautiful lobster, each bite dipped in melted butter. Or if it's lunch, have a plate full of cold cuts, or a big bacon cheeseburger with a blob of whipped cream in your coffee as a finish. And treat yourself by eating it in your most favorite place. *Bon appetit!*

17

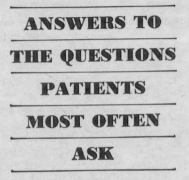

ANSWERS TO THE QUESTIONS PATIENTS MOST OFTEN ASK

I find that the questions my ten thousand patients have asked fall into a somewhat similar pattern. Here are the subjects most often brought up, arranged alphabetically with my answers.

A—AGING, PREMATURE

Q. *Is there any connection between a disturbed carbohydrate metabolism and premature aging?*

A. Yes, indeed. Premature aging—and the fatigue commonly associated with it—is a symptom of a disordered carbohydrate metabolism just as much as obesity. So when I treat this disturbance I feel I am helping arrest the progression of premature aging as well as overweight. Dr. Irving Perlstein, of the Louisville School of Medicine, demonstrated that the type of thickening of the blood vessels seen in normal aging people of seventy and over, can also be found in a high percentage of obese people, even those in their twenties.

A—ALCOHOL, CALORIES, AND CARBOHYDRATES

Q. *Does alcohol have calories? Is there anything different about them? Does it have carbohydrates?*

A. Most nutritionists assume that energy is available from alcohol. The rule of thumb for counting the calories in distilled spirits is if you know the proof, you know the number of calories per ounce. But it's not the calories in alcohol that need worry you. Alcohol calories are very closely related to carbohydrate calories in that alcohol also inhibits the fat mobilization—and is a potent producer of low blood sugar.

There are no studies to show just *how* inhibiting alcohol is on a low carbohydrate diet, but my clinical impression is that alcohol is almost as FMH-inhibiting as starches. Therefore, after the first weeks of the diet, I am only able to allow alcoholic drinks *in modest quantities*. But when a person is accustomed to drinking large quantities, allowing him just a few can be a harder rule to follow than allowing none at all.

A—ALCOHOL: HARD TO GIVE UP

Q. *I'm not an alcoholic, but I can't give up drinking. What do I do?*

A. If you *can't* give up drinking, then you'd be better off to admit you have "a drinking problem." It is unlikely that your weight problem will be solved if your drinking problem is not. Experience shows that when an alcoholic succeeds in getting off alcohol he usually substitutes sweets. This is because almost all alcoholics are hypoglycemic, and sugar provides the same temporary lift that alcohol once did.

B—BEER

Q. *What about that no-carbohydrate beer? Any limit on that?*

A. One can of it counts as one liquor unit; the same as one four-ounce glass of wine. It isn't only the carbohydrate in the beer that slows the speed with which you burn your fat, it's the alcohol, the readiest of all body fuels.

B—BITTER LEMON

Q. *Why can't I drink Bitter Lemon? The label says it only contains quinine and lemon flavoring—not a word about sugar.*

A. The sugar is there, even though the label doesn't say so. There's sugar in quinine water too (unless it's No-Cal or some other dietetic variety). Deceptions of this sort are the reason for need to refer constantly to one of the carbohydrate gram counters that give brand names.

B—BREAD

Q. *Is diet bread less full of carbohydrate than other kinds?*

A. At the present writing, none of the diet breads are significantly lower in carbohydrates than regular breads. A virtually carbohydrate-free bread has been made, but is not yet commercially available. Until that becomes available, the bread lowest in carbohydrate content is gluten bread: 5.6 grams in one slice of it.

B—BREATH

Q. *Is it true that with ketosis you have bad breath?*

A. Yes, if you're burning up your own fat at a very fast clip. So it is a mixed nonblessing. Drinking more water helps. Chlorophyll tablets help. Carry around Sen-sen or one of those purse-sized aerosol mouth fresheners, and you can have sweet breath and burn fat at the same time.

C—CALORIES

Q. *Don't calories play any role?*

A. There's no question—of course they do. A 1,500-calorie, ten-gram diet will take more weight off—and more quickly —than a 2,000-calorie ten-gram diet. If the carbohydrate levels remain unchanged, then the extra caloric intake does make a difference. People who eat out of force of habit and don't cut their quantities lose more slowly because of their high caloric intake.

If you can cut down on your quantities, you are better off to do so—but not when it gets to the point where you have to put up with discomfort or hunger. Then it just doesn't pay. However, as a traditional overeater you may have built up a mistaken impression of how much food it takes to satisfy you. On this diet there is a new level of satiety to become familiar with—try eating less and you'll find you are just as comfortable as when you ate more on a higher carbohydrate diet.

I'm not saying that "calories don't count." I'm saying that a low calorie diet is a second-best diet.

C—CARBOHYDRATE

Q. *What contains carbohydrates?*

A. Fruits, vegetables, grains—all the foods from the plant kingdom. The biggest concentration of refined carbohydrate is in sugar and flour; they're our worst poison, our biggest killers. But milk contains milk sugar. Lemons and limes contain carbohydrates, too, even though they aren't sweet. See the booklets, carbohydrate gram counters, and books mentioned in chapter 9.

Q. *Are all carbohydrates the same, gram for gram?*

A. According to the recent work of Dr. Walton Shreeve and his associates in Brookhaven, they are not. A simple sugar has more long-term fattening tendencies than a complex carbohydrate, such as starch. Because fruit is a simple sugar, it can only be added with great caution.

C—CARBOHYDRATE DEFICIENCY

Q. *Don't I need some carbohydrate for my body's requirements? Wouldn't I be suffering some deficiency without it?*

A. Absolutely not. I have stated this before but I wish to repeat it. Only an underweight person has need to eat carbohydrates. If you have fatty tissue on your body, that fatty tissue will be converted by your body into sugar. A total of 58 *percent of dietary protein is converted by the body into sugar.* Fat and protein foods have the advantage of being converted into sugar fuel more slowly than carbohydrate. They provide less hunger, more satisfaction for the same number of calories. And far from needing to eat carbohydrate in order not to damage the body, those people who have a disturbed carbohydrate metabolism (and that's about 80 to 90 percent of my patients) need to avoid eating carbohydrates. To them eating sugar, flour, even unrefined carbohydrate, is pure poison. There is one other exception; in competitive sports or in a strenuous exercise some people can't convert fat into energy *fast enough* for such pursuits without taking in some carbohydrates.

C—CEREALS

Q. *What kind of cereals can I add for the reduction diet?*

A. Basically, none. One ounce (one cup) of cornflakes, for instance, with three-fourths of a cup of milk and no sugar, contains around thirty-two grams of carbohydrate. This is certainly more than you should be taking in at any one meal, even on maintenance. It may well be that it's more than you can have healthily during any one day. Remember, if your carbohydrate metabolism is out of kilter, you can't eat as if it weren't . . . any more than a diabetic can.

C—CHEATING

Q. *Why can't I cheat on this diet?*

A. Because on this diet, cheating means adding carbohydrates, and carbohydrates stimulate the appetite and make you eat considerably more than you would have otherwise. In other words, a higher carbohydrate intake almost always leads to a higher caloric intake.

C—CHOCOLATE

Q. *Why is it every time I eat a piece of chocolate, I'm off on a binge?*

A. Chocoholism is a specific kind of addiction, one of the most common varieties of sugar addiction. Like its fellow addictives, heroin and alcohol, just one taste can lead to a prolonged bender. Why this specific reaction to chocolate flavor exists, I have never been able to learn, but I have never seen a vanillaholic. The treatment? *Don't take that first taste.* However, there are some good chocolate-*flavor* extracts, which, when mixed with heavy cream and a good artificial sweetener, can produce a very satisfying chocolate mousse.

C—CIGARETTE SMOKING

Q. *Why did I gain so much weight when I stopped smoking?*

A. The nicotine in cigarettes is pharmacologically somewhat related to amphetamines, and in each case weight gain is apt to take place on stopping their use. Nicotine has a direct effect on the stomach's secretions and motility, and this acts as an appetite suppressant.

Q. *Should I go back to smoking from the standpoint of controlling my weight?*

A. Why start up again with something that makes you gain so much when you stop?

C—COCKTAILS

Q. *How will I ever manage without a predinner cocktail? I really* need *it.*

A. Many people drink before dinner because it gives them temporary relief from low blood sugar. There's such dramatic improvement in nervousness, fatigue, irritability that they value that drink a great deal. While the blood sugar disturbance is being corrected by the diet, this biological need for a drink does not exist. The person who doesn't really have this biological need—the person who just drinks for sociability—mainly just misses the *idea* of having a drink along with others. But not for long, as a rule. For one thing, not drinking is increasingly "in"— the young being the bellwethers in this.

C—COFFEE

Q. *Does caffeine aggravate low blood sugar?*
A. Yes. People with a high caffeine intake almost always have low blood sugar. But which came first? Few people get clinical symptoms on less than three cups of coffee a day. And for those who take more and are caffeine dependent, it can be useful to mobilize the extra energy required for digestion.

C—COMPULSIVE EATING

Q. *I eat when I couldn't possibly be hungry—right after a big meal. Doesn't that mean I'm a compulsive eater?*
A. *Au contraire;* this represents a common metabolic disturbance among overweight people. The big meal, containing carbohydrate, triggers an excessive insulin response and the blood sugar starts plummeting down, in some people, before they can leave the dinner table.
Q. *Whenever I get upset, I go to the refrigerator and eat. How can you possibly help a compulsive eater like me?*
A. Great! I think that's wonderful! I want you to go straight ahead and eat some protein. I don't want to take away the role that food plays as a salve of injured feelings or a lifter of depression. I merely want to make sure that the food you eat is not carbohydrate. But I think going to the refrigerator is exactly what you should do when you're upset. Eat a piece of cold fried chicken or have a slice of the pot roast left over from yesterday. Or have some

cheese. Or cut yourself a piece of your homemade cheese-cake. Or have some Baken-ets.

What some people fail to realize is that proteins and fats have satiety value, whereas carbohydrate has hunger-provoking qualities. So if you eat the food with satiety value—protein and fat—when you're upset, the thing that will happen is that when mealtime comes around you won't be hungry. And if you do your "upset" eating at night, you'll end up not being hungry the next day. Because on a protein/fat diet satiety has a carry-over of twenty-four or even forty-eight hours. So that even over-eating on this diet one day is not so terrible, because there's almost always a diminished appetite the following day.

C—CRAMPS (LEG)

Q. *What do I do if I get leg cramps on the diet?*

A. This symptom usually comes at night and is probably due to calcium deficiency. I treat it with calcium supplements and Vitamins E and C. Sometimes magnesium and potassium have to be added. Lily Daché, who lives on this diet and looks twenty years younger than her actual age, always tells me that the thing she appreciates most is that "you cured my leg cramps."

C—CREAM CHEESE

Q. *Can I have cream cheese and cream cheese mixes?*

A. Yes; in the same quantity as is recommended for hard cheese, and if you are *certain* that no carbohydrates have been added to the mixes.

C—CURE

Q. *When could you pronounce me cured? After five years, as is sometimes mentioned in relation to cancer studies?*

A. Overweight is never cured. Even if there is no recurrence after five years, we know that the underlying pathology of the metabolism remains within the body.

D—DIABETES

Q. *Is low blood sugar the opposite of high blood sugar—or in other words, diabetes?*

A. Oh, no. The opposite of diabetes is normal. Low blood sugar, in fact, is probably the earliest manifestation of diabetes. In my opinion, they are different stages of the same disease, and they both have many of the same symptoms. The symptoms of early diabetes can be attributed to the low blood sugar that can be found in most early diabetics.

D—DIET CLUBS

Q. *Aren't there diet clubs where you don't count calories?*

A. There are clubs where *you* don't count calories; someone else has counted them for you. All you do is *weigh* your portions. At present there are no clubs dedicated to low-carbohydrate dieting, but after the Diet Revolution they should be plentiful.

D—DIET DRINKS

Q. *Is there any harm in bottled diet drinks?*

A. Not unless they contain sugar. Some still do. Read the label *carefully*. To a sweetoholic even a little sugar can have much the same effect as a little martini on an alcoholic.

D—DIURETICS

Q. *Is there any harm in taking diuretics for water retention?*

A. Well, taking a diuretic seems to be a favorite way of cheating with overweight. Remember, it takes the water off, but leaves the fat behind. As a matter of fact, the low-carbohydrate diet *acts as a natural diuretic.* I don't see any point in taking diuretics over a long term. Patients who do frequently complain of leg cramps, stomach pains, and a feeling of limpness and depletion. And they are depleted . . . of vital minerals and vitamins. That's what diuretics do when taken over any length of time. Worse yet, the most commonly used type of diuretics tend to aggravate diabetes and the prediabetic type of carbohydrate intolerance that most overweight people have. Also, the water loss only shows on the scale for two or three days and then you're right back where you started from.

D—DOCTORS

Q. *How do I know whether to see a doctor for my weight problem?*

A. It is always a good idea to visit a doctor if you have a weight problem, because if you do there is a good probability that something else may be wrong. If you have some of the symptoms mentioned in this book, they could probably be better diagnosed with a medical checkup. If you follow this diet and don't seem to be losing, a doctor might help, as would be the case if you don't feel your best while dieting.

D—DOCTORS, CHOOSING

Q. *How do I go about choosing a good doctor?*

A. This, as you might imagine, is the most difficult question of all. There are certain points to look for. He must profess *interest* in your weight problem and in obesity problems in general. He should be interested in testing you to search for the *causes* of your overweight. He should not be dispensing appetite suppressants or shots. *His dietary advice must be something you can follow.* He should be a doctor you feel you could trust to treat a serious chronic illness, or at least have the professional respect of the doctor to whom you entrust your general health.

E—EDEMA

Q. *How can I go off water pills? I fill right up with edema!*

A. Chances are that you are a woman and that you have

"idiopathic edema of women." This is a rather common condition, described by Dr. Edgar Gordon, of the University of Wisconsin, as "characterized by depression, nervous irritability, mild to severe overweight, by rapid gains and losses of weight, and usually by a large accumulation of emotional problems." This condition is thought to be a disorder of carbohydrate metabolism and in my experience the depression and irritability are probably due to the low blood sugar almost invariably found with it. This diet will provide the most effective treatment you've ever been exposed to.

E—EGGS

Q. *Won't having eggs every day raise my cholesterol?*

A. I tell my patients, "Eat all the eggs you want." The reason is that while eggs tend to raise the cholesterol level in theory, eating two eggs a day, seven days a week, theoretically would raise it only a few points. Studies have shown that you cannot absorb more cholesterol than is in two eggs each day. More importantly, there is a feedback control mechanism in your body so that the more cholesterol you eat, the less you manufacture. And three-fourths of your body's cholesterol comes from what you manufacture yourself, usually from dietary carbohydrates.

On the other hand, in actual practice, cutting out carbohydrates on the diet lowers the cholesterol sometimes as much as 200 points. We have had case after case in which the cholesterol level has come down 100 points or more in just a few weeks on the diet, with no other variable. I should say that cholesterol levels remain the same or go down in eight out of ten patients. Anticholesterol medication is needed by no more than one patient in ten. Also, one cannot evaluate changes in the blood cholesterol without knowing what is happening to the triglycerides as well. When the cholesterol does go up, it is more often than not offset by a greater fall in the triglyceride level.

E—EXPENSIVE

Q. *Isn't a low-carbohydrate diet expensive?*

A. It's true that the starchy stuffs are poor people's food all over the world, but Americans spend billions on Cokes, candy bars, cookies, crackers, and cereals. On a low-carbohydrate diet you can buy the less expensive cuts of meats, pork chops, chuck, ribs, and the like because you can have fat. Chicken is reasonable in price. So are a good many varieties of fish. But the best diet bargain of all is eggs.

E—EYESIGHT

Q. *I have read that sugar is essential for proper eyesight—something called "normal retinal function"—as well as for the brain and nerves. Is this true?*

A. Let me ask you a question. If sugar is essential for this, how did man see during all those millions of years of his existence before 1800 when sugar came into his diet?

As I have said elsewhere, what the eyes, brain, and central nervous system need is not sugar in the diet but sugar in the *bloodstream*. And the body has a more than adequate capacity for converting stored fat into glucose.

F—FASTING

Q. *What do you think about fasting as a method of losing weight?*

A. What's good about fasting is that after forty-eight hours you're not hungry; but it's hardly a permanent way of life. And three fairly recent studies show that between 59 percent and 66 percent of what is lost is not fat tissue, but vital, lean tissue taken from the muscles and vital organs—tissue that you need.

F—FATS, POLYUNSATURATED

Q. *Are polyunsaturated fats better for this diet than the saturated?*

A. I have not made a big point of this, but using polyun-saturates can prove advantageous in controlling certain people's cholesterol levels. It doesn't work for everyone because most of the protein we would eat occurs in natural combination with saturated fats, and a diet without them might be somewhat monotonous and unlivable.

F—FOREVER

Q. *Will I never be able to have my favorite carbohydrate dish?*

A. Sure, any time you'd like to *gain* three or four pounds. All you would have to do is diet until you're three pounds *under* your ideal weight, eat whatever you like, gain the three pounds, and end up at your ideal weight. But you must avoid your old "Gain now—diet later" philosophy.

G—GRAPEFRUIT

Q. *Why not grapefruit? The grapefruit diet is very successful.*

A. Despite the success of this forty-five-gram diet (each half-grapefruit contains around fifteen grams of carbohy-drate) no special qualities of the grapefruit in promoting weight loss have ever been scientifically shown, but the ability of restricting oneself to forty-five grams of carbohy-drate per day in *retarding* weight gain has been demon-strated time and time again.

H—HEARTBURN

Q. *I get heartburn on diets. What do I do?*

A. Go on this diet immediately. Nothing clears up on this diet more predictably than does heartburn.

H—HYPOGLYCEMIA, OTHER DIETS FOR

Q. *I've read about other diets for hypoglycemia . . . the original Seale Harris diet, more recent ones, too. They all seem to allow a lot more carbohydrate than you do. Are they just as effective in treating hypoglycemia?*

A. Depends on whether you're talking about thin hypoglycemics or overweight ones. The big difference is that this diet is ketogenic; the Harris diet is not. The Seale Harris type of diet is more suitable for those less frequently seen cases of *underweight* people who suffer from low blood sugar.

But if you are overweight, the diet in this book is cause for hypoglycemics to rejoice. The Seale Harris diet contains too much carbohydrate to allow the fat mobilizing hormone to get into the act. Therefore, the only energy that thin hypoglycemics have is what they get from the small amount of carbohydrate they eat.

On this diet, the absence of adequate carbohydrate causes a constant mobilization of the FMH, thereby tapping the great storehouse of energy your fat depots contain. This steady supply of fuel is what prevents low blood sugar, and tends to keep it stabilized at a near-normal level.

I—INCHES

Q. *How can I be losing inches if I'm not losing pounds?*

A. This is what happens almost every time. It demonstrates that water can be retained while fat is being used up. The loss of fat allows inches to melt off but the increased fluid retention neutralizes the loss of poundage.

C—CATSUP

Q. *Why can't I use catsup? It's only a condiment.*

A. Yes, but a condiment that has 14.4 grams of carbohydrate in a common two-ounce serving. Instead, try a dash of

Worcestershire sauce with a few drops of Tabasco. Or for seafood, try mayonnaise with horseradish or with mustard.

K—KIDNEY DISEASE

Q. *Isn't this diet harmful for someone who has kidney disease?*

A. It could be harmful for the patient who has chronic kidney insufficiency so far advanced that a low protein diet is recommended. The diet is safe even if there is a mild kidney malfunction. It is highly unlikely that you would have a serious chronic kidney ailment without knowing it as long as you follow the simple advice of seeing a doctor if you don't feel well.

L—LAST POUNDS

Q. *Why is it so much harder to lose those last few pounds?*

A. There are several reasons. Your diet has evolved to become less stringent than at first. You may be more complacent, or at least less desperate, and thereby take a few more liberties with the diet. Most important, the farther you are from your peak weight, the farther you are from the weight that has become natural for your now distorted metabolism and you have less readily mobilizable fat left on your body.

M—MAINTENANCE

Q. *Once I get the weight off and am a normal person again, why can't I maintain this normal weight by merely eating normally?*

A. Because you only *look* normal; *inside* your body is the same metabolic abnormality that made you overweight in the first place. This, by the way, is one of the key points of the whole book.

M—MEDICATIONS

Q. *How can you make me lose weight without medication?*

A. (This is the commonest question posed to me.) I can't

make you lose weight. I can only show you how. But no medicine (as of 1972) can make you lose weight, except temporarily, and that weight loss cannot be sustained without persisting in taking what has always proven to be a dangerous drug.

M—MILK

Q. *If I can have cheese, why can't I have milk?*

A. Milk contains milk sugar, called lactose. In the process of being made into cheese, most of milk's lactose gets fermented. What's left is largely protein and fat.

N—NIGHT EATING

Q. *I am so good on my diet all day; why do I louse it up with an eating binge every night?*

A. Night eating is the commonest disorder of the eating pattern due to a metabolic disturbance; it almost always signifies an abnormal blood sugar response. If you have been hungry every night in the past, there's one thing you can be sure of: you'll be hungry tonight, also.

Why don't you prepare for it by eating enough (non-carbohydrate) food today during *the day* rather than your skimpy daytime diet, so that for once you are satiated when nighttime comes.

Every year I see at least two hundred patients who have been night eaters. Their eating pattern is little or no breakfast, a small lunch, followed almost by continuous eating from late afternoon or dinner on into the night. The clinical experience of treating patients like this on the zero-carbohydrate diet is both gratifying and dramatic. This diet is infinitely better for night eaters than any other diet. I've seen many hundreds of patients whose night hunger disappears with carbohydrate restriction. Yet if they start eating carbohydrates, the night eating begins again.

Q. *I wake up from a sound sleep and can't get back to sleep until I eat something; that's psychological, isn't it?*

A. Wrong. Nothing could be more physical. There is a 99 percent probability that it is nocturnal *low blood sugar* that wakes you up and sends you to the kitchen. Don't even hesitate, just arrange for your glucose tolerance test next week.

O—ORANGE JUICE

Q. *You really don't expect me to go without a glass of orange juice for the rest of my life?*

A. If you have the type of low blood sugar that causes symptoms, I would. A cup of orange juice contains 25.6 grams of carbohydrate; more of a jolt than your pancreas can take without flooding your blood with insulin. And if all you have is a weight problem, you must still reckon with the fact that twenty-five grams of fruit sugar can put on up to a pound when you're on strict carbohydrate restriction.

O—OVEREATING

Q. *If I hate being overweight so much,* why *do I overeat?*

A. Most probably because you're overhungry. After you go on this diet for a while you won't be hungry, and your dislike of being overweight will carry the day.

O—OVEREATING, PSYCHOLOGICAL

Q. *What could be more psychological than the fact that I eat when I'm upset?*

A. What could be more physical than the fact that anxiety increases your insulin output, which in turn lowers your blood sugar and makes you hungry?

P—PREGNANCY

Q. *Can I follow this diet during a pregnancy?*

A. I recommend this diet to all my pregnant patients; I certainly cannot recommend to them that they load up on carbohydrates. Most obstetricians do a good job, however, of preventing an undue weight gain during pregnancy.

R—REFRACTORINESS

Q. *I have never been able to lose on a very low calorie diet; what do I do if I can't lose on this diet?*

A. People like you do exist; I've seen many. You do need a thorough medical evaluation. If your doctor cannot find the answer, may I respectfully suggest to him a clinical trial on synthetic thyroid hormone. Undetectable antibodies to your thyroid gland is the commonest cause of this phenomenon.

R—REGAINING WEIGHT

Q. *What's so good about a diet where you gain the weight back rapidly as soon as you go off the diet?*

A. I concede that the WORST feature about this diet is the rapidity with which you gain if you abandon it. But the BEST feature is that you don't HAVE to go off this diet, and its most important feature is that THIS IS A DIET YOU CAN LIVE WITH FOREVER IN COMFORT AND LUXURY.

S—SALT

Q. *Why do you allow salt? Doesn't salt hold weight?*

A. Yes it does, but the weight is water weight and does not represent fat. When salt is restricted, you run the risk of a low sodium syndrome, which causes a feeling of weakness and exhaustion. (Diuretics do the same thing.) When a severe degree of fluid retention takes place, then salt restriction might be a good idea. Remember that this diet can be a potent diuretic in itself.

S—SCALES

Q. *How often should I weigh myself?*

A. Every day. It never hurts to be *aware*. This is a good

habit to begin before you get to maintenance, because if you ever notice a small weight gain you would be likely to respond by promptly getting stricter with your diet.

S—SLOW LOSER

Q. *I'm losing very slowly; could this diet be wrong for me?*
A. Usually if you're a slow loser on this diet, you're a slow loser on any diet. Being a slow loser doesn't mean you're not going to get thin, just that it may take longer. After all, not everyone can run the hundred-yard dash in ten seconds, but most people *can* run a hundred yards.

S—STOMACH

Q. *Wouldn't it be a good idea to keep filling up on salad and vegetables so my stomach never gets empty? And I would never get hungry?*
A. No, because hunger results from what's in your blood-stream, not in your stomach.

S—SUDDEN GAIN

Q. *What does it mean if I gain four pounds overnight without cheating?*
A. Gaining without cheating invariably means water retention and does not represent accumulation of fat. It goes right away spontaneously, and is usually caused by temporary increases in salt intake or by being in a premenstrual state.

S—SWITCHING DIETS

Q. *Could I switch from this diet to another diet?*
A. Many people have used this technique successfully; many more have run afoul when they have tried it. There is no question that calorically restricted diets can allow you to lose weight also. The problem arises when, after being used to never feeling hungry, you reintroduce carbohydrates, which stimulate your appetite and make it difficult

to stick with your low-calorie diet. If switching diets is your personal choice, I advise you to avoid refined carbohydrates for health reasons, and not to switch too often because the day you switch you're eating a mixture, not a diet.

T—TEA

Q. *I love tea. Does it contain much carbohydrate? Is there a limit?*

A. It isn't the carbohydrate in tea (or coffee) that counts. It's an analogue of caffeine in tea called theobromine that does about what caffeine does (though it's not as potent). What both tea and coffee do is stimulate the secretion of insulin.

You're still allowed tea. But I caution a heavy tea drinker just as I would a heavy coffee drinker to make sure that it is *diluted*, and not a strong brew. Then you're fine.

Watch the instant teas. Even if they are said to be low calorie, they can contain malti-dextrin and have carbohydrates. Only by reading the label can you differentiate. Most luncheonettes will serve iced tea which is instant and does contain malti-dextrins. This can introduce enough carbohydrate (particularly in a hot, sweltering summer) to throw off your whole diet.

T—THYROID

Q. *I lose more slowly on your diet than other people seem to. Can it be my thyroid?*

A. It most certainly could be your thyroid. I have to administer thyroid to one patient out of five. A therapeutic trial of thyroid often pays off when the routine blood tests for thyroid seem to be normal. Dr. Irving Perlstein's excellent studies on antibodies to the thyroid hormone show how this can be. The medical pendulum is swinging back to the use of thyroid hormone in the treatment of overweight.

If you are a slow loser and suffer from lethargy or dry skin or inability to keep your body warm enough, you should see a doctor to have your thyroid evaluated by the newer, more sophisticated tests that show how much thyroid is actually present in the bloodstream (quite different from the old thyroid tests).

T—THYROID TEST

Q. *What happened to the old basal metabolism test?*

A. Basically inaccurate. Can be minus 20 one day and a plus 20 the next. A better way to determine thyroid performance is by tests that measure the amount of thyroid in the blood. In our office we also use the photomotogram, which measures the speed of relaxation of the ankle jerk reflex. This provides reproducible and, I think, meaningful information about thyroid function.

V—VITAMINS

Q. *Are vitamins important in your diet?*

A. Very. I believe their role in good health is generally underrated. We see certain beneficial clinical responses when Vitamins B, C, and E are ingested in megadoses —which means up to one hundred times the minimum daily requirement. One of the doctor's major problems in managing hypoglycemic patients is in maintaining a stabilized blood sugar level. Over years of experience I have found that megadoses of Vitamin E, in particular, appear to stabilize the blood sugar level.

V—VITAMINS, B

Q. *Couldn't I just take brewer's yeast (which is so much less expensive) to get my B vitamins?*

A. Because yeast also contains some carbohydrate (one ounce equals 3 grams) I would wait until the second week of the diet to add it, and would make certain by careful observation that the amount you take does *not* slow down your weight loss.

V—VOGUE DIET

Q. *In* VOGUE *magazine, you recommended this diet for only sixteen days, and in* COSMOPOLITAN *for only ten days; does this imply the diet is not advisable for longer periods of time?*

A. Not so. The purpose of the brief interval was merely to allow you to experience the advantages of this diet over the ones you previously had worked with, so that you could better decide which one seemed to you to be a better nucleus around which to build your *lifetime* dietary habits.

W—WILLPOWER

Q. *How can I diet if I have no willpower?*

A. Willpower in dieting is usually defined as the force of mind that enables one to withstand hunger. On a no-hunger diet it is not necessary. Willpower is also that quality that allows you to do something you don't want to do. If you *want* to be slim and healthy, you could do it by *choice*, not willpower.

18

WHY

WE NEED

A REVOLUTION,

NOT

JUST A DIET

I hope you read this chapter after you've been on the diet for a while. By that time—hopefully—you will feel the way that my patients and I do. You will find yourself thinking as I did, "How could I have been fooled all these years into thinking that to control my weight, I had to cut calories, starve myself, or stop eating?"

The fact that this monstrous misconception exists indicates that dramatic action must be taken on a nationwide scale to change things. Our laws must be changed to provide a proper way of eating for everyone.

I feel so strongly about this that I know my work will never be finished until a successful national Diet Revolution really is well on its way to being launched.

POLITICAL ACTION CAN CUT CARBOHYDRATES FOR YOU. Like any revolution, the Diet Revolution needs pressure from consumers that will be felt by the establishment. This is what leads to change.

Political action and protest on your part can help revolutionize the food industry, by forcing it to decarbohydrate many foods—just as it has de-calorized some foods—*but with a federal law to back this change!*

I think that by now you know that the calorie theory is wrong. It denies you the opportunity to eat as much varied, substantial food as you need to feel satisfied—and still keep your weight down, your blood sugar stable, and your energy high. Yet the calorie theory is the law of the land.

Yes, literally. By actual legislative act! Did you know that by federal law "diet" foods (a multimillion dollar industry) can be labeled "dietetic" only if they are reduced in calories? No law applies that they must be reduced in carbohydrates! There should be such a law. Because a reduction in carbohydrate is far more important not only in successful weight reduction, but in protecting us against some of our most killing diseases.

ROBBED OF CYCLAMATES! The most appalling example of the political power of caloric-theory proponents showed up in the abrupt and tragic withdrawal of cyclamates—the wonderfully palatable sugar substitute—from the market.

Those of us who were concerned and followed that drama are aware of the political influence that the sugar industry wielded to discredit the cyclamates, their relatively safe and palatable competitor. But this was accepted as profit-oriented self-interest, and, as such, compatible with the great American tradition.

Cyclamates had been consumed over two decades by millions of people—without restriction—and without a single known instance of harmful human reaction. Yet, when it was possible to trump up a single invalid, unreproducible study showing that cyclamates given selected, predisposed, laboratory rats, in totally unrealistic doses, could be implicated as a cause of cancer, the Secretary of Health, Education, and Welfare abruptly took them off the market.

Millions of people, of course, went back to drinking sugar-sweetened soft drinks. The Secretary's Medical Advisory Committee must have reasoned that the 144 calories contained in the two cans of sugar-sweetened diet cola that are the average dieter's daily intake couldn't have too much impact in an average 1,500-calorie reducing diet. What the calorie-oriented committee failed to note was that the thirty-six grams of sugar contained in the two cans *is sufficient to prevent weight loss in almost anyone using a low-carbohydrate diet.* Also it could precipitate any one of a million hypoglycemics in this country into a dizzying set of symptoms. In addition it could effectively prevent the remission of illness in several million early and borderline diabetics!

THE LOW-CALORIE-DIET THEORY STILL DOMINATES TOO MANY BIG MEDICAL GROUPS. The American Heart Association recommends reduced fat intake for overweight citizens but does not recommend carbohydrate reduction. The American Diabetes Association statement of diet policy does not even call for carbohydrate restriction *for diabetics*, despite the fact that carbohydrate restriction has long been known to alter the course of illness dramatically.

I HAD A DREAM . . . Martin Luther King had a dream. I, too, have one. I dream of a world where no one has to diet. A world where the fattening refined carbohydrates have been excluded from the diet. Our food technology has advanced to the point where we *can* make sweets without sugar and bread without starches. This has been done experimentally, but the marketplace should be full of such products so that everyone is able to buy them freely. This is part of the Diet Revolution I would like to see come about.

If we lived in a culture where carbohydrates were at a minimum, we could all eat all we wanted of anything, get youthfully slim again if we need to, and stay that way!

If my dream were to come true, there would exist for the dieter a world full of food he could eat and enjoy anywhere with anyone—foods that now are made of or with carbohydrates, but that would be modified to eliminate them.

In such a world, even the most careless overeaters could be thin. Right now, the dieter must function in a hostile world, full of people trying to get him to break his diet. And dieting can be a very lonely place.

HOW YOU CAN HELP GET THIS DIET REVOLUTION STARTED. If you follow the instructions outlined in this book, you will be successful in mastering your struggle against overweight, and you will know that I have helped you. In return, I ask you for your help in promoting the Diet Revolution.

When you hear a friend insist that one diet is as good as another, don't be silent. Talk! Talk to him until you have convinced him that it is not so. Help repeal the unfair legislation. Write your senators and congressman and ask them to rewrite the law banning artificial sugar substitutes. Help raise funds needed for medical research to prove the points that must be proved. Help see that school cafeterias stop filling up our children on a cheap diet of mainly refined carbohydrates. Lobby for them to eat more wisely than most of us did at their ages. And lobby for laws that require diet foods to be *low in carbohydrates as well as calories*.

With your help, there truly can be a Diet Revolution!

DESIRABLE WEIGHTS FOR MEN AND WOMEN AGED 25 AND OVER [1]
in pounds according to height and frame, in indoor clothing, and shoes

HEIGHT		SMALL FRAME	MEDIUM FRAME	LARGE FRAME
		MEN		
Feet	Inches			
5	2	112-120	118-129	126-141
5	3	115-123	121-133	129-144

[1] *Adapted from Metropolitan Life Insurance Co., New York. New weight standards for men and women. Statistical Bulletin 40.3, Nov.-Dec., 1959.*

DESIRABLE WEIGHTS (cont.)

HEIGHT		SMALL FRAME	MEDIUM FRAME	LARGE FRAME
MEN				
Feet	Inches			
5	4	118-126	124-136	132-148
5	5	121-129	127-139	135-152
5	6	124-133	130-143	138-156
5	7	128-137	134-147	142-161
5	8	132-141	138-152	147-166
5	9	136-145	142-156	151-170
5	10	140-150	146-160	155-174
5	11	144-154	150-165	159-179
6	0	148-158	154-170	164-184
6	1	152-162	158-175	168-189
6	2	156-167	162-180	173-194
6	3	160-171	167-185	178-199
6	4	164-175	172-190	182-204
WOMEN				
4	10	92- 98	96-107	104-119
4	11	94-101	98-110	106-122
5	0	96-104	101-113	109-125
5	1	99-107	104-116	112-128
5	2	102-110	107-119	115-131
5	3	105-113	110-122	118-134
5	4	108-116	113-126	121-138
5	5	111-119	116-130	125-142
5	6	114-123	120-135	129-146
5	7	118-127	124-139	133-150
5	8	122-131	128-143	137-154
5	9	126-135	132-147	141-158
5	10	130-140	136-151	145-163
5	11	134-144	140-155	149-168
6	0	138-148	144-159	153-173

STATEMENT OF
ROBERT C. ATKINS, M.D.
to the
SENATE SELECT COMMITTEE
ON NUTRITION
AND HUMAN NEEDS
April 12, 1973

It is my hope that, by setting forth at the outset the 10 basic points that I follow, I can help the members of this Committee view the details of my statement in the proper perspective.

1) First, obesity is one of the most serious nationwide health problems in the United States, and the medical profes-

sion should be cooperating on the development of fresh approaches for combating it instead of quarreling over every new suggestion that departs from the traditionally standard but unsuccessful recommendations of the medical establishment.

2) Second, although this nation has not been short of diets or dieters, obesity has continued to increase because, in my opinion, most unsuccessful dieters were struggling to follow a regimen, however sound and meritorious, that was simply beyond their mental and physical capacity to maintain.

3) Third, no diet works for everyone. No diet is right for everyone. Not all of my patients achieved success. But according to the carefully documented medical histories which any scientific investigator from this Senate Committee or the AMA should study before jumping to conclusions, the great majority of my patients have found it eminently safe, medically proper and exceedingly effective.

4) Fourth, while I understand the AMA's discomfort with the layman's language used in my book to make it more useable by the typical citizen, my desire was to combat obesity in this country, not to publish a treatise in technically precise but unreadable medical jargon.

5) Fifth, there are at least two *bona fide* dietary approaches for the overweight individual—restricting calories and restricting carbohydrates. Both approaches, in my opinion, are meritorious and generally beneficial to most persons who are overweight, and both represent a decided improvement over the use of amphetamines or other medications, useless gadgets or doing nothing at all.

6) Sixth, neither approach should be condemned by press releases in the absence of an impartial scientific evaluation of their comparative long-term and short-term effects based upon systematic clinical observations of a large sampling of individuals who have actually followed them.

7) Seventh, I fully understand the opposition to my diet from the manufacturers of sugars, starches and sugar- or starch-saturated foods; but I find it less easy to understand

the AMA's opposition in view of the large number of individual physicians who have recommended my diet for their families as well as their patients.

8) Eighth, although it has unfortunately not been unusual for the AMA to attempt to suppress the acceptance of these nutritional advances which challenge established medical dogma and commercial practices, it is remarkable that its attack has singled out my diet alone after decades of silence on the literally hundreds of low carbohydrate diets which have been published over the years by other physicians.

9) Ninth, much of the AMA attack on my diet is based upon studies of wholly different diets (for example, zero carbohydrate or fixed-quantity carbohydrate diets), or on irrelevant, inaccurate or unproven hypotheses, or on studies which in fact support my findings. Not one instance of a dangerous side effect attributable to my diet, even though it has been in widespread use for some time, was cited by the AMA statement.

10) Tenth, because every diet—like every medication, vaccination, surgical innovation or other medical advance—is potentially dangerous if misapplied, I have always recommended medical examinations and blood tests before and during various stages of my diet or any other. Symptoms of fatigue, lethargy, dizziness and hunger can occur in any diet; but the AMA is ironically correct in stating that anorexia, or loss of appetite, is a side effect of my diet.

It is my understanding that the purpose of this committee is to investigate frauds in nutrition and dieting, and it was in this context that I have been called before you to testify in defense of my actions. That this defense is necessary in what is considered to be a democratic society is incredible to me, as it is incredible to the millions of obesity victims who have achieved a new lease on life through the use of a sound physiological principle—carbohydrate restriction.

It is incredible that in 20th century America, a conscientious physician should have his hard-won professional reputation placed on the line for daring to suggest that an obesity victim might achieve some relief by cutting out sugars and starches.

To place my actions in historical perspective, let me state that I am a practicing physician who was taught in medical school to treat obesity by recommending a low calorie diet. In order to combat the hunger that invariably resulted, I soon learned to prescribe an amphetamine or some appetite-suppressant. When I achieved the same singularly poor long-term results that most of my colleagues were getting, I began to search for a better alternative. The medical literature of those days (1950's and early 60's) was replete with studies showing that carbohydrate restriction provided rather pre-dictably successful results. I began to work with this type of diet, first for my own personal needs and then with 65 AT&T executives. All of us achieved a substantial weight loss. Over the next 9 years I worked diligently in this field, ever learning, ever improving my approach. By 1966, I was work-ing to my office's capacity. By 1972, I had treated some 10,000 patients. I felt I had achieved an excellent reputation in my community. Doctors came to me, they sent their wives, children and their patients. Major corporations sent their exec-utives. Many popular magazines wrote about my dietary recommendations. The waiting list for new patient appoint-ments always numbered in the hundreds. I felt I had, by avoiding diet medications and by doing a thorough medical workup, including lipid profiles and a glucose tolerance test, EKG's and chest X-rays, evolved a diet which was no longer a theory, but an established, medically proven regimen, and achieved a measure of respect in my community. And with it, I felt I had evolved a diet which was no longer a theory, but a medically proven and predictable regimen. This vast experience with the diet enabled me to predict not only whether a patient could lose, but how much and when.

With the success that the vast majority of my patients enjoyed, my reputation achieved sufficient national prominence that several publishing houses urged me to write a book for the general public. I was absolutely convinced that the majority of unsuccessful dieters were failing because they were struggling to follow a diet that was beyond their mental and physical capacity to maintain.

I sincerely felt that the public should be allowed to benefit in the same gratifying way as my private patients. In no way did it seem fair to withhold this opportunity to solve such a frustrating problem as obesity from people who would never be able to visit my office. Although diet books were glutting the marketplace, they either advocated diets of a truly bizarre nature or else were rewrites of the same low calorie diet that could never be followed because of its constant companion, hunger. I thus was convinced that there was a definite need to publish a diet book which would present to the public a dietary regime which had been so carefully monitored by clinical observations on thousands of patients.

And so I wrote the Diet Revolution.

For nearly five months, the public (and professional) acceptance of the book was so great that the book was in constant short supply. It was sold by word of mouth, not by a vigorous advertising or promotional campaign. "The diet works," the public said, "and I feel great." It is a matter of public record that 97% of all respondants on phone-in TV and radio shows reported success upon following the diet. The acceptance of the book proved how sorely it had been needed.

But then, as if by a centrally contrived plan, there issued forth a barrage of public criticism through news releases, press conferences, magazine stories, radio and TV networks. "Medical groups declare Atkins diet dangerous" was the theme of the headlines. With an unprecedented news release and an unprecedented panel discussion the media were invited to carry the word to America that I was a quack, a faddist, a charlatan. Even the Chairman of this respected Committee was not averse to letting the wire services know that I was one of the first diet "frauds" to be investigated.

But I submit that these groups, such as the AMA's Council on Food and Nutrition, attacked the recommendation for the treatment of obesity, as set forth in my book, without a shred of evidence to support their contentions.

The fact remains that the Diet Revolution regimen is eminently safe, medically proper and exceedingly effective. I have found, after systematic study of over ten thousand patients, no persistently deleterious side effects attributable to the diet. And curiously enough, despite 56 references to scientific publications, published *prior* to my book, the AMA was unable to report a single instance of a dangerous side effect resulting from my diet, even though at the time of their press release thousands of Americans had followed it.

Perhaps the basis of the AMA's inaccuracy has been their concern with the idea that the diet is "neither new nor revolutionary." It is essential to note that while the program is neither absolutely new nor revolutionary, *it is different.* There is considerable clinical evidence that these differences are sufficient to explain the variations in reports of effectiveness and safety.

The Diet Revolution regime is neither a zero carbohydrate nor a fixed quantity carbohydrate diet; it is a program of progressive *levels* of carbohydrate intake, titrated to conform to an individual's metabolic response, taken along with a significant supplement of essential vitamins and minerals.

Nonetheless, the council has seen fit repeatedly to denounce this diet by reference to studies of other dissimilar diets which clearly do not pertain to the regime under question.

In other words, there is only one way to study the Diet Revolution regimen. This clearly was not done by the Council, either directly or secondarily.

The AMA allegation that the diet is "for the most part, unscientific" is clearly misleading. It should be noted that the book was designed for the lay reader, not the scientist. Therefore it was not footnoted with references to valid medical studies. But this is not to be construed to mean that these valid studies do not exist or that the scientific bases for the book are not accurate.

The Council made a number of points. Let us answer them seriatim:

1. Despite the recrudescence of a succession of low carbohydrate diets, "no nationwide decrease in obesity has been reported."

A. Is this not better explained by the fact that virtually all physicians have been taught to prescribe the low, notoriously difficult to follow, caloric diet rather than the low carbohydrate approach?

2. "Obesity is prevalent in North America, where the proportion of fat in the diet is higher than in most other countries."

A. This is true, but is it not also true that the intake of *sugar* here ranks among the highest in the world?

3. In Asia and Africa, "a majority of human beings remain lean on diets extremely high in carbohydrate and correspondingly low in fat."

A. Is this not explained by the low total caloric intake of these cultures? At no point do I deny that caloric restriction can also be effective for weight control by an individual or a culture.

4. No diet can defy the first law of thermodynamics and "be effective unless it provides for a decrease in energy intake or somehow increases energy losses." This cannot be explained by the excretion of ketones. The notion that sedentary individuals can lose weight on a diet containing 5,000 calories/day is incredible.

A. It is true that no studies of energy metabolism have been performed on individuals who lose adipose tissue on a high caloric, very low carbohydrate diet. In the absence of such studies, only idle speculation is in order. My office has observed a significant number of these "incredible" individuals. They do exist, and it is obvious that some of these individuals should be subjected to studies of total energy metabolism.

The data accumulated would be of great scientific interest to both parties in this dispute. It has always been my contention that the reason behind the metabolic advantage this diet offers would thus be made apparent.

5. A normal person can avoid weight loss on a carbohydrate free diet.

A. This may not be true, inasmuch as the data proferred to prove this point consist merely of the two subjects in the Stefansson study whose dietary carbohydrate intake was estimated to be as much as 50 grams, mainly liver glycogen. Furthermore, there is no evidence that weight loss can be avoided in an *obese* individual.

6. The weight loss is adequately explained by the "consumption of fewer calories."

A. The control of pathologic hunger patterns as well as the increased satiety value of this diet do, in general, lead to a significant decrease in caloric consumption. This, indeed, represents the principal advantage the diet provides, manifested by the extremely high percentage of the population who report that they are able to follow it easily. This is *only one* of the reasons by which the diet works.

7. The weight loss can be attributed to "temporary differences" . . . due chiefly to changes in water balance.

A. This favorable diuretic effect of the diet is a second reason for the effectiveness of the diet. It explains its remarkable usefulness in the treatment of edematous states. Significantly this effect allows for greater use of salt in the diet, which improves palatability and it diminishes the need in the dieters regimen for diuretics, most of which have an adverse effect on sugar and insulin metabolism.

Moreover it is clear from sampling the results of the many Americans who have followed the diet that the weight loss can be attributed to the loss of body fat, not water.

8. No scientific evidence exists to suggest that the diet has a metabolic advantage over more conventional diets.

A. To make this allegation, one must deny the validity

of the classic experiments of Kekurck and Powan, who showed that loss of body fat took place on diets of the same caloric value, when they were composed of fat or protein, but not when they were composed of carbohydrates.

The AMA tried to deny this work by references to studies done by Dr. Sidney Werner, but he studied a 52 gram carbohydrate diet—certainly a much higher level than that proposed in the Diet Revolution. Or by the work of Olesen and Qusade which their actual data showed that seven out of eight subjects on the low carbohydrate diet lost significant amounts of weight and the eighth was able to break even despite increasing her daily caloric intake by over 900 calories. Or by the work of Pilkington, where the calories were limited to only 1,000 and only 3 subjects were given less than 32 grams of carbohydrate.

There is a metabolic advantage and this represents a third reason that the diet works.

9. Fat cannot convert into carbohydrate.

A. While this is semantically true, the fact remains that fat is the primary source of the body's fuel when carbohydrate is absent more than two days. By entering into the anaerobic glycolytic metabolic cycle, it provides adequate fuel, in conjunction with the amino acids from the high protein diet. The significant observed fact is that it is extremely rare for any dieter's blood sugar level to fall *below* the normal range even after years of strict carbohydrate deprivation.

10. It is inaccurate to state that sugar has antinutrient properties.

A. There is scientific evidence that sugar increases requirements for thiamine and other B complex constituents. A variety of studies have been published indicating that sugar causes a significant increase in the body's requirements for thiamine and riboflavin, plus other B complex constituents. They form the basis for the statement that sugar is an antinutrient.

11. No such hormone as fat mobilizine hormone (FMH) has been established in man.

A. This statement seems to be deliberately inaccurate. There have been more than forty scientific papers on this substance. It has been recovered from the urine of humans subjected to carbohydrate deprivation and made to cause fat mobilization when injected into animals.

12. There is no good evidence that hypoglycemia causes depression or chronic fatigue.

A. This statement is so incredibly untrue as to preclude comment. There are millions of Americans who have suffered from depression and chronic fatigue, found they had hypoglycemia during a glucose tolerance test and saw their symptoms clear up when a high-protein, low carbohydrate diet was followed. Common medical logic would insist on concluding that symptoms which occur on a diet containing carbohydrates clear up when carbohydrates are withdrawn, and recur when carbohydrates are restored to the diet, must be carbohydrate-induced. This is the basis for the observation that hypoglycemia is indeed very prevalent in our culture.

More serious was the Council's allegation that the Diet Revolution recommendations were "potentially dangerous." It is important to point out that *any* diet, when misapplied, is "potentially dangerous."

But the implication as the AMA News Release was interpreted by the media across the country is that the diet is "dangerous." I cannot help but object to this deliberate measure to distort the public's understanding of the effects of this eminently safe and proven dietary regimen.

The dangers listed include such immediate side effects as fatigue, dehydration, postural hypotension, nausea, vomiting and anorexia.

What the report does *not* state is the rarity of such reactions when the diet is followed as directed. The general response to the regimen is an improvement in feeling of well-being either from the beginning of the diet or by the fourth day. In the less common eventuality that symptoms persist, the reader is instructed to increase his mineral, fluid or carbohydrate intake until the symptoms clear up. In this way, such immediate side effects rarely persist. It is not human nature for a person to persist in following a weight-reduction program that makes him feel bad.

Another point the Council *fails* to make is that these symptoms (especially fatigue, lethargy, dizziness and hunger) occur with *much greater frequency* on the 45% carbohydrate, low calorie diet espoused by the AMA.

Of especial curiosity is the inclusion of anorexia (loss of appetite), which does indeed occur with great frequency, as an "unwanted" side effect. It seems self-evident that this side effect can only be of *benefit* to the overweight dieter.

Of more serious concern in any medical evaluation of a dietary regimen is the possibility of insidious side effects—those which would go unnoticed by the dieter himself. Despite the Council's labeling of this diet as "potentially dangerous," they were able to cite no more than three areas of danger potential—impaired kidney function, elevations of uric acid levels, and elevation of serum lipid.

It is important to point out that if the book's recommendations to have blood tests done before and during various states of the diet are followed, all of these potential problems will be detected in susceptible individuals and the recommendations can be appropriately modified, thus reducing the possibility of "dangerous" consequences down to nil.

The specific areas under question may be analyzed as follows:

Normal or even moderately impaired kidneys have more than adequate capacity to handle the solute load imposed upon them by this diet's metabolic changes. *No case of impaired renal function attributable to this diet has ever been reported.* Significant elevations of blood urea nitrogen are occasionally seen, but when checked against other kidney function tests, it is apparent that they are not renal in origin. As a further precaution, the book clearly states that any patient with significant kidney disease should continue to follow the diet prescribed by his own physician.

The possibility of elevation of uric acid does represent a significant area of complication from this diet, as well as many others, especially those involving fasting or severe caloric deprivation. The book itself made a great point in stressing this potential difficulty.

Perhaps the greatest focal point of controversy rages over the question of "unlimited intake of saturated fats and cholesterol-rich foods." The Council is quick to point out that "*individuals* responding to such a diet with a rise in blood fats will have an increased risk of coronary artery disease and atherosclerosis." The latter statement would, of course, be true of *any* diet, even a low-fat diet.

There are always "individuals" who respond to a given diet in a manner opposite to the majority; this does not mean that the diet is bad for the majority, merely that it is incorrect for that individual.

What is important to determine are the statistical mean blood fat levels, both before and during various states of the diet. The AMA failed to gather any appropriate statistical studies on this particular varied-level carbohydrate regimen. Therefore, the only data which exist pertinent to the effects of this regimen upon the blood lipid levels are those gathered in my office. These data, which are currently undergoing computerized sampling analysis, show a definite tendency for the serum cholesterol levels to fall compared to pre-diet levels and for the serum triglyceride levels to fall with great regularity.

Another criticism of the diet has been the view that the ketosis occurring from severe carbohydrate restriction is potentially harmful. The confusion in this statement rests with the fact that ketosis signifies the utilization of fat for energy and is not the ketoacidosis of a diabetic out of control. Ketosis is a natural state produced by the body in response to either starvation or marked restriction of dietary carbohydrates. Ketoacidosis is a pathological state of severe insulin deficiency where catabolism (breakdrown) of fat occurs at an excessively rapid rate causing the body to become excessively acidotic (too much acid). Acidosis does *not* occur in the obese non-diabetic or in the obese non-insulin dependent diabetic on a low carbohydrate ketogenic diet.

Further, because of the progressive increments in carbohydrate intake most dieters are in ketosis in the early phases of the diet only.

Testimony has been given to suggest that this diet is dangerous during pregnancy.

I have made three statements in my book referable to my diet during pregnancy. 1) "I treat my pregnant patients with this diet." This is quite true, and there have been no cases of fetal damage incident to its use. 2) "I do not recommend an obese expectant mother to go back to eating a high carbohydrate diet." This is valid because of the high incidence of diabetes beginning during a pregnancy in the obese population group. 3) "Most obstetricians do a good job of preventing weight gain during pregnancy." This statement indicates that I fully expect any pregnant reader to be under the care of her own physician and following his diet. It also indicates that the goal of dieting during pregnancy should be to prevent weight gain, which means that the maintenance version of this diet is to be used.

Further, there exists not one shred of evidence that this diet causes any maternal or fetal complication.

The responsibility of this committee evaluating the usefulness of this dietary regimen is made considerably easier by the fact that this diet is easily amenable to comparison with the more conventional diet since both can be used by the same person for the same purpose and the results compared. Would it not be a shame if this committee were to form a conclusion on the basis of testimony by non-observers of the diet, by speculation or ivory-tower deductions, when the actual answers are so amenable to controlled scientific investigation, which could be commenced immediately?

I personally know what results such studies would yield;

I have seen the results so many thousands of times. But I know that an investigating committee would only be satisfied with independently-acquired data. I submit that these scientific facts should be assembled before arriving at even a tentative conclusion.

Dated, N.Y., N.Y.   Respectfully submitted,
     April 11, 1973
                                         Robert C. Atkins, M.D.

INDEX

acetone, 128–130
  see also ketones
acidosis, 12
Addison's disease, 81
adrenal cortical extract for
    hypoglycemia, 81
adrenaline:
  amphetamines and, 87
  secretion of, 60–61
age:
  carbohydrate sensitivity and,
    60, 64
  diabetes and, 50
aging, premature, 272–273
Air Force Diet, 11, 27
Albrink, Margaret J., 44, 87
alcohol, 146- 147, 263
  addiction, 265- 266
  calories and carbohydrates, 273
  cocktails, 277–278
  giving up, 273, 277–278
  units of, 147
allergy to carbohydrates, see
    carbohydrate sensitivity
American College of Physicians,
    99
American Diabetes Association,
    51, 296
American Heart Association, 296
American Medical Association,
    76, 81
amphetamines, 85–89
  discontinued before diet,
    123–124
  harmful effects, 88, 124

Antar, Mohamed A., 56
anxiety, carbohydrate sensitivity
    and, 60–61
appetite suppressants, see
    amphetamines
appetizers, see hors d'oeuvres;
    snack foods
apples, 107
Armenian food, 269
artificial sweeteners, see
    sweeteners, artificial
AT&T diet program, 27, 150
atherosclerosis, 48
Austrian soufflé, 196
avocados, 103

babies, overfeeding and
    overweight, 58–59
bacon, recipes:
  bacon and cheese balls, 250
  bacon and cheese soufflé,
    194–195
  bacon cheeseburger, 200
  quiche Lorraine, 188
balanced diet, conventional, 2
bananas, 107
Banting, William, 4
Basset, D. R., 44
bean sprouts, 139
Béarnaise sauce, 209
beef, recipes:
  bacon cheeseburger, 200
  dried beef rolls, 250–251
  hamburger fondue, 200–201

ABOUT THE AUTHOR

ROBERT C. ATKINS, M.D., was born in Dayton, Ohio, attended the University of Michigan and Cornell Medical College, and was a resident at St. Lukes Hospital, in New York, before entering private practice as a cardiologist.

DON'T MISS
THESE CURRENT
Bantam Bestsellers